Identity
in Modern Society

To Gilmar

Identity

in Modern Society
A Social Psychological Perspective

Bernd Simon

Blackwell
Publishing

350 Main Street, Malden, MA 02148-5020, USA
108 Cowley Road, Oxford OX4 1JF, UK
550 Swanston Street, Carlton, Victoria 3053, Australia

First published 2004 by Blackwell Publishing Ltd

Library of Congress Cataloging-in-Publication Data

Simon, Bernd.
Identity in modern society: a social psychological perspective / Bernd Simon.
p. cm.
Includes bibliographical references and index.
ISBN 0-631-22746-6 (alk. paper) – ISBN 0-631-22747-4 (pbk. : alk.paper)
1. Identity (Psychology) 2. Identity (Psychology)–Social aspects. I. Title.

BF697.S546 2004
302.5–dc21

2003007537

A catalogue record for this title is available from the British Library.

Set in 10/12$^{1}/_{2}$ Baskerville
by Kolam Information Services Pvt. Ltd, Pondicherry, India
Printed and bound in the United Kingdom
by MPG Books Ltd, Bodmin, Cornwall

For further information on
Blackwell Publishing, visit our website:
http://www.blackwellpublishing.com

Contents

List of Figures

List of Tables

Foreword

In this book Bernd Simon gets to grips with the problem of self and identity. He tackles it from a social psychological perspective and this is entirely appropriate since the problem *is* distinctively social psychological and it is in social psychology that important advances have been made in the past 30 years. The book is scholarly, original and beautifully written. He sets the scene for us, outlining the issues and background, provides an authoritative and lucid review of the three most influential traditions in contemporary social psychology (in both psychology and sociology), next attempts the task which nobody else has yet attempted, of bringing together the main insights of the major traditions into a unified and integrated theoretical framework, and then uses this theoretical formulation to generate a series of testable ideas which he and his colleagues explore in a variety of empirical studies across a range of important areas. In the course of this, he discusses the issue of the modernity or universality of the contemporary self and draws together the innovative ideas and findings which his studies have produced in different areas and which are already making an important contribution to current research. Simon's book is excellent both in providing a well-informed and coherent statement of what social psychologists know about the self and also in summarizing his own extensive programme of original research in terms of its key insights and findings.

Why does the self matter? In one sense the answer seems obvious, but in another, deeper, way the answer, I think, is still controversial. The self is a human universal. It is an undisputed given of human experience and life. It is found in all phenomena of human consciousness, feeling and action. We find it in the large scale, in the march of history and culture, in past and present arguments about the definition of our species, in conflicts between social groups, and we find it in the intimate, subjective and personal, in the deepest recesses of mental functioning. It is not possible to have a human mind, let alone be human, without self-awareness and without some identity (or identities) of which to be aware. It seems likely (I would say beyond doubt) that the human self-process is biologically distinctive, being more complex cognitively and socially than that of other animals. Self and identity, therefore, are not matters of idle philosophical speculation. They are central to the scientific problem of how the human mind works. They are central to the issue of the relationship between human psychology and society, to the question of whether and in what way the mind has a social nature.

These questions – how the mind works and how it is affected by society – are linked precisely because of the nature of the self-process. This is one of the things, one of the most important things, we have learned from a century of social psychology. In looking at and trying to make sense of psychological functioning in its natural social context we keep finding the self. There is probably not one idea, finding or theory in social psychology which is not related to the self in one way or another, covertly if not overtly, indirectly if not directly, at first or second remove if not immediately. It does not matter whether one ponders attitudes and attitude change, crowd behaviour, group processes, prejudice and intergroup relations, social cognition, social justice or personal relationships, there is no way to summarize or explain what we have discovered about these phenomena without invoking the self-process in one or more of its varying guises. Attitudes, values, norms, goals, motives, memories, emotions, intentions, attributions, commitment, beliefs, decisions, expectations, justifications, and so on and so forth, are all terms for describing mental structures or processes which involve the self. Social psychologists may not have set out to study the self – and indeed we know that there were those who for metatheoretical reasons sought determinedly to do without it – but the simple fact is that in seeking to unravel the interplay of psychology and social life all roads have led back to self. It has gradually become clear from decades of research and hard-won theory that it is 'self', not 'attitude', which is our indispensable concept. Understanding the way in which it works to connect the individual and the situation, the way in which it functions as a dynamic principle of psychological activity, transforming the psychological by means of the social, the way in which it translates social structure, products, relationships and place into psychological resources, perspectives and activities, is probably the defining task of our science. Slowly but surely the self has moved to the theoretical core of social psychology.

This does not mean that the science is awash with theories of the self or that it is explicitly addressed in the bulk of research. There is no doubt that there has been great progress in the past 30 years – this book is a witness to it. There are now well-developed and influential theories, a high level of research activity directed specifically to understanding the self, and ideas about the self are shaping the mainstream of the subject. But there is still an historically, ideologically and philosophically derived tendency to downgrade the importance of the self, to underestimate its centrality, to take it for granted in a way that dulls curiosity. Outside of social psychology there are still scientists and philosophers trying to build models of the human mind as if individuals were self-free computing or neurological systems functioning in a social vacuum. Inside social psychology, important phenomena are often discussed without any consideration of how they might relate to different views of the self. It is as if the researchers have never examined their assumptions about the nature of self, as if everybody already knows and agrees about the nature of the self, and of course, ideologically speaking, this can often be true. The self is sufficiently important that in one sense it has to be taken for granted, to be made a receptacle for the myths and prejudices of the dominant cultural and political understanding of human nature.

But good science is critical science and progress in understanding is marked by the clash between the scientifically new and the culturally orthodox. Amongst other things, Bernd Simon's book records the progress social psychology has made in rejecting some of the key myths about the self that have dominated psychology in the past and are still influential in social psychology and other fields. The 'axis of evil' in this regard is individualism, reification and reductionism.

In broad terms, individualism here means the tendency to define the self as a unique, purely individual property of the person, the idea that it is about one's personal identity as an 'I' or a 'me' (rather than one's shared collective identities) and that it is defined by or closely related to one's personality traits or other individual-difference factors. The alternative view deriving from self-categorization theory is that there are many levels of self-categorization (from the intra-personal to the individual to the group and collective levels), of which personal identity is only one, and that group selves are not idiosyncratic but shared and normative, constructed *inter alia* through social interaction and influence.

Reification is the tendency to define the self as a thing, a mental entity stored in the cognitive system, rather than as a dynamic social psychological process. In perceiving how individuals and groups behave in particular situations we abstract summary judgements from our descriptions which we then unjustifiably transform into underlying causal principles; these principles in turn are transmogrified into fixed psychological structures which supposedly cause the behaviour from which they were inferred. Thus we think of the self as a relatively stable and fixed system of cognitive structures somehow and somewhere stored in memory which causes the experience of self when somehow and somewhere 'activated'. What is self? It is a mental system, a mental homunculus, which we call 'self'. This attempt at explanation is wonderfully elastic and satisfying, since every self-response can be traced back to a stored self-structure, but unfortunately it is completely circular.

Even worse, it complicates the task of investigation by directing theory away from the idea of complex dynamic principles into the dead-end of Aristotelian 'essences' (as was pointed out by Kurt Lewin in the 1930s). The self is not a fixed thing; it is a complex social psychological process defined above all by a functional rather than a structural property, that is, reflexivity.

Reductionism here is the tendency to seek to reduce the self-process to the functioning of simpler, more elementary processes. It is in particular the tendency to deny that something special, new and qualitatively different emerges in human mental functioning and social life because of the way in which the self connects the psychological and the social. Individualism and reification are both examples of reductionism and go with it in this context. We see human beings solely as individuals, the content of whose selves is fixed and given in some pre-social essence. We act supposedly on the basis of our self-interest, our motives, drives, traits, likes, dislikes, needs, fears etc., as if these were fixed in our character independent of and prior to social inter-action. Rather than explore or think about the interplay between our personal and collective selves, about how, for example, political ideologies and the position of one's group in the social structure create, sustain and influence people's personality traits through shaping their contemporary self-identities, the pervasive fashion is to reify the traits into fixed psychological structures and allude vaguely to socialization, genetics or even evolution to account for their origin and deny their sensitivity to current social forces (see Turner & Reynolds, in press). We fail to see that individuality is socially structured through the self, not pre-social, not prior to self. To allude to socialization, genetics and evolution to avoid confronting the complexity and malleability of the human self is inevitably to push a reductionist view of these phenomena as well as of psychology.

Social psychology has made a big contribution to the refutation of a reductionist view of the human mind. Four ideas about the self seem to me particularly important in this context. I shall express them in my own way and perhaps too cryptically, but they should still give the reader a good idea of why the self matters.

1. The self is the process by which individual psychology is socialized, by which individual psychology and society interact. Self-identities are social definitions of the perceiver (deriving from and produced by society, reflecting group memberships, social relationships and one's social place) which ensure that all cognitive, emotional, motivational and behavioural functioning take place from a socially defined vantage point and are regulated and mediated by socially produced anchor-points.
2. The adaptive flexibility of human behaviour, the capacity to vary what we think, see, do and feel from situation to situation in a way that is

reality-oriented, functional and appropriate, is made possible by our capacity to construct self-regulating self-identities in light of and on the basis of
changing social circumstances. The self shapes how we act and can react
and it is a dynamic, varying representation of the perceiver precisely
because it is a social representation of the perceiver. The variability,
heterogeneity and flux of social life are translated by the self into the
cognitive and behavioural flexibility of the perceiver.

3. Human psychology and social life are characterized by emergent processes
   and properties made possible by the functioning of the self and irreducible
   to principles unaffected by a self-process. For example, if I may refer to my
   own work, we know that psychological group formation transforms the
   mutual orientation of group members by enhancing the relative salience of
   a higher-order, shared social identity (a collective self) compared to individuals' personal identities and that the former makes possible qualitatively
   different social relationships and psychological capacities. Human tendencies to sympathy, empathy, trust, cooperation, altruism and so on follow
   from seeing self as other than purely personal and egoistic and from
   including others within a shared collective self. Egoistic theories of altruism
   and other pro-social orientations, theories with a much reduced view of the
   human self, only explain these phenomena by defining them out of existence. The self-process explains why human individuals are not purely
   'individualistic'.

4. The same self-process which enables humans to act as other than purely
   individual personalities is at the root of social influence processes which
   make possible the psychological reality of values. Human cognition is not
   purely individual, neutral, asocial, but takes place within a social field in
   which individuals always, implicitly or explicitly, test the validity of their
   beliefs against the views of others with whom they share a relevant social
   identity. The judgement of this collective self generates norms, rules, values
   and standards (of truth, correctness, virtue) whose validity is felt to be
   independent of the judgement of any individual perceiver. The collective
   self is therefore the basis of morality and perceived truth. What psychologists and non-psychologists alike refer to as 'self-esteem' is one psychological consequence of the functioning of social values in self-regulation. By
   means of the self, individual behaviour is compared to and shaped by
   internalised standards derived from group interaction.

In the following chapters Bernd Simon describes research which illustrates,
tests, qualifies and extends these and other important ideas about self and
identity. One of the great pleasures of this book is the effortlessness with which
Simon moves between general analysis and detailed experimental work.
Another is the fact that in one research topic after another he provides

compelling evidence for a perspective which contradicts received wisdom in the area. I think most attractive of all, however, is the way that thorough scholarship, excellent writing, imaginative theory and cutting-edge research are so seamlessly combined. One expects as much from someone who is immersed in and familiar with contemporary research on self and identity and who has already made original, important and influential contributions to the field, but it is a pleasure nevertheless.

John C. Turner
School of Psychology
Australian National University

Canberra, April 2003

REFERENCE

Turner, J. C. & Reynolds, K. J. (in press). Why social dominance theory has been falsified. *British Journal of Social Psychology*.

Preface

The writing of this book has been motivated by my intellectual fascination for identity which, I suspect, is not free from biographical roots. Since I know myself as a thinking being, I have been fascinated by the question of 'how the social gets into, and is in turn made possible by, the individual'. The dualism alluded to in this question may have an experiential basis – not least in my own biography – but I always sensed that it was more apparent than real. This book on identity is an interim report on my attempt both to answer this fascinating question and to overcome the dualism it seems to imply. I am sure I am not there yet, but at the same time I feel some progress has been made.

Writing this book, as well as conducting the research on which it draws, has been a breath-taking intellectual adventure for me which I would not have been able to undertake without the company and support of many people. I am indebted to my academic teachers Amélie Mummendey, Rupert Brown and Tom Pettigrew for suggesting and introducing me to a social psychological answer to my question. I may not have been always a faithful student of theirs, but I suspect I owe even this '*esprit de révolte*' to their wisdom. Tom Pettigrew deserves special thanks for reading the entire manuscript and for providing many helpful comments. John Turner and Penny Oakes also played invaluable roles in the process leading to this book. Without their ground-breaking work on self and identity (together with other admirable colleagues), their intellectual inspiration and sincere passion for science, I would have felt too lonely to write this book.

As is apparent from the publications cited in this book, most of the research on identity I was involved in during the last 15 years or so resulted from collaboration with others, among them Claudia Hastedt, Giuseppe Pantaleo, Michael Loewy, Claudia Kampmeier, Birgit Aufderheide, Stefan Stürmer, Markus Lücken and Ludger Klein. Most of them were my students, and over the years some of them became colleagues and even friends. I am grateful to all of them. I also wish to thank my colleague Rainer Mausfeld here at Kiel for suggesting interesting reading outside social psychology and for our hopefully continuing discussions about psychology and beyond. Maggie Ribeiro-Nelson deserves credit for proofreading the manuscript and Kristina Hauschildt for preparing the indexes.

Finally, I would like to express my very special thanks and love to Gilmar Iost, simply for everything. Please keep bringing cups of tea when I again slam the door because words are hiding from me while I try to write the next book!

Kiel, March 2003

Chapter 1

Introduction

Identity is fashionable. Everybody wants to have one, many promise to provide one. Lifestyle magazines advertise identities, fashion stores purport to sell them and pop psychology aspires to discover people's 'true' identities. It seems that interest in identity is particularly strong in our times, which are characterized by processes of accelerated modernization and globalization. For some of us, this interest is spurred by hopes, for others by fears. The former welcome or hope for an invigorating and playful 'anything goes' that liberates identity from the restrictions of tradition, the latter fear and caution against the anomie of 'nothing counts any more' that threatens to undermine the very essence of identity.

In any case, the general popularity of (the notion of) identity suggests that most people, irrespective of their hopes or fears, are fascinated by identity and what it does to and for themselves and others. For example, most of us would agree that identity is responsible for how we feel about ourselves and that a lack of identity or an identity crisis jeopardizes our well-being or even our physical existence. Also, identity is thought to underlie much, if not all, of our behaviour. Different people are thought to behave differently because they have different identities. We go to different buildings called churches, synagogues or mosques because we have different religious identities as Christians, Jews or Muslims. Alternatively, we may stay at home because we identify ourselves as atheists (or because as hedonists we are simply too tired to enact any religious identity after that wonderfully sinful party last night). Identity is also assumed to be at work in the soccer stadium when thousands of people in blue shirts try to scream louder than thousands of other people in red shirts. Similarly, but more dramatic in its consequences, identity is obviously involved when a majority group stigmatizes, mistreats or even annihilates a minority group. However, identity is also often praised for its socially desirable consequences. For example, it is difficult to imagine how loyalty, solidarity or social cooperation could be achieved and maintained without a sense of shared identity.

Hence, identity is not just a fashionable commodity that people strive to have or think they have to have; it is also intuitively very appealing as an explanatory concept. The present book respects this intuition as a fruitful starting-point, but aspires to go beyond popular thinking and discourse upon identity. The book is a more disciplined, scientific effort to employ the notion of identity as a social psychological concept in order to improve our understanding of the complexities and regularities of human experience and behaviour. Throughout this book, I use the notion of identity in a rather broad sense to cover also phenomena and processes which are often discussed elsewhere under the heading of 'self'. For the present purposes, the integrative potential of this broader use justifies the neglect of conceptual nuances and terminological traditions. However, where necessary, additional clarifications are added in subsequent chapters.

Approaching Identity as a Scientific Concept

Identity is a seductive concept. It can easily foster 'homuncular regression in our thinking' (G. Allport, 1968) in that we are easily at risk of reifying identity as an explanans (or independent variable). To avoid this fallacy, two measures are necessary, and hopefully, sufficient. First, we must also take into account the role of identity as an explanandum (or dependent variable). To understand the dual role of identity as both a social psychological explanans and a social psychological explanandum means to understand its role as a social psychological mediator in people's experiences and behaviours in the social world. Identity results from interaction in the social world and in turn guides interaction in the social world. This must not be misunderstood as logical circularity. Rather, it describes a causal chain in which identity serves as a critical mediating link (see figure 1.1). The assumption of such a mediating role of identity is the basic premise underlying the perspective developed in this book.

The second precautionary measure to avoid the homuncular fallacy is a more radical one. It prescribes that we need to entertain the possibility that

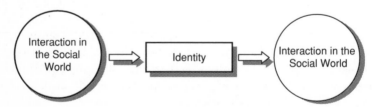

Figure 1.1 Identity as a social psychological mediator between input from and output in the social world.

identity could eventually turn out to be an analytic fiction. At best, the search for the essence of identity as a 'thing', say, in the form of a physiological or hard-wired mental structure, would then be a futile effort. But I fear worse. I suspect that such a search would be a misleading endeavour that diverts our efforts from a more promising *process-oriented* course. It may be convenient and common for lay persons, but not only for lay persons, to imbue identity with essentialistic meaning, but this tendency should itself be an object of scientific study and explanation (Medin & Ortony, 1989). It must not be reproduced in scientific discourse. This is not to say that systematic research on identity along the lines suggested in figure 1.1 is pointless. On the contrary, my conviction is that even if identity turns out to be an analytic fiction, it will prove to be a highly useful analytic fiction in the search for a better understanding of human experiences and behaviours. If used as a shorthand expression or placeholder for social psychological processes revolving around self-definition or self-interpretation, including the variable but systematic instantiations thereof, the notion of identity will serve the function of a powerful conceptual tool. It is the purpose of the subsequent chapters to demonstrate this power of identity by theoretical argument and empirical evidence. In addition to research conducted in controlled experimental settings, the chapters also build on research conducted in a variety of different field contexts of high social relevance, including minority–majority relations, intercultural encounters and contexts of socio-political mobilization and participation, in order to underline the ecological importance of the proposed identity processes.

Identity is a multifaceted phenomenon. Accordingly, it has attracted the interest of scholars from a wide spectrum of scientific disciplines. This spectrum includes, *inter alia*, philosophy (e.g. Flanagan, 1994; Popper & Eccles, 1977; Strawson, 1997), anthropology and cultural studies (e.g. Hall, 1992; Holland et al., 1998), political science (e.g. Preston, 1997), sociology (e.g. Stryker & Statham, 1985) and psychology (e.g. Baumeister, 1986; Turner et al., 1987; for overviews, see also Ashmore & Jussim, 1997; Hoyle et al., 1999). This book presents a social psychological approach to identity. It is therefore rooted primarily in the fields of psychology and sociology, whose major contributions to the social psychological analysis of identity are discussed in detail in the next chapter. At the same time, the particular approach presented in this book has also been informed and enriched in important ways by insights I gathered from the other disciplines indicated above. However, because I can by no means claim to be an expert in those disciplines, their influences are necessarily selective and I have most likely underused their potential contributions. In many cases, I would be unable even to pinpoint clearly the respective influences and correctly trace their sources because they have slowly built or bubbled up over many years of my scattered reading of

the relevant literature. I will therefore refrain from any archaeological endeavour to rediscover these influences.

In the remainder of this chapter I will instead delineate the wider multidisciplinary context of my scientific inquiry into identity. More specifically, I
will discuss two important issues which can be thought of as markers pointing
to two different poles of the wider spectrum of scientific disciplines contributing to the study of identity. These issues are (a) human consciousness and (b)
the social conditions of human existence. The former points to the contributions to the study of identity made by philosophy, and more recently cognitive
neuroscience, with their focus on intrapersonal processes, while the latter
points to the contributions of anthropological and cultural studies, with their
focus on the social relations between people or groups of people and the
broader social processes affecting those relations. The following discussion
reflects my understanding of these disciplines' promising attempts to illuminate the issues of human consciousness and the social conditions of human
existence. Although I concede that the respective insights probably allow for a
variety of different social psychological approaches to identity, I believe that
no such approach should build on premises that ignore these insights. I
certainly accepted the latter as important guidelines for the development of
my own approach to identity.

Human Consciousness

Streamlike consciousness

Building on James (1890/1950), Flanagan (1994) suggests that the master
metaphor that helps us to understand human consciousness is that of a stream:
'all individual consciousnesses are streamlike' (p. 155). This metaphor is meant
to capture the phenomenology of human consciousness, that is, how consciousness seems or feels from the first-person point of view. It is not meant to
imply that the physiological and brain processes that underlie consciousness
are also streamlike. Nor is the suggestion that consciousness has a subjective
streamlike character at odds with the reasonable assumption of special purpose processors and parallel mental processing (e.g. Calvin, 1990; Johnson-
Laird, 1988). In an objective sense, consciousness may well be less streamlike
and more 'gappy' than its phenomenology suggests (Dennett, 1991), but the
phenomenology or subjective side of consciousness remains an important
feature of human mental life in need of explanation. Moreover, as Flanagan
(1994, p. 170) points out, even if 'consciousness is in fact realized like a movie
reel consisting of individual images, the moments of consciousness, with small
separations between them, the gaps', . . . 'a continuous impression may well

be what the system is designed to do'. Thus, rather than being an obstacle to scientific progress, attention to the streamlike phenomenology of consciousness is likely to contribute to an adequate specification of the explanandum and eventually to a full understanding of human consciousness.

It is the phenomenology of human consciousness that should concern us here because the subjective streamlike quality of consciousness seems to play an important role in grounding a person's sense of self or identity (Erikson, 1968; James, 1892/1961). Flanagan (1994) specifies several interrelated characteristics of the subjective stream of consciousness which facilitate such a role. First, consciousness and each thought in it are 'owned' because persons usually experience their experiences as their own. Although thoughts can be shared in the sense that they can be communicated and that similar thoughts can be thought in different minds, each person has to think his or her own thought and can experience only his or her own mental states and no one else's. Thereby consciousness supports the divide between self and non-self.

Second, although constantly in flux, consciousness feels continuous. From an objective point of view, our consciousness is constantly changing even over short intervals of time. We are always in a new state of mind characterized by a different neural pattern. However, from a subjective point of view, consciousness clearly seems continuous because 'even where there is a time-gap the consciousness after it feels as if it belonged together with the consciousness before it, as another part of the same self' and 'the changes from one moment to another in the quality of the consciousness are never absolutely abrupt' (James, 1890/1950, p. 237). From an objective point of view, consciousness may be interrupted by non-conscious periods such as periods of sleep. But, each normal consciousness bridges such gaps and reconnects to its past. As a subjective consequence, it feels unbroken and flows. In this connection, Flanagan (1994, p. 163) cautions us against confusing the contents of consciousness with consciousness itself. Of course, the latter is partly constituted by its contents, which are discrete and discontinuous. However, no qualitative contrast between different contents breaks the stream of consciousness. Every content of consciousness is embedded in consciousness itself. Even unexpected thunder becomes conscious as 'thunder-breaking-upon-silence-and-contrasting-with-it' (James, 1892/1961, p. 26). This unbroken flow of consciousness supports the subjective sense of self-continuity.

Finally, this flow reveals a third characteristic of the subjective stream of consciousness that helps to ground a person's sense of self or identity. In accordance with James (1892/1961), Flanagan (1994) reminds us that we should not focus exclusively on the contents or 'substantive resting places' of consciousness. Instead, closer examination of the transitory flow of consciousness reveals 'the "penumbra," the "fringe," the "halo of relations" that is carried in the flow and is partly constitutive of the substantive state, that frames or washes over the contents of consciousness' (Flanagan, 1994, pp. 163–4). The notion of the fringe of consciousness is meant to capture the idiosyncratic or unique character of a person's conscious stream which impregnates and is then carried on by every substantive state or thought that flows in it. The fringe reflects past experiences and guides expectations about the future. It provides people with differential routes and readiness to arrive at certain experiences. Along with the two other characteristics of human consciousness (i.e. consciousness as owned and continuous), the unique fringe of each consciousness supports the divide between self and non-self as well as the subjective sense of self-continuity. More specifically, it further strengthens the foundations of a person's identity in that it furnishes the divide between self and non-self with the experience of distinctiveness of self and adds the experience of sameness to the subjective sense of self-continuity.

The 'Me' and the 'I'

Kant (1781/1997) introduced the distinction between self as object or the empirical self and self as subject or the pure ego which was further pursued by Schopenhauer (1819/1995) as the distinction between 'the known' or content of self-consciousness and 'the knower' who as such cannot be known (see Viney, 1969). A similar distinction was made by James (1890/1950) between the empirical self or 'Me' and the pure ego or 'I'. His approach had a particularly strong influence on psychological theorizing and research on the self and identity (G. Allport, 1961, 1968). More specifically, James (1890/1950) further divided the empirical self or 'Me' into the material self, the social self and the spiritual self. The material self centres on the body as its core, but it is usually extended to include also one's family (e.g. mother, father, spouse and children) as well as important places and possessions (e.g. one's home). The social self reflects one's ties with various groups of people and the recognition one gets from them. According to James (1890/1950), 'we have an innate propensity to get ourselves noticed, and noticed favorably, by our kind' (p. 293) so that '*a man has as many social selves as there are individuals who recognize him* and carry an image of him in their mind' (p. 294, emphasis in the original). Furthermore, 'as the individuals who carry the images fall naturally into classes, we may practically say that he has as many different social selves as there are distinct *groups* of persons about whose opinion he cares' (James, 1890/1950, p. 294, emphasis in the original). The spiritual self refers to 'a man's inner or subjective being, his psychic faculties or dispositions, taken concretely' (James, 1890/1950, p. 296). It becomes visible when we think of 'our ability to argue and discriminate, of our moral sensibility and conscience, of our indomitable will' (James, 1890/1950, p. 296). The experience of the spiritual self thus derives from a reflective process, from thinking of subjectivity as such, from thinking about ourselves as thinkers. However, once the spiritual self is turned into its active mode, it no longer belongs to the empirical self or 'Me', but has become the pure ego or 'I' (Flanagan, 1994, p. 181).

It is tempting to postulate a pure ego or a mind's 'I' that, as the cognizing self or knower, is separable from and transcends the known, that is, the empirical self or 'Me'. Some philosophers, including Kant and Schopenhauer (see Viney, 1969), adopted this position. Similarly, psychologists like G. Allport (1961, 1968) argued that the 'I' as the knower should be sharply segregated from the 'Me' as the known because, unlike the 'Me', the 'I' cannot be an object of direct knowledge (see also Markus & Wurf, 1987, p. 314). In fact, G. Allport (1961, 1968) suggested a radical surgery, claiming the problem of the 'Me' for psychology while consigning the problem of the 'I' to philosophy.

Conversely, the philosopher and psychologist James (1890/1950) argued against the separation of the 'I' and 'Me', though not necessarily against an analytic distinction between the two. He rejected both the substantialist view of the 'I' (or soul) that he ascribed to Plato and Aristotle as well as to Hobbes, Descartes, Locke, Leibnitz, Wolf and Berkeley and the transcendental view proposed by Kant. For James, the words 'I' and 'Me' are grammatical constructions designed to indicate and emphasize different interpretations of the same stream of consciousness, namely interpretations either as thinker or as thought about oneself. In the final analysis, however, these interpretations would be inseparable because 'thought is itself the thinker' (James, 1890/1950, p. 401). Thoughts are the thinkers because current thoughts, including thoughts about oneself, are appropriative of past thoughts, which make themselves felt on the fringe or in the penumbra of consciousness, and consti-tutive of future thoughts. Thereby, unity in and between thought and thinking is found and fashioned. Flanagan (1994) shares and elaborates on this view. In particular, he sees no need to postulate a separate mind's 'I' that presides over or stands behind the objective person experienced as 'Me' because 'what there is, and all there is, is the stream of experience' (Flanagan, 1994, p. 178). It is the whole human organism with its functional nervous system and the organ-ism's active involvement with the external world that enables and guides the stream of experience from which the self emerges as experience accrues. The organically connected mental life of human beings includes the capacity for self-representation and self-interpretation, both in the active agent mode and in the passive object mode (i.e. both as thinker and thought). This is also an attractive view for psychologists. It fits in with the interactionist meta-theoretical assumption, widely shared in the field of psychology, according to which psychological phenomena can be understood as a joint function of the personal organism's mind and its environment.

Activity and self-control

Like James (1890/1950) and Flanagan (1994), Popper (Popper & Eccles, 1977, especially pp. 100–209) rejects the transcendental view of a pure ego and is critical of the notion of unique psychical substances or matters (e.g. air as 'soul-stuff' as in Greek philosophy; see Popper & Eccles, p. 160). In addition, there exist several other similarities between Popper's analysis and the positions of James and Flanagan. For instance, Popper suggests that 'being a self is partly the result of inborn dispositions and partly the result of experience, especially social experience' (p. 111). He also acknowledges the psychophysical nature of self and consciousness as well as the phenomenological or *experienced* quality of self as an essence or 'quasi essence' (see also Strawson, 1997), while, again like James and Flanagan, he successfully avoids falling prey to homuncular regression and essentialistic thinking. Moreover, Popper advocates a process-oriented view that partly overlaps with James's (1890/1950) metaphor of consciousness as a stream.

However, the same stream metaphor is also a bone of contention. Popper sharply criticizes James's (1890/1950) notion of streamlike consciousness because, in Popper's opinion, it suggests passivity instead of activity. Hence, he wants to see it replaced by the metaphor of the self as 'the active programmer to the brain (which is the computer)', as 'the executant whose instrument is the brain', whereas '[t]he mind is, as Plato said, the pilot' (Popper & Eccles, 1977, p. 120).

Activity and self-control are indeed important characteristics and powers of the human organism and its mind (see also G. Allport, 1968), but, as Flanagan (1994) has argued convincingly, they are by no means incompatible with James's notion of streamlike consciousness. Two quotes, one from Popper and one from James, may help to illustrate that the gap between the two positions is in reality not too wide. Popper posits:

> Our mind . . . is never a mere 'stream of consciousness', a stream of experiences. Rather, our active attention is focussed at every moment on just the relevant aspects of the situation, selected and abstracted by our perceiving apparatus, into which a selection programme is incorporated; a programme which is adjusted to our available repertoire of behavioural responses.
>
> *(Popper & Eccles, 1977, p. 128)*

Similarly, James was convinced that the personal conscious stream enables flexible action and adaptive responses in novel situations by loading the dice in favour of the stream's owner:

Loading its dice would mean bringing a more or less constant pressure to bear in favor of *those* of its performances which make for the most permanent interests of the brain's owner; it would mean a constant inhibition of the tendencies to stray aside. Well, just such pressure and such inhibition are what consciousness *seems* to be exerting all the while. And the interests in whose favor it seems to exert them are *its* interests and its alone, interests which it *creates* . . . Every actually existing consciousness seems to itself at any rate to be a *fighter for ends*, of which many, but for its presence, would not be ends at all.

(James, 1890/1950, pp. 140–1, emphasis in the original)

Thus streamlike consciousness enables and supports useful and interest-guided activity such as distributing attention, planning or goal setting. The stream of consciousness does not condemn us to passivity, as Popper fears, but invites and encourages activity, as Popper demands, because it is never a *mere* stream of consciousness, but one that has evolved with a function. Its function is to fight for the system that houses it. Consciousness may not be involved in all of the system's fights, nor may it be involved in a given fight all the time. However, many important fights require consciousness, at least at certain stages. Then, action is often initiated and self-control executed by entering certain representations of self or identities into the stream of consciousness and thus into the motivational and regulatory circuit (Flanagan, 1994). This view is fully in line with the premise underlying this book, and summarized in figure 1.1, that identity plays an important mediating role in people's experiences and behaviours.

The idea that identities can enter into the motivational and regulatory circuits allows for a parsimonious view of self-control that does not require us to postulate a separate *centre* of control. Thus, Flanagan (1994, p. 189) doubts that 'mind *must* have a control center and that the conscious self must be *the* control center in the mind' (emphasis in the original). According to his alternative centreless view, 'conscious experience emerges seriatim, in a streamlike fashion, because the recurrent network of parallel processors declares one winner at a time in the competition among all its tracks' (Flanagan, 1994, p. 191). In other words, a specific identity that enters into the motivational and regulatory circuit and consequently has motivational bearing and behavioural effects is only one of a person's many possible identities. However, it is the one that has currently been elected by the brain, in interaction with the environment, to take the driver's seat and therefore also the likely 'center of narrative gravity' (Dennett, 1989, 1991). While in the driver's seat the particular identity is expressed, but it is also responsive to new experiences which may eventually lead to its replacement by another identity and the opening of another chapter in the narrative about oneself.

Consciousness, identities and narratives

All experiences that enter into my stream of consciousness are subjective experiences because they involve some sense of awareness that they are *my* experiences, happen to *me*, occur in *my* stream and relate to *my* personal existence, but they are not necessarily accompanied by an 'I think that . . . ' thought. When my experiences are not accompanied by this thought, I am, according to Flanagan (1994, pp. 193–5), self-conscious in a weak sense, whereas when I am also very well aware of the fact that it is *I* who is doing the thinking I am, according to Flanagan, self-conscious in a strong sense. Interestingly, it seems to me that both the weak and the strong form of self-consciousness involve, at least in a weak sense, identity experiences because both the experienced 'mine-ness' of the thought and the experience of myself as thinker have to be anchored in some kind of self-representation or self-interpretation. Note that this should be true even when *my* thought, in the case of weak self-consciousness, or what *I* think, in the case of strong self-consciousness, is not directly about myself.

However, as argued above, identities can and also often do enter directly into the stream of consciousness. This should then result in identity experiences in a strong sense. Such strong identity experiences combined with weak self-consciousness (i.e. when I think about myself without explicit awareness that I think this thought) should play a rather efficacious mediating role in the motivational and regulatory circuits, whereas strong identity experiences combined with strong self-consciousness (i.e. when I am acutely aware that I think this thought about myself) may be too intrusive or overly self-absorbing for efficacious planning and (self-)regulation. At the same time, the combination of strong identity experiences with strong self-consciousness should be a very likely cause and consequence of extended soliloquies or dialogues with others, during and through which we attempt to construct coherent and comprehensive narratives about ourselves. Such narratives seem to follow a 'one self to a customer' principle, taught and practised since earliest childhood, in order to bind together the variety of our identities that typically emerge from interaction with(in) our heterogeneous environment (Dennett, 1989; Flanagan, 1994).

The Social Conditions of Human Existence

Sociality and sociability

For most of the 80,000 to 120,000 years of their history as a biological species, humans (*homo sapiens sapiens*) lived together in bands of about 30 to 100 members who shared a habitat (Barchas, 1986; Diamond, 1992). The small group served as a basic survival medium which facilitated the production of the means of life as well as reproduction of human life (Caporael, 2001; Tice & Baumeister, 2001). Having a collective place as a group as well as one's own individual place in the group was and still is crucial for survival. Like other social animals, people could not exist as isolated individuals because survival, both as a species and as an individual, requires coordinated and often cooperative action.

As a consequence, the evolutionary past has conditioned human existence to be social in at least two fundamental respects. First, humans are social in that they are dependent on each other for physical and psychical well-being or even survival. Second, they are social, or more precisely, sociable in that they are able to initiate and maintain functional relationships with each other (Esser, 1993; see also Campbell, 1985; Harris, 1987). Human sociality and human sociability are thus complementary conditions of human existence. The former constitutes the problem or challenge of human existence, while the latter is (part of) the solution to this problem or challenge. Human sociality is most obvious in the prolonged and marked dependence of the human child on its social environment, but also manifests itself throughout our entire life because the lack of genetic determination makes effective self-regulation dependent on social mechanisms, such as social norms and social validation. Human sociability builds on important abilities, such as the ability to engage in symbolic communication (language) and mutual perspective taking, which in turn make the development and participation in social mechanisms of self-regulation possible.

It should be noted that the complementary relation of sociality and sociability does not imply that human relationships are necessarily harmonious. As humans, we are fundamentally dependent on each other, but we have by no means identical interests. However, our sociality requires us, and our sociability enables us, to pursue our different, or even opposite, interests in and through networks of both positive and negative interdependencies. In fact, owing to the scarcity of many valuable resources, human interaction often takes the form of 'antagonistic cooperation' (Esser, 1993). Although there is competition for scarce resources among people, a single person is rarely in the position to get access to such resources without the support of others. Hence, we also need to take the interests of others into account and to cooperate with them on some level. The success of such cooperation crucially depends on the availability of social mechanisms of self-regulation, and it is the task or function of social organizations and their institutions to make these social mechanisms available and thus to sustain social order. Society is usually ascribed this role as it is considered the ultimate frame in which social order is constituted.

Required by their sociality and afforded by their sociability, humans are thus bound together by relationships of interdependence. These relationships exist at different levels of social inclusiveness engaging the entire spectrum of social entities, ranging from dyads (e.g. husband–wife relationships) through social groups and categories (e.g. ethnic, religious or national groups) to supranational associations (e.g. European Union) or other superordinate units (e.g. entire cultures). It is the involvement in such relationships and the associated positions and perspectives that make people social and from which their identities emerge (Mead, 1934/1993). Any truly social analysis of people's identities must take this into account. Moreover, the way in which their relationships are organized and interpreted reflects and affects people's identities. The remainder of this chapter therefore revolves around the discussion of recent social and cultural developments that have important implications for the organization and interpretation of human relationships and thus for (the analysis of) identity in modern society. The next section starts this discussion with a brief overview of prominent conceptions of identity that have been put forward in response to these developments.

The social and cultural context of understanding identity

In a review of modern concepts of identity, Hall (1992) suggests that modernity is associated with three very different conceptions of identity: the identity of the 'Enlightenment subject', the identity of the 'sociological subject', and that of the 'post-modern subject'. According to Hall (1992, p. 275), the identity of the Enlightenment subject was conceptualized as the essence of a 'fully centred, unified individual, endowed with the capacities of reason, consciousness and action, whose "centre" consisted of an inner core which first emerged when the subject was born, and unfolded with it, while remaining essentially the same – continuous or "identical" with itself – throughout the individual's existence'. However, the growing complexity of the modern world precipitated a different conception of identity, one that placed greater emphasis on the interactive nature of identity. Hence, the identity of the sociological subject was construed as one that revolved around the interaction between individual and society. This identity was able to mediate the individual's active exchange with her social environment as well as her acceptance or internalization of socially significant meanings and values which made her part of society (see also chapter 2). Hall (1992, p. 276) emphasizes that this conception of identity still assumes an inner core or essence, but one that is 'formed and modified in a continuous dialogue with the cultural worlds "outside" and the identities which they offer'. Finally, as the result of further structural and cultural changes in late-modernity, the postmodern subject was postulated who no longer possesses a single essential identity that serves as *the* centre of the individual. Instead, the postmodern subject is conceptualized as being fragmented and her identity as permanently shifting, as one that is 'formed and transformed continuously in relation to the ways we are represented or addressed in the cultural systems which surround us' (Hall, 1992, p. 277).

The view that in (post)modern society identity no longer serves as *the* centre of the individual, but possesses a high degree of multiplicity, variability and flexibility, has also informed the integrative approach to identity presented in this book, although not without qualifications (e.g. concerning the social psychological adequacy of the postmodernist interpretation of identity as 'depthless' identity; see chapter 3). This de-centring view has emerged from several strands of modern thought and social theory. More specifically, Hall (1992) discusses five major perspectives and the corresponding advances in modern thought and social theory that represent important steps towards the de-centring view. The first four perspectives are associated with the works of Karl Marx, Sigmund Freud, Ferdinand de Saussure and Michel Foucault, respectively, while the fifth is closely related to feminism. Let me briefly summarize the critical features of each of the five perspectives and the associated advances in modern thought and social theory (for further details, see Hall, 1992, pp. 285–91).

First, Marx's writings and the rediscovery of his work, especially in the 1960s, was a forceful blow to the 'Enlightenment' view that each individual is endowed with an essential identity as her inner centre. Marx's alternative position was that 'the human essence is no abstraction inherent in each single individual', but '[i]n its reality it is the ensemble of the social relations' (Marx & Engels, 1978, p. 145). Consequently, '[i]t is not the consciousness of men that determines their being, but, on the contrary, their social being that determines their consciousness' (Marx & Engels, 1978, p. 4). Questioning the existence of an essential identity centre, inherent in each individual, also led to an important qualification of the notion of individual agency because now the socio-historical circumstances were entered into the equation:

> Men make their own history, but they do not make it just as they please; they do not make it under circumstances chosen by themselves, but under circumstances directly found, given and transmitted from the past.
>
> ***(Marx & Engels, 1978, p. 595)***

Second, Freud's 'discovery' of the unconscious challenged the notion of identity as the fixed and stable centre of the rational individual. Freudian and post-Freudian thinkers emphasize that identity is formed dynamically in relation to others and, more specifically, that it emerges from an ongoing learning process which involves complex unconscious psychic negotiations

between the individual and the powerful fantasies she has of important others.
Parental figures play a key role, especially in early phases of the process of
identity formation (i.e. during childhood). However, the search for identity
continues throughout adult life and is critically affected by contradictory and
unresolved feelings experienced during childhood, such as the splitting of love
and hate for the father, the conflict between the wish to please and the impulse
to reject the mother or the compartmentalization of one's good and bad parts.
Owing to these persisting difficulties and unresolved issues, identity never
actually reaches a state of complete unity. Instead, it is always in the process
of formation, driven by and striving towards a fantasized image of unity.

The third perspective with important de-centring implications for the
theorizing about identity revolves around the role of language in identity
construction and is associated with the work of the structural linguist
Ferdinand de Saussure. This perspective emphasizes that language is indispensable to identity formation and identity expression, but also that language
is a social system that pre-exists the individual. Words and their meanings are
not private property, but belong to entire language and cultural communities.
Statements always carry echoes and trigger off meanings above and beyond
those intended by the speaker. Hence, identity cannot be formed or expressed
without participation in more inclusive language communities, and just as we
are never the sole authors of our statements, so identities are never our
isolated, innermost centres, of which we are the sole owners. And our attempts
to create fixed and stable identities are subverted in the same way in which the
meanings of words and statements slip away from us.

Fourth, the work of Michel Foucault had important de-centring effects
because it revealed the role of disciplinary regimes or institutions in the
process of individualization and identity construction. Large-scale collective
institutions, such as schools, workshops, hospitals, barracks or prisons, exert
disciplinary power assisting the regulation and surveillance of the individual
and the body as well as the government of entire populations. The actual aim
of disciplinary power is stricter discipline and control, but, quite paradoxically,
the organized nature of the institutions, their meticulous documentary appar-
atuses and the ensuing accumulation of individual documentation also
contribute to greater individualization and the construction of specific identities. Thus, there is again a crucial shift in the conception of identity because
important roots of identity are now relocated away from the centre of the
individual into the outside world and its institutions.

Finally, Hall (1992) lists feminism as another step towards the de-centring
view of identity. Alongside other new social movements (e.g. the civil-rights
movement or the peace movement), feminism, as a theoretical critique and a
social movement, fostered and reflected the break-up of traditional (class)
politics and its fragmentation into or replacement by identity politics. More

specifically, questioning the classic distinction between 'private' and 'public', feminism politicized subjectivity and identity ('the personal is political') and thus pushed identity out of the private centre of the individual into the political arena.

In conclusion, by emphasizing different social dimensions or social mechanisms (i.e. socio-historical circumstances, unconscious learning and socialization processes, language, disciplinary power of institutions and the politicization of subjectivity), all five perspectives have contributed to a novel interpretation of the social conditions of modern human existence which has important de-centring implications for the understanding of the individual and her identity. As successful intellectual, and often also political, enterprises, they had, and still have, a major impact on the identity discourse and on identity politics in modern society, and possibly on the very construction of identity as well (Sampson, 1993). In this sense, they have in fact become components of the more comprehensive cultural or political-cultural identity (or identities) of modern society itself (see also Preston, 1997).

Nation, culture and globalization

In the modern world, the nation into which a person is born is an important source of her identity (Assmann, 1994; Billig, 1995; Habermas, 1992; Hall, 1992; Wimmer, 2002). National belonging affects identity because it gives access to a national culture which is 'a way of constructing meanings which influences and organizes both our actions and our conception of ourselves' (Hall, 1992, pp. 292–3). Although 'objective' criteria, such as language, religion or geography, play a role in the definition of nation and national culture, nations are in an important sense also 'imagined communities' (Anderson, 1983). That is, the boundaries between nations do not necessarily converge with the boundaries of language, religion or geography. Instead, national boundaries and national essences are typically 'imagined' in the sense that they are social constructions (with very real consequences, to be sure) which involve, *inter alia*, the naturalization of the nation as a primordial and pure community, foundational myths and the invention of traditions, symbols and rituals (Hall, 1992; Hobsbawm & Ranger, 1983). To ensure a nation's imagined singularity, history and the specific national narrative are constantly revised in a social process during which different elites or interest groups compete for social influence, trying to 'sell' their own version of the nation and its culture and thus to affect the identity of all members of the imagined national community (Dekker, Helsloot & Wijers, 2000).

However, despite their close interrelation, nation and culture should not be equated with each other. Although it is widely acknowledged that the modern nation functions as an important institutional and cultural frame (e.g. Assmann, 1994; Billig, 1995; Habermas, 1992; Hall, 1992; Wimmer, 2002), culture is often also construed in a broader sense that transcends national boundaries (see also Popper's notion of World 3 in Popper & Eccles, 1977, p. 359). For example, Preston (1997) identifies three key areas or regions within the global system that seem to provide their inhabitants with a distinct cultural and political background (see also Huntington, 1996). Two of these regions clearly transcend national boundaries, while all three of them are economically rooted in industrial capitalism. These regions are the European Union, Pacific Asia and the USA. For each of them, Preston (1997, pp. 13–15) suggests a list of characteristic political and cultural elements. These are, for the European Union: 'a political economy in which state and market interact, with the state having a directive role; a social-institutional structure which affirms an idea of the importance of community, and sees economy and polity acknowledging the important role of the community; and a cultural tradition which acknowledges established institutions, a broad humanist social philosophy and a tradition of social-democratic or Christian-democratic welfare politics'. The key elements for the Pacific Asian region are: 'the economy is state directed; state direction is top-down style and pervasive in its reach; society is familial and thereafter communitarian (thus society is non-individualistic); social order is secured by pervasive control machineries (sets of social rules and an extensive bureaucratization of everyday life) and a related hegemonic common culture (which enjoins submission to the demands of community and authority); and political debate and power is typically reserved to an élite sphere (and political life centres on the pragmatic pursuit of overarching economic goals)'. The key elements for the US region are: 'a public commitment to an open market economy; a public commitment to republican democracy; and a strong preference for individualism, a tradition which celebrates the achievements of ordinary people and a cultural tradition of liberal individualism'.[1] Because there is no one-to-one relation between culture and nation in the modern world, the concept of culture requires a separate definition. Although the reference to society in the following definition given by Triandis (1989) is reminiscent of the close relationship between culture and nation (or nation-state), this definition is sufficiently flexible to allow also for the specification of different cultures above (and below) the national level of inclusiveness:

> Culture is to society what memory is to the person. It specifies designs for living that have proven effective in the past, ways of dealing with social situations, and ways to think about the self and social behavior that have been reinforced in the past. It includes systems of symbols that facilitate interaction . . . , rules of the game of life that have been shown to 'work' in the past. When a person is

socialized in a given culture, the person can use custom as a substitute for thought, and save time.

(Triandis, 1989; pp. 511–12)

To further specify different cultures, two constructs have become very popular, especially in psychology, namely the notions of collectivism and individualism (e.g. Cousins, 1989; Hofstede, 1980; Markus & Kitayama, 1991; Triandis, 1989, 1990, 1995; Triandis et al., 1988). Key elements typically ascribed to collectivism are subordination of individual goals to group goals (or the equation of the former with the latter) and achievement aimed at improving the position of one's group, whereas primacy of individual goals and achievement aimed at improving one's own position as an individual are usually considered key elements of individualism. However, cross-cultural research has revealed considerable ambiguity and complexity around the collectivism–individualism distinction (e.g. concerning its dimensional structure), so that an undifferentiated and static classification of nations or transnational regions into individualistic and collectivist cultures appears highly problematic (e.g. Triandis et al., 1988).

Globalization further undermines the alleged cultural unity of nations and sets additional limits to the usefulness of a collectivist–individualist classification. Cutting across national boundaries, globalization processes result in 'integrating and connecting communities and organizations in new space–time combinations, making the world in reality and in experience more interconnected' (Hall, 1992, p. 299). As a result, cultural ties and allegiances above and below the level of the nation are strengthened. That is, transnational cultural zones emerge (e.g. Preston, 1997), and in a particular nation, more and more people live in 'cultures of hybridity' regarding language, religion, custom, traditions etc. (Hall, 1992, p. 310; see also Giddens, 1990, 1991; Harvey, 1989; McGrew, 1992). This is the complex cultural context in which identity in modern society takes shape (Chryssochoou, 2000).

A Brief Overview of Subsequent Chapters

The following chapter discusses the major contributions of sociology and psychology to the social psychological analysis of identity. With regard to sociological contributions, the focus is on symbolic interactionism, role theory and identity theory. With regard to psychological contributions, a distinction is made between 'North-American' and 'European' approaches, with the social cognition perspective as the leading paradigm of the former and the social identity or self-categorization perspective as the leading paradigm of the latter.

Chapter 3 then provides the theoretical foundation for the subsequent chapters. It introduces an integrative social psychological approach to identity that revolves around a self-aspect model. Here the distinction between individual and collective identities is elaborated as well as their relationship and respective conditions in (post)modern society. This chapter also includes a discussion of major functions and processes of identity.

Chapter 4 is a review of research guided by the self-aspect model of identity (SAMI) on important antecedents or sources of individual and collective identity. Research is presented that examines the role of various person and social context variables as well as the dynamic interplay between individual and collective identities in modern society.

Chapter 5 focuses on identity in the context of minority–majority relations. More specifically, it discusses the consequences of minority and majority membership for self-interpretation, social information processing, well-being and (discriminatory) intergroup behaviour. Although the discussion starts from a numerical definition of minority and majority membership, status and power asymmetries are considered as well.

Chapter 6 deals with identity in intercultural contact. It first provides an overview of the most influential social psychological models of intergroup contact and then proceeds to issues of contact and identity in the context of immigration. Avenues and obstacles to the social integration of immigrants into the society of settlement are discussed, including processes of politicization of the collective identities of immigrants and indigenous people. The chapter concludes with a comment on the discourse upon cultural differences and racism.

Chapter 7 is concerned with the role of identity in social mobilization and participation in collective behaviour. Its major part revolves around the role of collective identity in social movement participation, which is an important collective strategy for members of disadvantaged groups to improve their lot. In addition, it is shown that both collective and individual identity can also play a facilitative role in less controversial forms of collective behaviour, such as intragroup or organizational cooperation and volunteerism.

Finally, chapter 8 summarizes the major conclusions, but also identifies open questions and suggests new directions for future research.

Summary

In this chapter, I introduced the phenomenon of identity as a scientific issue and delineated the role of identity as a crucial mediator variable between input from and output in the social world. Moreover, outlining the wider multidisciplinary context of the study of identity, I discussed two important issues, namely human consciousness and the social conditions of human existence. The discussion of these issues highlighted the contributions to the study of identity made by philosophy, on the one hand, and by anthropological and cultural studies, on the other. It was argued that human consciousness can be understood, at least in its phenomenological or subjective aspects, in terms of William James's stream metaphor, according to which human consciousness is experienced as owned, continuous and unique. The whole human organism, with its functional nervous system and active involvement with the external world, underlies human consciousness, and we do not need to postulate a pure ego or separate 'I' that stands behind human consciousness and does the thinking. Even without a separate control centre, human consciousness allows for activity and self-control in that variable self-representations or identities can enter into the stream of consciousness and thus into the motivational and regulatory circuits where they function as mediators in line with the causal chain depicted in figure 1.1. Human consciousness affords self-consciousness and identity experiences which in turn feed into the self-reflexive construction of narratives about oneself.

Turning to the social conditions of human existence, it was pointed out that our evolutionary past has conditioned us to be social in at least two funda-mental respects. We are social in that we are dependent on each other, but we are also social or sociable in that we are able to initiate and maintain functional relationships with each other. Our identities emerge from our involvement in such relationships at various levels of social organization, and they are critically affected by changes in the organization and interpret-ation of these relationships. Thus, in response to modern changes and developments, a number of influential strands of social theory (including the works of Marx, Freud, de Saussure and Foucault as well as feminist thinking) have argued for a de-centring view of identity such that identity should no longer be viewed as the fixed and stable centre of the individual. Instead, important roots of identity can be found in the social world. This view concurs with the rejection of homuncular thinking and the proposed role of identity as a mediator (see figure 1.1). In addition, the nation was acknowledged as an important institutional and cultural frame for social relationships and thus for identity. But nations are not identical with cultures. Especially due to global-ization processes, we see the emergence of broader, transnational cultural zones as well as the emergence of cultural hybridity within nations. Thus, culture influences social relationships and associated identities not only at the national level, but also at levels above and below the nation. The chapter concluded with a brief overview of the remaining seven chapters of the book.

NOTE

1. Preston (1997, pp. 15–16) also discusses what has in the post-war period been called the Third World. However, owing to its heterogeneity, he does not consider it a distinct political-cultural region.

Chapter 2

The Social Psychology of Identity: Sociological and Psychological Contributions

There exist two fairly distinct subtypes of social psychology (Graumann, 1996). One subtype is rooted primarily in the field of sociology (sociological social psychology, SSP) while the other is rooted in the field of psychology (psychological social psychology, PSP). Accordingly, social psychological approaches to identity also fall into two broad classes or categories, with one being more sociologically oriented and the other being more psychologically oriented. Like all categorizations, the SSP–PSP distinction inevitably entails the accentuation of inter-category differences and intra-category similarities. Consequently, the following discussion of the sociological and psychological contributions to the social psychological study of identity centres on the major or (proto)typical contributions which characterize each subtype (see also Côté & Levine, 2002).

Sociological Contributions

The distinctive contributions of sociological thinking to social psychology revolve around the insight that social life is structured, and that this structure affects the development of the social person and the production of social behaviour. Sociologically oriented social psychologists therefore build on the premise that social structure and person mutually constrain, if not presuppose, one another (Stryker, 1977). Several sociological frameworks have been developed to conceptualize this society–individual reciprocity. Symbolic interactionism and (structural) role theory have been particularly influential (Stryker & Statham, 1985). I will first summarize these two frameworks and then turn to identity theory (Stryker, 1980, 1987) as an attempt to synthesize the most important insights concerning self and identity derived from the symbolic interactionist and role-theorectical perspectives.

Symbolic interactionism

Symbolic interactionism was critically shaped by Mead's (1934/1993) conceptualization of mind, self and society and their interrelationships. According to Mead (1934/1993), people form and use significant symbols in the course of social interaction within society. The mind emerges as symbolic representations are practised and communicated during social interaction. The mind is thus a product of symbolic social actions mediated by language and so is the self, which develops via the same process. More specifically, the self is an outcome of the reflexive cognitive activity of role taking during cooperative social activity. By viewing herself reflexively from the standpoint of others, the individual becomes a meaningful object to herself. Both mind and self are thus fundamentally social and interactive. Society and its structure shape social interaction and thus both mind and self, but society is also continuously re-created through social interaction in which the individual (in Mead's terms, the 'I') responds to the expectations of others (in Mead's terms, the 'Me').

The evolution of symbolic interactionism beyond Mead led to internal differentiation and even to the development of different 'schools' of symbolic interactionism (e.g. Blumer, 1969; Kuhn, 1964). However, we need not concern ourselves with this heterogeneity any further. I shall rather review the core of interrelated basic concepts that is essential to most current symbolic interactionist theorizing (Stryker & Statham, 1985).

Like other social animals, people do not and could not exist as isolated individuals. Reproduction of human life as well as production of the means of life depends on coordinated, and often cooperative, human action. Accordingly, social interactionists emphasize that human action is often, if not always, social interaction. That is, people act with reference to other individuals who are also actors. The different actors thus take each other into account. In order to be able to do this, people need to understand each other and the meanings of their respective acts. An act is meaningful when it includes a gesture which is indicative of other parts of the act yet to occur in the sequence of social interactions. When the gesture is understood in the same way by the people involved in the interaction, the gesture has become a significant symbol. Significant symbols emerge from social interaction and organize social interaction. From the perspective of symbolic interactionism, language is probably the most important system of significant symbols. It serves as the primary vehicle of communication, which is virtually synonymous with social interaction for many symbolic interactionists.

Meanings, significant symbols and social interaction are interdependent. Meanings and significant symbols emerge from social interaction, but they are also necessary for successful social interaction. Without meanings and significant symbols, social interaction breaks down. The interactive situation must be defined through the assignment of meanings and significant symbols. Habit and culture facilitate this process. In novel situations, tentative definitions permit the interaction to begin and are then tested and, if necessary, revised in the course of the social interaction. However, revision or reconstruction of definitions is by no means restricted to novel situations. These are general features of the symbolization or definition process, and the definition of a situation is typically (re)negotiated in the course of social interaction. Among the most important aspects of the interactive situation that need to be defined are the other actors involved in the social interaction. To achieve this, people use socially meaningful categories or positions such as 'teacher', 'son', 'intellectual' and so forth. These positions refer to 'the kinds of people it is possible to be in a given society' (Stryker & Statham, 1985, p. 323). Positions are associated with specific expectations called roles and thus help to organize social interaction. Positions and roles are inherently social. They are relational, making reference to complementary or opposite positions and roles (e.g. teacher vs. student), have socially shared meanings, are (re)produced in the course of social interaction, and in turn shape social interaction. Moreover, especially in modern society, persons can be defined in terms of multiple, and sometimes even contradictory or conflicting, positions and roles.

However, it is not just other people that are defined as part of the interactive situation. People also define themselves in terms of multiple positions and associated roles. For symbolic interactionists, this reflexive activity is the self. Self-definition in terms of positions and associated roles ensures that the self incorporates the expectations of others, which in turn facilitates social interaction. The specific expectations of others are learned through role taking or other socializing experiences which involve anticipating the responses of others with whom one is implicated in social interaction.

Role theory

Whereas symbolic interactionism emphasizes the processual and negotiated nature of social interaction and the social person, the emphasis of role theory is on the import and impact of social structure. From a role-theoretical perspective, social interaction, irrespective of whether it takes place between persons, groups, organizations, institutions or even total societies, needs to be explained in terms of the larger social system in which social interaction is embedded and of which the interaction partners are interdependent and functionally related parts. For most social interactions, groups are the immediate structural context, but are themselves functional substructures of a given society or culture. Group members interact with each other, holding differentiated positions as interdependent parts of an organized whole. The expectations or roles associated with these positions are rather fixed societal or cultural products. They are firmly rooted in values and norms, exist before the specific interaction and thus leave little room for negotiation. People learn roles through socialization and are then expected and pressured to act out the appropriate scripts. Accordingly, the set of important social psychological phenomena investigated by role theorists includes issues of socialization, role conflict, role relationships and role transitions.

Identity theory

Dissatisfaction with role theory's normatively deterministic view of social life as well as with symbolic interactionism's insufficient recognition of social structural influences has motivated several attempts to articulate both frameworks (for a detailed review, see Stryker & Statham, 1985). Identity theory will be described here as an illustrative example because it has informed the development of my own approach, presented in this book in important ways.

As a more balanced framework for the analysis of the self–society reciprocity, identity theory (Stryker, 1980, 1987) builds on the introduction of role theory into symbolic interactionism and allows for the incorporation of both interactionally constructed and social structural aspects of the social person. A basic premise of identity theory is that modern society is a complex and multifaceted mosaic of interdependent but highly differentiated parts. In keeping with the reciprocity between self and society, it is further postulated that in modern society the social person is equally differentiated and complex. More specifically, identity theory proposes that people have multiple identities which result from participation in multiple sets of structured role relationships (see also Wallman, 1983).

Together with the concept of identity, defined as a set of internalized role expectations, the concepts of identity salience and commitment form the conceptual cornerstones of identity theory. The multiple identities of a particular person are conceived as organized in a hierarchy of salience. This hierarchy is defined by the probability of the various identities to come into play within or across situations. Identity salience is the location of an identity in that hierarchy. It affects the threshold of invocation of a given identity and becomes particularly important if, owing to various other situational or person variables which are not yet systematically specified by identity theory, multiple identities are implicated in a situation. The distribution of identities in the salience hierarchy, in turn, reflects the different levels of commitment to the social roles underlying the various identities. Commitment is defined as the costs to the person could she no longer participate in a particular social relationship and thus no longer play the corresponding role or have the corresponding identity. A person is committed to a social role to the extent to which her social relationships are built around the role. Characteristics of the larger social structure, such as organizational principles based on class, gender or age, affect commitment, and thus constrain identity, in that they either facilitate or impede entry into and exit from social relationships.

The central proposition of identity theory that relates these key concepts to each other asserts that 'commitment impacts identity salience impacts role performance' (Stryker, 1987, p. 89). Regarding the link between identity salience and role performance, it is claimed that variation in role performance is determined by the location of the identity reflecting the particular role in the identity salience hierarchy. Under the condition that the social structure actually allows for behavioural choice, this claim has received good empirical support. The identity salience–role performance link is further explicated in terms of validation processes. Identities are assumed to motivate behaviours that reaffirm that one is the kind of person defined by the identities. The more salient an identity, the more sensitive a person should be to opportunities for behaviour that could confirm the identity and the stronger her motivation actually to perform such behaviour. Moreover, in line with the altercasting process (Weinstein & Deutschberger, 1963), a salient identity can also lead the person to actively cue her interaction partners so that they enable her to act out her identity. While the emphasis concerning the identity salience–role performance link is clearly on the directional effect of identity salience on role performance, it is not denied that the relationship can also be reciprocal. Actors are also observers of their own actions and they often observe what they do in order to learn who they are (Bem, 1972). Observations of one's own behaviour can therefore lead to inferences about the salience of one's identities. In particular, diagnostic information about the relative salience of one's identities can be obtained from behavioural choices in situations in which activation of alternative identities is possible.

Regarding the link between commitment and identity salience, it has been argued that two related but distinct types of commitment can be distinguished. Interactional commitment derives directly from one's embeddedness in social networks. It reflects the extensiveness of relationships that would be lost were one no longer to play a given role. Affective commitment reflects the subjective importance of the others to whom one relates in one's social networks. In other words, it captures the emotional costs attached to departure from a given role. Both high interactional commitment and high affective commitment can lead to high identity salience. Whether or not one likes the people with whom one must deal, frequent interaction with them endorses one's role relationship with them as well as the associated identity, which is continuously cued and practised. Repeated interaction in terms of the particular identity thus increases the salience of that identity. Conversely, even if interactional opportunities are momentarily blocked, the expectation that it might eventually be possible to develop role relationships with attractive and important others can ensure a relatively high salience of the (possible) identity. Reverse effects of identity salience on interactional and affective commitment are also acknowledged. For instance, people tend to value others who allow them to express a salient identity. Also, people tend actively to integrate others implicated in the role relationship that underlies their salient identity (e.g. spouse) into their additional social networks and thus increase the extensiveness of the original role relationship.

In conclusion, identity theory as a promising, albeit not yet fully realized, programme for the integration of symbolic interactionism and role theory offers a number of important insights that ought to be incorporated into any comprehensive theory of identity in modern society (see also Stryker & Burke, 2000). First, identities are *relational*. They reflect people's differentiated positions *vis-à-vis* each other. Second, identities are *socially constructed*. They have socially shared meanings which are constantly (re)negotiated during social interaction. Third, identities are *socially structured*. They reflect the structured social context of social interaction which is also the context of their construction. Fourth, people typically have *multiple identities*. This multiplicity reflects the multiplicity of differentiated positions and roles available, especially in modern society. Fifth, identities have *social consequences*. They are a source of motivation, shape social interaction, direct individual and collective behaviour and can thus also impact on social structure. Taken together, the concept of identity serves to bridge social structure (society) and social person (self). It is necessary for an adequate understanding of the social person, whose experiences and behaviours are shaped and constrained both by the structure of the immediate social interaction and by the structure of the wider societal context, but who, at the same time, is not merely a passive recipient of these influences. Identity mediates between structural forces and the social person's responses. Therefore, the social person is able to interfere by way of active participation in the construction and selection of identities as well as through creative resolution of conflicts between multiple identities. I can now turn to the psychological contributions to the social psychological study of identity and associated processes.

Psychological Contributions

In keeping with philosophers and early psychologists, including Dewey (1890), Royce (1895) and James (1890/1950), Gordon W. Allport (1955, 1968) convincingly argued for the inclusion of the concept of self (or 'proprium') in a modern science of psychology. However, he demarcated the self as 'the known' (James's 'empirical self' or 'Me') from 'the knower' (James's 'I' or a 'pure ego') and consigned the latter to philosophy (see chapter 1). In order to support his plea for the self as a vital and central concept of psychology, G. Allport listed seven key phenomena or themes that should be analysed in terms of a psychology of the self. These themes were (1) self-image, (2) continuity of self over time, (3) self-awareness (with particular reference to bodily sense), (4) self as agent and regulatory system, (5) self-enhancement and self-esteem, (6) motives of self-actualization and growth ('propriate striving') and (7) self-extension. Therewith, G. Allport anticipated, and most likely prompted, many important trends in modern psychology. This listing can therefore serve as an organizing scheme for the discussion of the most important psychological contributions to the social psychological study of identity.

In addition, the following discussion reflects two broader traditions or trends, one of which is primarily of North-American origin whereas the other started as a distinctly European endeavour. Within the North-American psychological tradition, the term 'self' is usually preferred to the term 'identity' and the self is typically conceptualized in rather individual(istic) terms. This is especially true for the social cognition perspective which has served as the leading paradigm of this tradition since about the 1970s (e.g. Markus, 1977). To be sure, the social cognition perspective does not deny the social dimension of the self, but it grounds its variant of the social self primarily in interpersonal relationships, while intergroup relations play a minor role. If a person's group membership is actually taken into account, it is construed as just another individual feature that, together with the person's numerous other individual features, makes up her unique cognitive self-representation which in turn feeds into information processes. Conversely, the European tradition, with the social identity or self-categorization perspective as its leading paradigm (Tajfel & Turner, 1979, 1986; Turner et al., 1987) and its preference for the term 'identity' over the term 'self', emphasizes the role of group memberships and intergroup relations. It adds another distinct social dimension to identity (or self) in that it focuses on the antecedents and consequences of collectively shared identities (or selves). This focus resonates with G. Allport's (1968) self-extension theme, which explicitly acknowledges group identifications, while G. Allport's other themes have been pursued mainly within the North-American tradition.

The self in 'North-American' psychology

The self-concept   G. Allport's (1968) suggestion that people have self-images, including, *inter alia*, images of their abilities, status, roles and aspirations, can be seen as a precursor of a more formal definition of 'the self-concept as a set of self-schemas that organize past experiences and are used to recognize and interpret relevant stimuli in the social environment' (Markus, Smith & Moreland, 1985, p. 1495). Self-schemas, in turn, are defined as 'cognitive generalizations about the self, derived from past experience, that organize and guide the processing of self-related information contained in the individual's social experiences' (Markus, 1977, p. 64). In her seminal article introducing the social cognition perspective on the self, Markus (1977) operationalized the notion of self-schema in terms of both high perceived self-descriptiveness and high perceived importance to self-description of a given feature (e.g. independent or friendly). She demonstrated that such self-schemas facilitate schema-relevant judgements and decisions about the self as well as the retrieval of schema-consistent behavioural evidence and the confident self-prediction of behaviour on schema-relevant dimensions. Self-schemas also strengthened individuals' resistance to counter-schematic information. Additional research (Markus et al., 1985) also testified to the role of self-schemas in the perception of others, demonstrating that self-schemas are often used to comprehend the thoughts, feelings and behaviours of others. Moreover, the self-concept seems to be characterized by a high degree of multiplicity and malleability, so that it is difficult to refer to *the* self-concept. Instead, it has been suggested to distinguish between core aspects of the self (i.e. one's self-schemas), which are chronically accessible and therefore relatively unresponsive to changes in one's circumstances, and other aspects of the self, the accessibility of which depends on motivational and social context variables (Markus & Kunda, 1986). Therefore, the actual working self(-concept) should consist of rather stable core self-aspects that are embedded in a more flexible layer or belt of self-aspects tied to the immediate circumstances. The working self can also include future-oriented components or 'possible selves' (Markus & Nurius, 1986) which concern ideas of what one may become, would like to become (G. Allport's 'aspirations') or is afraid of becoming.

Linville (1985, 1987) proposed a definition of the self-concept which is very similar to that of Markus and colleagues. She suggested that the self can be thought of as being cognitively represented in terms of self-aspects. A self-aspect is a cognitive category derived from social experience which serves to process and organize information and knowledge about oneself. Self-aspects can concern, *inter alia*, physical features, roles, abilities, preferences, attitudes, traits or explicit group or category memberships. The notion of self-aspect is broader than the notion of self-schema because the former is not necessarily limited to the core components of one's self-concept. More importantly in the present context, Linville's approach places particular emphasis on the structure of the self-concept, whereas the approach of Markus and colleagues focuses more on the content of the self-concept. According to Linville, people differ in self-complexity, which is defined as a joint function of the number of self-aspects and the degree of their relatedness. High self-complexity occurs with a large number of independent self-aspects, whereas low self-complexity occurs with a small number of self-aspects that are highly interrelated. This structural aspect of the self-concept has primarily been examined with respect to its implications for mental and physical well-being. Research indicates that a complex self-structure can protect the individual from emotional turmoil (Linville, 1985, 1987), although these effects may be more limited than initially assumed (Morgan & Janoff-Bulman, 1994; Woolfolk et al., 1995). I will return to the idea of self as a structured ensemble of different self-aspects in chapter 3 because it plays an important role in my own approach to identity.

Finally, it should be noted that several other representational models of the self have been suggested in the literature. They define the self-concept in terms of either hierarchies, prototypes, associative or distributed connectionist networks or spaces (for an overview, see Markus & Wurf, 1987; also Smith, Coats & Walling, 1999). Moreover, different models have been suggested to account for cultural variations in content and structure of people's self-concepts (Kashima, Kashima & Aldridge, 2001; Markus & Kitayama, 1991). Despite these variations, however, most, if not all, pertinent models concur with the approaches of Markus and Linville that the self-concept is a multifaceted dynamic cognitive representation that is implicated in a wide variety of social information processing phenomena with important social consequences.

Continuity of self   Most of us are pretty certain that the person we see in the bathroom mirror in the morning is the same person we saw in the mirror the night before (although, depending on nocturnal happenings, we might not particularly like our image in the mirror the day after). Otherwise, our sense of self would be seriously shattered. Uninterrupted existence or continuity of self over time, or more precisely the perception thereof, is therefore considered an important defining criterion of the self (Baumeister, 1986). (Perceived) self-continuity over time, in turn, presupposes memory. Today I need to remember what I experienced and did yesterday, and tomorrow I need to remember important experiences and behaviours of both yesterday and today. In other words, self and memory are highly interdependent and not completely separable from each other (Klein, 2001). The self builds on memories of one's past, but the act of remembering one's past is similarly dependent on a sense of self because the past must be identified as one's own past.

To further illuminate this special relationship between self and memory, Klein (2001) draws on two important distinctions suggested in the memory literature. First, procedural memory can be distinguished from declarative memory (e.g. Schacter & Tulving, 1994). Procedural memory makes possible the acquisition and retention of motor, perceptual and cognitive skills, while declarative memory consists of facts and beliefs about the world. Second, declarative memory can be further divided into a semantic and an episodic memory. The former is concerned with general knowledge, whereas the latter is concerned with experienced events. Unlike the contents of semantic memory, the contents of episodic memory include a reference to the self in subjective space and time (Tulving, 1993). Episodic memory should therefore be closely linked to self-continuity. Reviewing evidence from developmental, clinical and neuro-psychology, Klein (2001) concluded that a breakdown of the sense of self-continuity indeed causes serious disruptions in episodic memory. Interestingly, the reverse relationship does not seem to hold to the same degree. A loss of episodic memory typically diminishes people's capacity to recollect their personal past, but people are still able to know things about themselves. This ability is most likely due to an intact semantic memory which may after all enable people to know things about themselves without consciously having to recollect the specific experiences on which that knowledge is based. Nevertheless, it appears to be the episodic memory, though normally in interaction with the semantic memory, that is chiefly responsible for the ability to construct a personal narrative and to perceive oneself as existing through time (Klein, 2001).

Self-awareness   Each of us has his or her own body which James (1890/ 1950, p. 292) considered to be 'the innermost part of our material self'. The bodily sense and the self are intimately interwoven. G. Allport (1968) provides a juicy illustration by way of a brief thought experiment:

> Think first of swallowing the saliva in your mouth, or do so. Then imagine expectorating it into a tumbler and drinking it! What seemed natural and 'mine' suddenly becomes disgusting and alien . . . What I perceive as belonging intimately to my body is warm and welcome, what I perceive as separate from my body becomes, in the twinkling of an eye, cold and foreign.
>
> *(G. Allport, 1968, p. 28)*

This exercise also illustrates that, although we might not constantly be aware of our bodies, we can easily be made aware of them. The bodily sense thus provides us with a lifelong anchor for self-awareness (G. Allport, 1968).

However, awareness of one's body is not the only source of self-awareness. Self-awareness can result from conscious attention on a variety of aspects of the self, such as physical appearance, behaviour, mood, thoughts and so forth (Hoyle et al., 1999). Moreover, when people are reminded of themselves as social objects or recipients of other people's reactions, self-awareness is also referred to as objective self-awareness (Duval & Wicklund, 1972). Self-awareness can be created by environmental factors, such as the presence of a video or tape recorder, a mirror or an audience, but also by internal factors, such as transitory emotions (e.g. negative mood) or even chronic tendencies to focus attention on oneself (Fiske & Taylor, 1991; Hoyle et al., 1999). In order to distinguish chronic tendencies to engage in self-awareness from temporarily induced tendencies, the chronic tendencies are often referred to as self-consciousness. They are further separated into public and private self-consciousness (Fenigstein, Scheier & Buss, 1975). Public self-consciousness results from a heightened attentional focus on publicly observable aspects of the self (e.g. physical appearance or behaviour), while private self-consciousness results from a heightened attentional focus on aspects of the self that are covert and hidden from other people (e.g. one's feelings or thoughts). The correlation between public and private self-consciousness is modest, so that a particular person can be high with respect to one form of self-consciousness and at the same time low with respect to the other form of self-consciousness.

A related personality variable is the construct of self-monitoring (Snyder, 1987). It captures differences in the extent to which people observe and regulate their public appearances in social situations and interpersonal relationships. High self-monitoring people regulate their public appearances in line with cues they receive from the social environment, whereas low self-monitoring people behave in ways that express their internal attitudes and feelings. There is some empirical relationship between (high vs. low) self-monitoring and (public and private) self-consciousness. For example, high self-monitoring people also tend to be higher in public self-consciousness than low self-monitoring people. Conceptually, however, self-monitoring and self-consciousness have different foci. The former places particular emphasis on self-presentational skills, whereas the latter emphasizes focus of attention (Fiske & Taylor, 1991; Hoyle et al., 1999).

Self as agent and regulatory system   People must continually regulate their behaviour in order to survive, or, less dramatically, in order to reach desired goals. The self is implicated in this process because an understanding of who or what one is and an understanding of what one wants are important guidelines or even requirements for a successful synthesis of 'inner needs and outer reality', irrespective of whether this synthesis is achieved by rational planning or rationalization (G. Allport, 1968, p. 29). Moreover, because people usually recognize themselves as the origin of their thoughts and actions, the self is directly experienced as an influential agent (Bruner, 1994; deCharms, 1968).

Self-regulation generally refers to ways in which people control and direct their own actions. More specifically, it involves goal setting, cognitive preparations for behaving in a goal-directed manner and the ongoing monitoring and evaluation of the goal-directed activities (Fiske & Taylor, 1991; Hoyle et al., 1999; Markus & Wurf, 1987). Goals depend on needs, motives and values which are in turn instantiated in terms of the person's working self. For example, the self-enhancement or self-actualization motives are more likely to prompt a person to set ambitious artistic goals for herself if she currently or chronically defines herself as an artist as opposed to a scientist (see also the discussions below concerning self-enhancement/self-esteem and self-actualization/growth). Similarly, goals are derived from ideas of what one should be, would like to become or is afraid of becoming (e.g. 'self-guides' or 'possible selves'; Higgins, 1987; Markus & Nurius, 1986). Other determinants of goal setting are control-related beliefs or expectations that people hold about their abilities to accomplish certain tasks (e.g. 'self-efficacy', Bandura, 1997; see also Fiske & Taylor, 1991, pp. 197–204). Once particular goals are set, people cognitively prepare for goal-directed behaviour by drawing on their procedural memory to select effective strategies. Although strategies are likely to be evaluated and selected in the light of their benefits and costs for the self, particular strategies such as scripts (Schank & Abelson, 1977) are closely linked to the working self so that these strategies are readily available and often executed without much prior deliberation or calculation. Actual performance execution leads to the next step in self-regulation. Here people typically monitor their behaviour, judge it against a goal-relevant criterion or standard and reward or punish the self via feelings of approval or disapproval or via more tangible consequences.

Self-regulation is also responsive to attentional processes. Research indicates that (situationally) heightened self-awareness can prompt the activation of a behavioural criterion or standard or make an existing standard more salient. In addition, heightened self-awareness can activate the process by which a current state is compared against a given standard. A perceived discrepancy then motivates corrective behaviour. As a final consequence, behavioural conformity to given standards tends to increase with heightened self-awareness (for a review, see Hoyle et al., 1999; but also Markus & Wurf, 1987, pp. 312–14). There also seem to be differences between people who are chronically high in public and low in private self-consciousness and people who are chronically high in private and low in public self-consciousness. The former seem to give particular weight to externally provided standards, the latter to internal standards. Similar differences emerge between high and low self-monitoring people. The former plan and enact their behaviour more in response to their social environment, whereas the latter self-regulate more in line with internal cues (Hoyle et al., 1999).

Finally, it is noteworthy that, in the context of social interaction, people also engage in self-regulation in order to manage their impressions and present themselves (to others as well as to themselves) in ways that are consistent with their beliefs about themselves. To this end, people not only select specific behavioural strategies, but they also strategically select situations and other people with whom to interact (Schlenker, 1980).

Self-enhancement and self-esteem   Self-love is a well-known phenomenon. Certainly it is noticed, and criticized as selfishness, mainly in other people, but this may be just a particularly effective means to convince ourselves and others how much more loveable we are ourselves. There is indeed a solid body of psychological research which shows that people usually think, or wish to think, positively of themselves in self-relevant respects. In other words, most people have, or want to have, (high) self-esteem and are motivated to secure or achieve this through self-enhancement (Hoyle et al., 1999).

Self-esteem and the self-enhancement motive most likely have evolutionary roots. A propensity to high self-esteem or self-love is likely to be selected in evolution because it fosters self-care, which in turn increases the likelihood of survival and reproductive success (see also Greenwald & Pratkanis, 1984). Self-esteem can also be recast in more interpersonal or intragroup terms and thus linked with the evolutionary importance of social group membership for survival and successful reproduction (Trivers, 1985). More specifically, self-esteem may have developed, and may still function, as a measure ('sociometer') of one's interpersonal or intragroup connections such that low self-esteem reflects or signals (the danger of) social rejection, whereas high self-esteem is a response to (the prospect of) social acceptance by others (Leary et al., 1995; Leary & Baumeister, 2000). Moreover, self-enhancing strategies may be adaptive because they seem to promote successful life adjustment and mental health (e.g. feelings of happiness and contentment or the ability to engage in productive and creative work), even if self-enhancing perceptions do not conform to reality (Taylor & Brown, 1988; but see also Hoyle et al., 1999, pp. 117–18).

Self-enhancing strategies are possible because the social world is a heterogeneous, though socially structured, pool of perspectives. The social world can thus be looked at, and social information processed and interpreted, from various different perspectives (which may often involve 'distortion', or better, mutual accusations of distortion among people with conflicting perspectives). Accordingly, damage to self-esteem can be prevented or undone, for example, by self-serving causal attributions (e.g. 'The exam was too difficult'), rationalizations (e.g. 'I'm sure those [unattainable] grapes are sour anyway'), downward social comparisons (e.g. 'My friend did even worse in the exam'), compensatory self-affirmation (e.g. 'I might have failed the maths exam, but I am a very good swimmer') or defensive pessimism (e.g. 'I'm sure, I will do very badly in the exam. Simply passing would be sufficient for me').

In addition to such motivated cognitive tactics (Fiske & Talyor, 1991), the social world and one's social relationships can also actively be manipulated or managed in order to prevent or undo damage to one's self-esteem (Hoyle et al., 1999). For example, being afraid that one will fail the maths exam, one might engage in behavioural self-handicapping by heavy partying the night before so that failure on the following day comes as no surprise and does not threaten one's self-esteem as a (potentially) capable student. Self-esteem or positive self-evaluation can also be maintained by increasing the social distance to friends who perform better than oneself in self-relevant areas as well as by further increasing one's closeness to a friend who performs exceptionally well in an area that is not directly self-defining ('This famous piano player is a very good friend of mine'). Similarly, one can bask in reflected glory by actively associating, rather than comparing, oneself with successful groups or teams (Cialdini et al., 1976; Tesser, 1988).

The self-enhancement motive is pervasive and often stronger than the motive to assess oneself accurately, that is, to find out how good one 'really' is (Sedikides, 1993; Sedikides & Strube, 1997; but see also Trope, 1983). However, the self-consistency motive is often cited as a potential competitor of the self-enhancement motive (Fiske & Taylor, 1991). Research has shown that people are motivated to maintain a consistent image or concept of themselves because self-consistency strengthens perceptions of control and predictability concerning one's individual fate (Swann, 1996). People therefore think and behave in ways that verify their self-concepts and thus sustain self-consistency. More often than not, the self-consistency motive may operate in harmony with the self-enhancement motive because, as indicated above, most people have a reasonably high self-esteem.

However, there is also research on people with relatively low self-esteem. This work suggests that, like most other people, people with low self-esteem also tend to react with more negative affect to unfavourable feedback than to favourable (i.e. self-enhancing) feedback. But the cognitive responses of people with low self-esteem show the opposite pattern. They indicate greater cognitive acceptance of unfavourable (i.e. self-consistent) as opposed to favourable feedback. Interestingly, it seems that such 'cognitive–affective crossfire' is eventually resolved because the affective reaction gradually recedes or is transformed in accordance with the cognitive response (Swann et al., 1987). Although such a resolution mechanism underlines the importance of the self-consistency motive, this motive must not be misconstrued as a general obstacle to self-enhancing self-concept change. On the contrary, there is an intriguing possibility for articulation or synthesis of the self-consistency and self-enhancement motives which revolves around the full development of the potential of one's existing self-concept. On the one hand, the improvement or growth inherent in such development satisfies self-enhancement needs. On the other, the trajectory of change is a direct function of the potential of one's existing self-concept which ensures sufficient overlap between successive stages so that self-consistency needs are satisfied as well. This possibility has been discussed in the psychological literature in connection with the striving for self-actualization and growth to which I will now turn.

Self-actualization and growth   Motives of self-actualization and growth ('to become what one has the potential to become') have been stressed particularly by psychologists with a humanistic perspective (e.g. Rogers, 1959; Maslow, 1970) in opposition to the rather negative views of the psychoanalytic and behaviourist perspectives. Humanistic psychologists maintain that human beings are endowed with an inherent tendency to develop, grow and improve and that they will actually do so as long as their more fundamental needs are met or other circumstances do not hinder them. G. Allport (1968, p. 30) also criticized reductionist views of motivation that revolve solely around 'a disposition to act, by instinct or by learning, in such a way that the organism will as efficiently as possible reduce the discomfort of tension'. Instead, he argues, the characteristic feature of 'propriate striving', such as striving for self-actualization and growth, 'is its resistance to equilibrium: tension is maintained rather than reduced' and such striving 'makes for unification of personality' (see also White, 1959). More recently, other theorists have acknowledged similar intrinsic motivations related to the development of competence and mastery (Deci & Ryan, 1985, 1995; see also Baumeister, 1986). Similarly, the notion of possible selves as components of the existing self-concept that possess a self-improvement potential to be realized in the future resonates with the central idea of the humanistic perspective that self-actualization and growth refer to a process of becoming what one has the potential to become (Markus & Nurius, 1986). The idea that possible selves can function as guides for self-improvement thus builds an important bridge between the humanistic perspective and the social cognition approach (see also Higgins, 1987).

Identity in 'European' social psychology

The six themes discussed so far (i.e. self-concept, self-continuity, self-awareness, self as agent and regulatory system, self-enhancement and self-esteem, self-actualization and growth) represent the cornerstones of the

'North-American' psychology of the self. The remaining theme of self-extension revolves around the variable 'range and extent of one's feeling of self-involvement' (G. Allport, 1968, p. 29). G. Allport (1968) actually considered it a mark of maturity that the self can be extended to include concrete objects, other people or abstract ideals which then become matters of high importance and are valued as 'mine' (see also Kohlberg, 1976). He particularly emphasized the human capacity to identify with groups at different levels of inclusiveness (e.g. family, neighbourhood, nation). Although the past decade has seen a steady growth in the interest of North-American psychologists and social cognition researchers in the theme of self-extension in general and group identification in particular (Aron, Aron & Norman, 2001; Sedikides & Brewer, 2001; Smith & Mackie, 2000), the major theoretical and empirical contributions in this area have been made, or were critically inspired, by European social psychologists. Most notably, these contributions crystallized into the social identity theory of intergroup relations (Tajfel & Turner, 1979, 1986) and self-categorization theory (Turner et al., 1987). I will now discuss each of these highly influential theories, which are often also referred to collectively as the social identity perspective, in greater detail.

The social identity theory of intergroup relations (SIT)   SIT is a theoretical framework for the social psychological analysis of intergroup relations, with a particular emphasis on intergroup conflict (Tajfel & Turner, 1979, 1986). The development of SIT received its critical impulse from the now classic 'minimal group experiments' which attempted to provide a social psychological answer to the question of why members of different groups discriminate against each other (Tajfel, 1970; Tajfel et al., 1971; also Tajfel, 1982). In contradistinction to Sherif's (1967) work, the minimal group experiments demonstrated that negative interdependence of members of different groups with respect to scarce material resources was not a necessary condition for intergroup discrimination or conflict. Instead, the results pointed to the critical role of social categorization processes in intergroup discrimination. This observation was further developed into the idea that categorization into ingroup and outgroup provides the germ for the development of a group or social identity, which in turn can spur intergroup discrimination. More specifically, SIT proposes that, when acting as group members, people have a need for positive social identity and are therefore motivated to positively differentiate their ingroup from relevant outgroups. Intergroup discrimination is then explained as a means, though not the only one, to establish such positive ingroup distinctiveness.

Notwithstanding the critical role of these paradigmatic findings in theory development, SIT is more than just a theory of intergroup discrimination. 'It provides a comprehensive theory of intergroup relations and social change in socially stratified societies' (Turner & Reynolds, 2001, p. 134). It systematically relates characteristics of the intergroup situation (e.g. status differences between ingroup and outgroup) to people's cognitive, affective and behavioural reactions (e.g. individual mobility or collective protest), while social identity is viewed as the critical intervening mechanism and defined as 'that *part* of an individual's self-concept which derives from his knowledge of his membership of a social group (or groups) together with the value and emotional significance attached to that membership' (Tajfel, 1978a, p. 63, emphasis in the original).

A typical application of SIT can be found in the analysis of the social psychology of low-status minorities or otherwise disadvantaged groups (Tajfel, 1981). According to SIT, the disadvantaged social position of such groups is likely to confer an unsatisfactory social identity on the respective group members. This identity problem should then motivate group members to adopt subjectively appropriate coping strategies. These strategies can range from individualistic strategies of social mobility to collective or group strategies of social change. Individualistic strategies involve leaving the disadvantaged ingroup physically or at least psychologically. People who adopt individualistic strategies act as individuals and not as group members because no deliberate attempt is made at finding a solution for the entire ingroup. Instead, positive social identity is sought through assimilation or actual admission to the advantaged outgroup. Conversely, when people adopt group strategies of social change, they seek to achieve a positive social identity through actual changes in the objective social structure (e.g. a revolutionary reversal of status relations) or at least in the relative positions of the ingroup and outgroup on salient comparison dimensions (e.g. economic success). Such strategies typically involve direct confrontations or at least competition with the outgroup.

Another group strategy is called social creativity. Like all group strategies, it involves acting in terms of one's group (Tajfel, 1974), but it does not necessarily involve any actual change in the ingroup's social position relative to that of the outgroup. Instead, group members seek a positive social identity by redefining or altering elements of the comparative situation (e.g. by changing the comparison outgroup or by changing or reinterpreting the comparison dimension). According to SIT, the selection of a particular strategy is critically determined by collectively shared beliefs about the nature of the social structure, such as beliefs about its legitimacy and stability or beliefs about the permeability of group boundaries. For example, group strategies of social change should be preferred to individualistic strategies when status inferiority of the ingroup is perceived as illegitimate and unstable and the boundaries between ingroup and outgroup are perceived as impermeable.

There is now an impressive body of empirical evidence that supports major predictions of SIT, especially with respect to the effects of important characteristics of the intergroup situation, and associated beliefs, on intergroup conflict and harmony and on group members' choice of identity management strategies (for reviews, see Brown, 2000; Ellemers, 1993; Ellemers & Barreto, 2001; Simon, Aufderheide & Kampmeier, 2001; Wright, 2001a). However, researchers have also claimed to have uncovered a number of anomalies and lacunae which concern, for example, the relationship between group identification and intergroup discrimination (Brown et al., 1992), the role of self-esteem as either an antecedent or consequence of intergroup discrimination (Abrams & Hogg, 1988) or the dimensionality of social identity (Ellemers, Kortekaas & Ouwerkerk, 1999; Jackson & Smith, 1999). As a reaction, there have been various suggestions for further theoretical elaboration of SIT and refinement of its key concepts, but controversies still persist (for overviews, see Brown, 2000; Turner & Reynolds, 2001). I suspect that the continuing controversies are due at least in part to an insufficient appreciation of the limited focus of SIT. It was deliberately developed with a focus on social identity which involves only 'limited aspects of the self' and is 'relevant to certain limited aspects of social behaviour' (Tajfel, 1978a, p. 63). That is, SIT is primarily a theory of the *consequences* of social identity for intergroup conflict and harmony. It is not, and was probably never intended to be, a general theory of self or identity which systematically analyses and compares the different variants of identity (e.g. social vs. personal identity) and their specific antecedents and consequences. In recognition of these inherent limitations, self-categorization theory was developed as a more comprehensive theoretical framework for the analysis of identity to which I will now turn.

Self-categorization theory (SCT)   The distinction between personal identity and social identity (Turner, 1982) marks the beginning of SCT which was then elaborated in greater detail by Turner et al. (1987). Personal identity means self-definition as a unique individual in terms of interpersonal or intragroup differentiations, whereas social identity means self-definition as a group member in terms of ingroup–outgroup differentiations. As this broader basis indicates and the following discussion will further illustrate, SCT is a more general theoretical framework than SIT. SCT specifies the antecedents and consequences of personal and social identity and can thus provide explanations for both (inter-)individual and (inter)group behaviour as well as an explanation for the transition from one form of behaviour to the other. Hence, although SIT is the older theory, it can be considered a logical derivation from SCT (or SCT an extension of SIT) because SCT also encompasses SIT's analysis of intergroup relations.

According to SCT, both personal and social identity derive from self-categorizations which are 'cognitive groupings of oneself and some class of stimuli as the same . . . in contrast to some other class of stimuli' (Turner et al., 1987, p. 44). Self-categorizations exist as part of a hierarchical system of classification so that identities can be construed at different levels of abstraction related by means of class inclusion (Rosch, 1978). That is, despite the paradigmatic status of the distinction between personal and social identity, SCT explicitly acknowledges that there always exist different layers of nested identities. For example, one's social identity as a resident of the city of Berlin is more abstract than, and thus includes, one's social identity as a resident of a specific neighbourhood in Berlin. At the same time, one's social identity as a German citizen, a European citizen or a human being is even more abstract and includes one's lower-level social identities as well as one's very exclusive personal identity. It is further postulated that identities are relative constructs that are compared with, and evaluated relative to, contrasting identities at the same level of abstraction, but in terms of the next more inclusive identity. For instance, one's identity as a resident of a specific neighbourhood in Berlin would be compared with, and evaluated relative to, (the identity of) residents of other neighbourhoods in Berlin with respect to attributes that characterize residents of Berlin in general (e.g. witty). By the same token, one's identity as a resident of Berlin would be compared with, and evaluated relative to, say, residents of Cologne or Munich with respect to attributes that characterize German citizens in general (e.g. efficient).

However, identities vary not only along the dimension of abstraction or inclusiveness. Another source of variation is the multiplicity of a given person's group memberships even on similar levels of abstraction (e.g. groupings based on gender, sexual orientation, profession or political orientation). People are usually members of many different groups, but not all group memberships are salient at the same time. The analysis of identity salience is therefore a central component of SCT. It builds on the adaptation of Bruner's (1957a) work on the functioning of categorization in perception. Accordingly, a particular group membership and the associated identity is said to be salient to the extent to which it is 'functioning psychologically to increase the influence of one's membership in that group on perception and behaviour, and/or the influence of another person's identity as a group member on one's impression of and hence behaviour towards that person' (Turner et al., 1987, p. 118). Identity salience is assumed to be a joint function of people's *readiness* to adopt a particular identity and the extent to which that identity *fits* as a meaningful self-definition in the given social context.

Readiness to adopt a particular identity depends on people's general values, changing motives, current goals, prior experiences and so forth. For example, prior experiences of being mistreated because of a particular group member-ship likely reduce one's readiness to define oneself in terms of the correspond-ing social identity in order to escape further mistreatment. Conversely, if one's current goal were to draw public attention to one's mistreatment, readiness for such self-definition should increase. Also, readiness to adopt a particular identity may be influenced by the relative strengths of one's needs for assimilation or differentiation (Brewer, 1991). The fit of a particular identity as a meaningful self-definition increases with the degree to which observed similarities and differences between people (including oneself) are perceived to correlate in an expectancy-consistent manner with a social division into 'us' and 'them' (or 'me' and 'you'). For example, gender identity fits well and is meaningful in a situation in which women and men discuss issues of rape and sexual violence and most women plead for harsh punishment of rapists or sexual offenders whereas most men disagree with them and plead for more lenient measures.

At this point it is important to note that, although SCT has so far focused primarily on the antecedents and consequences of the salience of social identity, SCT posits that the salience of personal identity is also governed by the same general principles, but with opposite consequences. The salience of personal identity is thus analogously construed as a joint function of readiness (e.g. a high need for individuality) and fit (e.g. a high degree of perceived intragroup variation paired with little perceived intra-individual variation). Yet, whereas a salient social identity is assumed to enhance the perception of self as similar to, or even interchangeable with, other ingroup members, but different from outgroup members, a salient personal identity should enhance the perception of inter-individual differences and intra-individual similarity or consistency. According to SCT, it is this mechanism of depersonalization, associated with a salient social identity, or personalization, associated with a salient personal identity, that is responsible for group behaviour or individual behaviour, respectively.

SCT has generated an impressive body of empirical research to test its central tenets (e.g. concerning the antecedents and perceptual consequences of social identity salience) and has also been applied to the theoretical and empirical analysis of a wide variety of important social psychological phenomena, such as social influence, social stereotyping and prejudice, group cohesiveness, group polarization, social cooperation, collective action and organizational behaviour. Overall, research has provided good support for SCT, both for its central tenets and its various applications (Haslam, 2001; Oakes, Haslam & Turner, 1994; Turner, 1991; Turner et al., 1987). At the same time, SCT offers a number of new insights into, and often provocative perspectives on, G. Allport's (1968) 'classic' themes of the psychology of self (Onorato & Turner, 2001; Turner & Onorato, 1999).

First and foremost, SCT suggests a more process-oriented view of the self-concept as 'a dynamic process of reflexive social judgment' (Onorato & Turner, 2001, p. 159). According to this view, the self is not represented in terms of fixed, absolute properties such as self-schemas (Markus, 1977) or self-aspects (Linville, 1985), but in terms of relational, varying self-categories. This view allows for more fluidity because both the inclusiveness and the content of these self-categories are assumed to be critically influenced by elements of the comparative context such as the comparison other or the comparison dimension. For example, identity as a German should be filled with different content, and thus also acquire a different meaning and receive a different evaluation, depending on whether German identity is constructed in the context of German–Israeli relations, in which Germany's fascist history is particularly salient, or in the context of German–Austrian relations, in which the image of Germany as 'the more powerful brother' is salient.

Second, SCT acknowledges that the self can be experienced as stable, but suggests that such self-continuity reflects stability in the parameters (resources, conditions and objects) of reflexive judgement rather than a fixed underlying cognitive structure. For example, conditions of stable social relations and hence stable self–other (interpersonal, intragroup or intergroup) comparisons may greatly facilitate feelings of self-continuity.

Third, the distinction between personal identity and social identity broadens the scope of the remaining self-themes in important respects. Reflexivity and self-awareness can no longer be limited to a self defined primarily in terms of personal identity with the bodily sense as a lifelong anchor (G. Allport, 1968). Social identity can also be the object or focus of self-awareness, and such self-awareness can involve both private and public aspects of one's social identity (e.g. one's private feelings and thoughts as a group member or one's public appearance and behaviour as a group member). The distinction between personal identity and social identity has also helped to uncover the active, regulatory role of self in group contexts. There is often a sharp difference or even a discontinuity between people's feelings, thoughts and actions as group members, on the one hand, and how they feel, think and act as individuals, on the other (R. W. Brown, 1954; R. J. Brown & Turner, 1981; Schopler & Insko, 1992). SCT has demonstrated the explanatory power of social identity as a regulatory system in group contexts. This reassures researchers that group perception and group behaviour need not, and must not, be dismissed or discredited as unpredictable or irrational phenomena simply because they cannot be explained in terms of personal identity processes. Moreover, it has been suggested by self-categorization researchers that the analysis of self-esteem and the self-enhancement motive can fruitfully be extended from the level of personal identity to the level of social identity (e.g. Long & Spears, 1997; see also Luhtanen & Crocker, 1992) and that social identity may serve as a phenomenologically equally valid platform for self-actualization and growth (Oakes & Reynolds, 1997; Oakes et al., 1994).

Finally, with respect to G. Allport's (1968) self-extension theme, it is important to highlight that, according to SCT, social identity is not merely personal identity projected on to other ingroup members (cf. Cadinu & Rothbart, 1996), nor is it personal identity presented to and incorporating the views of others (cf. Stryker & Statham, 1985). Rather, social identity is an extended self in the sense that it is a more inclusive, social categorical 'we'. It extends beyond the individual 'me' to include and define as self other ingroup members who do not simply reflect 'me', but participate in a higher-level social entity (Turner & Onorato, 1999).

In conclusion, there are undeniable differences and disagreements between SCT, or more generally the 'European' social identity perspective, on the one hand, and the 'North-American' social cognition perspective on the self, on the other. Explication and elaboration of these disagreements play a product-ive role in current theory development and empirical research (Sedikides & Brewer, 2001; Tyler, Kramer & John, 1999). At the same time, the discussions and debates proceed, and are in fact only possible, on the basis of a shared appreciation of identity as a crucial social-cognitive mediator that enables people to comprehend and act in their social worlds as self-conscious and motivated agents.

Summary

In this chapter I reviewed sociological and psychological contributions to the social psychology of identity. With regard to sociological contributions, the focus was on symbolic interactionism, role theory and identity theory. Sym-bolic interactionism emphasizes the emergent quality of identity as the out-come of continual social construction and negotiation processes during social interaction. Conversely, role theory places greater emphasis on the import and impact of social structure and people's positions and roles in that structure. Identity theory synthesizes the insights derived from both symbolic interac-tionism and role theory. It emphasizes the relational, socially constructed and socially structured nature of identity and further elaborates on the possi-bility and necessity of multiple identities in modern society, their differential invocation and social consequences.

With regard to psychological contributions, a distinction was made between 'North-American' and 'European' approaches, with the social cognition per-spective as the leading paradigm of the former and the social identity or self-categorization perspective as the leading paradigm of the latter. Seven major psychological themes were identified: (1) self-concept, (2) self-continuity, (3) self-awareness, (4) self as agent and regulatory system, (5) self-enhancement and self-esteem, (6) self-actualization and growth and (7) self-extension. Theorizing and research concerning the first six themes has been influenced and dominated primarily by the social cognition perspective, whereas the self-extension theme, which mainly revolves around the role of group identifications, has been guided primarily by the social identity or self-categorization perspective. Besides various conceptual and theoretical disagreements between the different psychological perspectives, they share a fundamental appreciation of identity as a crucial social-cognitive mediator that operates between people's social environment and their perceptions and behaviours. The sociological and psychological contributions reviewed in this chapter provide the theoretical platform for the integrative approach to identity presented in the next chapter.

Chapter 3

Identity in Modern Society: An Integrative Approach

Theoretical Background and Levels of Identity Analysis

In this chapter, I develop an approach to identity that builds on important insights provided by the different sociologically oriented and psychologically oriented perspectives reviewed in the previous chapter. The synthesis of these insights allows for an integrative approach that articulates micro-, meso- and macro-level analyses of identity (Esser, 1993; Pettigrew, 1996). The micro level of analysis concerns the individual person and her perceptions, feelings, thoughts, motivations, actions and so forth. This level of analysis is the traditional domain of psychology because it is the individual person who perceives, feels, thinks, has motivations, acts and so forth. Although higher-level social factors and processes are undoubtedly implicated in psychological processes and the ensuing behaviour, it is the individual person who ultimately executes psychological processes and behaviours. Early attempts at assigning higher-level social entities, such as crowds or groups, their own unique psyche (Le Bon, 1903; McDougall, 1920) have therefore rightfully been rejected as metaphysical speculations (F. Allport, 1924; see also Reicher, 1982). Accordingly, the identity approach presented in this chapter is fundamentally psychological in the sense that the individual person serves as the basic unit of analysis and that it is his or her identity that is at stake. With respect to this micro level of identity analysis, the present approach has been informed in important ways by the social cognition perspective on the self. As specified in greater detail below, the approach revolves around a self-aspect model of identity that incorporates important insights provided by the social cognition perspective concerning the cognitive representation of the self and the role of motivated cognition in self-representation (Fiske & Taylor, 1991; Kunda, 1990).

At the other extreme, the macro level of analysis focuses on society and its social structure. This level of analysis is the traditional domain of sociology. In line with role theory (Stryker & Statham, 1985), the identity approach presented in this chapter explicitly acknowledges that each individual person is also part of society as a larger socially structured system and that her position and role in society critically affects her identity and the associated psychological functioning. The approach also incorporates the insight that, especially in modern society, people have multiple positions and roles and can therefore have multiple identities with differential consequences for their psychological functioning. However, macro-level social structural and micro-level psychological factors and processes never meet in the abstract. It is always concrete people who meet and interact with each other under concrete circumstances. Therefore, a truly social psychological analysis, which focuses on the meso level of the situation or immediate context of social interaction, is required as well. It is in the meso-level interaction situation that macro-level and micro-level factors and processes meet and affect each other. People do not experience social structure *per se*, but in or as socially structured interaction situations. It is in such interaction situations that (meso-level) social psychological processes take shape and translate (macro-level) social structure or processes into (micro-level) psychological experiences which in turn guide the interaction, with possible consequences for the (macro-level) social structure as well as for (micro-level) psyche.

By the same token, it is in the socially structured interaction situation that identity takes shape through constant (re)negotiation among the interaction partners. Identity is thereby rooted in socially structured practice, and people are (inter)active participants in the process of identity construction. These insights, derived from more sociologically oriented perspectives (Stryker & Statham, 1985), are integrated into the present identity approach, as is the observation emphasized by more psychologically oriented social identity and self-categorization theorists (Tajfel & Turner, 1986; Turner et al., 1987) that groups frequently provide the immediate situational context for social interaction. Social interaction then takes place in either an intergroup or intragroup context. In the latter case, the group may often remain implicit, so that intragroup relations are experienced more as interpersonal or interindividual relations.

However, the important point is that because groups are social entities which usually have an internal social structure and are themselves part of the larger social structure, they import social structure into the interaction situation, into the process of identity construction and therefore eventually into identity itself. The resulting notion of identity as socially structured self-representation is an important bridge between the more psychologically oriented social identity or self-categorization perspective (Tajfel & Turner,

1986; Turner et al., 1987) and more sociologically oriented perspectives on identity (Stryker & Statham, 1985), and it is also assigned a prominent role in the integrative social psychological approach to identity presented in this chapter. Finally, this approach incorporates two additional characteristics of identity which are stressed especially by self-categorization theorists (Oakes et al., 1994). These are the relational nature of identity and its situation- or context-specificity. Both characteristics are closely related and derive from the importance of the situation of social interaction, and its comparative elements, as a meso-level variable for the process of identity construction. Identity is relational because it serves to define and reflect one's own position or part in the interactive relationship relative to that of one's interaction partner, and it is situation-specific to the extent to which one's part in a given relationship, or the 'to-be-represented' relationship as a whole, varies with the interaction situation.

A Self-Aspect Model of Identity (SAMI)

The integrative approach to identity developed in this chapter revolves around a self-aspect model of identity (Simon, 1997, 1998a, 1998b, 1999). This model builds on the premise that, as active meaning seekers, people engage in self-interpretation, which refers to the social-cognitive process whereby people give coherence and meaning to their own experiences, including their relations with the physical and social environment. Through self-interpretation, people achieve an understanding of themselves or, in other words, an identity, which in turn influences their subsequent perception and behaviour. The central working assumption of the model is that self-interpretation involves a varying number of self-aspects. Borrowing from Linville (1985), a self-aspect is viewed here as a cognitive category or concept that serves to process and organize information and knowledge about oneself. Self-aspects can refer, *inter alia*, to generalized psychological characteristics or traits (e.g. introverted), physical features (e.g. red hair), roles (e.g. father), abilities (e.g. bilingual), tastes (e.g. preference for French red wines), attitudes (e.g. against the death penalty), behaviours (e.g. 'I work a lot') and explicit group or category membership (e.g. member of the Communist Party).

The development of self-aspects is a function of a person's experiences in various social roles, relationships and situations. The relation between a self-aspect (as a cognitive concept) and experiences (as empirical examples) is analogous to the relation between theory and data (Medin, 1989). Self-aspects help people to interpret or explain their experiences (e.g. 'I don't like parties. That's because I am introverted') in a way very similar to the use of more formal theories to explain scientific observations (e.g. the use of genetic theories to explain a physical or mental handicap). Yet, scientific observations or data can also force us to modify our theories. Similarly, experiences can lead to a change in one's self-aspects (e.g. 'I come to like parties more and more. Maybe I am not so introverted after all'). Finally, theories guide data collection or data production. In a similar way, self-aspects can increase the likelihood of certain experiences (e.g. 'I am an extraverted person, so perhaps I should do something to cheer up this crowd'). In this sense, self-aspects may also be viewed as theories or mini-theories about oneself (Epstein, 1973).

A number of other interrelated characteristics of self-aspects, and hence of identity, are noteworthy. First, self-aspects are of a truly social-cognitive nature because they are both cognitive and social products. They are constructed as cognitive representations of oneself, but they are also social products in that their meanings emerge from social interaction with other people which is in turn embedded in wider societal and cultural contexts (Kashima et al., 2001; Stryker & Statham, 1985).

Second, self-aspects are never absolute features of an isolated monad, but relational features of social beings embedded in a context of social relationships (Oakes et al., 1994). For example, the self-aspect 'young' helps to interpret oneself, and only makes sense, relative to older people with whom one participates in particular social relationships, such as 'son–father' or 'pupil–teacher' relationships. Third, self-aspects reflect one's social positions *vis-à-vis* others and in society at large (e.g. one's membership in a subordinated minority group). Self-aspects thus import social structure into the individual mind (Tajfel & Turner, 1986).

Fourth, people usually have access to multiple self-aspects. The multiplicity of self-aspects reflects the complex web of social relations that has evolved, especially in modern society (Stryker & Serpe, 1982).

Fifth, self-aspects are interrelated to varying degrees and thus provide a cognitive structure for self-interpretation (Linville, 1985, 1987). For example, the self-aspect 'student' is more likely to be related to the self-aspect 'young' than to the self-aspect 'father'. Together with 'young' and other related self-aspects (e.g. intelligent, critical, poor), the self-aspect 'student' then serves as a coherent cognitive structure for self-interpretation. The interrelation of self-aspects reflects the overlap of social relations (e.g. 'Students are usually young people, but rarely fathers') as well as people's lay theories or stereotypes.

Sixth, the salience or role of a particular self-aspect in self-interpretation varies with the immediate situational context. For example, the self-aspect 'skinny' should increase in salience and play a more important role in self-interpretation while one is in the gym as opposed to the lecture room (Turner et al., 1987).

Finally, although self-aspects may become chronic owing to high personal importance and/or prolonged periods of social contextual invariance, they need not be understood as hard-wired cognitive structures. Self-aspects can also be constructed 'on-line' in working memory based on both specific information salient in the concrete situation and more general knowledge retrieved from long-term memory (Barsalou, 1987; Onorato & Turner, 2001).

A metaphor serves to further illustrate these characteristics. Self-aspects can be understood metaphorically as places that one occupies in the social world. For example, ascribing to oneself the self-aspect 'tall' can be understood as placing oneself near the top of the height dimension, away from short people. Similarly, ascription of any other self-aspect concerning roles, abilities, behaviours, tastes, traits, attitudes, explicit category or group memberships or something else implies self-placement on a specific dimension in a social space or landscape. Such places are social and relational because people find their places in the social world in interaction with other people and relative to other people. That is, places are created, assigned and taken by way of a social negotiation process and demarcated from other people's places ('My place is my place because it is not your place'). Moreover, the social landscape is not homogeneous. It is socially structured so that some people have good, comfortable, attractive and well-respected places that provide them with lots of important resources, whereas others live in bad, uncomfortable, unattractive and less respected places with fewer resources. Especially in highly developed social landscapes, it is possible for people to have multiple places, provided they have the means to move around in the social landscape. Usually the distances between one's multiple places vary, and it is easier to visit those places that are nearby than to visit the more distant ones. In any case, a good map of the entire ensemble of one's multiple places and their interconnections is important for self-orientation. The multiplicity of one's places also allows for the possibility that at different times one may feel at home in different places. Finally, although people may often have rather stable homes because they have been staying in the same place for a long period of time, changing circumstances can prompt them to change places and build new homes. In order to construct their new homes, people may use the building material available in the new situation as well as bring old material with them from their former homes.

Self-interpretation in terms of self-aspects (or 'places') that possess these characteristics provides people with identities that are equally social, relational, complex, socially and cognitively structured and context-dependent. Identities are therefore inherently dynamic and, depending on the interplay of various person variables and social context variables, different identities can be at work at different times, which does not exclude the possibility, however, that identities can also solidify and function as rather stable self-definitions under appropriate conditions (e.g. prolonged periods of social contextual invariance). In the following section, I will elaborate on two variants of (working) identity that are of particular social psychological relevance.

Defining collective and individual identities

More than a hundred years ago, Sigmund Freud (1922/1989, p. 6) insisted that any individualistic psychology inevitably at some point confronts the challenge 'to explain the surprising fact that under a certain condition this individual, whom it had come to understand, thought, felt and acted in quite a different way from what would have been expected. And this condition is his insertion into a collection of people which has acquired the characteristic of a "psychological group".' Later, the relationship between the individual and the group was even declared a 'master problem' of social psychology (F. Allport, 1962; Brown & Turner, 1981). Today, most scholars in the field of social psychology acknowledge what appears to be a 'discontinuity' between the perception and behaviour of people acting as individuals, on the one hand, and the perception and behaviour of people acting as group members, on the other (Brown, 2000; Schopler & Insko, 1992; Smith & Mackie, 2000). As explained in the previous chapter, self-categorization theory (SCT, Turner et al., 1987) introduced the distinction between personal identity and social identity as a conceptual tool which helps researchers to better understand the transition from individual to group perception and behaviour and vice versa. Personal identity was identified as the critical psychological basis of individual phenomena, that is, patterns of perception and behaviour characterized by inter-individual variation, whereas social identity was identified as the psychological basis of collective or group phenomena, that is, patterns of perception and behaviour characterized by inter-individual uniformity (see also Marx & Engels, 1978, p. 199, for a similar, but more specific, distinction between the personal individual and the class individual).

The current self-aspect model of identity builds on and incorporates the distinction between personal identity and social identity. It further elaborates these two important identity variants and analyses their interrelationships with a particular emphasis on their functioning in modern society. Owing to their traditional focus on group phenomena, social identity and self-categorization theorists have so far invested most of their conceptual and empirical efforts in promoting our understanding of social identity, whereas the concept of personal identity has received only scant attention. The following analysis thus also serves to correct this imbalance. Before turning to this analysis, a few comments on terminology are in order.

First, social psychologists, especially European social psychologists, have traditionally used the term '*social* identity' to refer to the identity that people derive from their memberships in social groups, whereas the term '*personal* identity' is usually reserved for people's self-definitions as unique individuals (Tajfel & Turner, 1979, 1986; Turner et al., 1987; see also Luhtanen & Crocker, 1992, p. 302). However, I prefer to use the attributes 'collective' and 'individual' instead of 'social' and 'personal' in combination with identity in order to preclude the misinterpretation that, by implication, (personal) identity as a unique individual would be asocial and/or that it would more authentically represent some inner or private self, such as one's 'true personality'. As I shall show in detail later, such conclusions would be incorrect and were certainly never intended by the original self-categorization theorists (see Turner et al., 1987, p. 46).

Second, I need to clarify that the notion of collective identity is used here as a (social) psychological concept and not as a sociological concept in a Durkheimian sense (Durkheim, 1895/1976; Rucht, 1995). That is, collective identity in the present sense is the identity of a person derived from membership in a collective or group and not the identity of a group as a *sui generis* entity.

The final comment concerns the use of the terms 'self' and 'identity'. A cursory inspection of the social psychological literature suggests that the term 'self' is typically used in the social cognition literature where the emphasis is on the working self-concept as a cognitive representation (e.g. Fiske & Taylor, 1991; Markus & Wurf, 1987), whereas the term 'identity' seems to be preferred by perspectives that place greater emphasis on the social structural context, such as identity theory (Stryker & Statham, 1985), social identity theory (Tajfel & Turner, 1986) or self-categorization theory (Turner et al., 1987). These different traditions have also left their traces in the terminology used in the present integrative approach. The term 'self' is retained in the designation as 'self-interpretation' of the critical social-cognitive process assumed to underlie people's identities, while the use of the term 'identity' for the output of this self-interpretation process can be viewed as a tribute to the perspectives that emphasize the role of social structure.

Collective identity: self-interpretation focused on a socially shared self-aspect   I suggest that a collective identity is constructed whenever self-interpretation is based primarily on a single self-aspect that one shares with other, but not all other, people in the relevant social context. In short, collective identity results from self-interpretation that centres on a socially shared (collective or social categorical) self-aspect. It is therefore basically one-dimensional (e.g. 'First and foremost, I am a Christian'). Inter-individual differences on other dimensions or self-aspects become irrelevant and the similarity or interchangeability of oneself with other people sharing the same self-aspect moves into the psychological foreground. By the same token, perceived ingroup homogeneity increases (Turner et al., 1987).

The critical psychological process underlying collective identity is therefore the process of focusing or concentrating self-interpretation on a single socially shared self-aspect. Accordingly, factors that facilitate this process also facilitate collective identity. In chapter 4, I will review research that supports this assumption and that has identified several person variables (e.g. personal importance and valence attached to self-aspects) as well as social context variables (e.g. numerical distinctiveness and social contextual fit of self-aspects) that are likely to play such a facilitative role. Two other points need to be made. First, although collective identity is conceptualized here as being focused or centred on a single dominant self-aspect, it is not maintained that, beyond this focal self-aspect (e.g. Christian), no additional self-aspects can be involved in collective identity. They certainly can. The important point is, however, that such 'secondary' self-aspects (e.g. pious, honest, virtuous) are typically implied by the focal self-aspect. They are stereotypically associated or correlated with it and, in this sense, they are redundant. Second, it may be somewhat misleading to speak of *the* collective identity of a given person. At least hypothetically, a person can have as many different collective identities as she has socially shared self-aspects. This view is similar to James's (1890/1950, p. 294) conviction that a person has 'as many different social selves as there are distinct *groups* of persons about whose opinion he cares' (emphasis in the original).

Individual identity: self-interpretation based on a complex config-uration of self-aspects   I suggest that an individual identity is constructed whenever self-interpretation is based on a more comprehensive set or config-uration of different, non-redundant self-aspects (e.g. 'I am female, a Christian, musical, a lawyer, have brown hair, like French cuisine and so forth'). The more comprehensive and complex this set or configuration, the more pronounced one's individual identity, and the less likely it is that another person possesses an identical set of self-aspects. As a consequence, one's distinctiveness or uniqueness as an individual moves into the psychological foreground.

Another consequence concerns the experience of individual freedom or independence. The more complex the configuration of self-aspects that informs self-interpretation, the less likely it is that one single self-aspect monopolizes this process and the ensuing perception and behaviour. Instead, the very existence of many different self-aspects assures psychological variabil-ity, flexibility and ultimately independence (Linville, 1985; Thoits, 1983, 1986). For example, being a family man in addition to being a soccer player makes a person less dependent on the approval of his team mates because he has access to an alternative source of positive self-evaluation or self-esteem. That is, the more aspects are available for self-interpretation, the greater the choice and therefore the less one's dependence on each single self-aspect for (psychological) need satisfaction.

Similarly, multiple self-aspects make it easier to escape unwanted obligations associated with each particular self-aspect. For example, being a volunteer for the Red Cross may allow a person to avoid some disliked family event, while at other times his role as father may allow him to excuse himself from less attractive volunteer activities. Hence, a complex configuration of self-aspects, together with the ensuing tension or even conflict between the different self-aspects, augments and highlights one's independence as an individual (see also Stryker & Statham, 1985, p. 359). This observation also points to an interesting, almost paradoxical, interrelation of sociological and psychological phenomena in that the psychological experience of individual independence seems to be predicated, from a sociological point of view, on the individual's participation in a complex web of social relationships and hence on an extension of the 'chains' of social interdependence (Elias, 1988, 1990). Taken together, it can be suggested that individual identity comprises at least two distinct, but related components, namely self-interpretation as a distinct individual (see also Turner et al., 1987) and self-interpretation as an independent individual (see also Deci & Ryan, 1991; Markus & Kitayama, 1991).

This two-component conception of individual identity corresponds to a distinction made by Georg Simmel almost 100 years ago. He suggested two components or ideal-types of individuality, namely individuality as self-determination or independence and individuality as differentiation or distinctiveness (Simmel, 1908, pp. 527–73, 1984, pp. 212–19; also Schimank, 1996, pp. 44–53). According to Simmel, individuality as self-determination is predicated on people's freedom from restrictions or constraints imposed by their groups. To the extent to which people are free and do not have to conform to group norms, their individuality can and will unfold. In the final analysis, such individuality also means universal equality among people as the removal of all external social constraints or restrictions will reveal the essential similarity of all people or, in other words, their shared human identity. Simmel traced the ideological and material roots of this individuality component back to the era of the Enlightenment and the economic liberalism of the eighteenth century ('free enterprise'). Conversely, individuality as differentiation is, according to Simmel, predicated on differences from other people. Unlike the independence component of individuality, the differentiation component implies fundamental inequality among people and is ideologically and materially rooted in the nineteenth century, characterized by the ideas of Romanticism and the then prevalent economic principle of 'division of labour' (see also Baumeister, 1986).

Irrespective of whether the emphasis is on its distinctiveness component or its independence component, the critical process underlying individual identity is the process of 'de-centrating' or 'de-monopolizing' self-interpretation.[1] Again, this process is a joint function of person variables and social context variables. More specifically, it increases in strength with a person's readiness, deriving from her values, motives, goals, prior experiences and so forth, to extend her self-interpretation beyond a single social categorical self-aspect and heed additional self-aspects. At the same time, the social context also needs to afford sufficient opportunities for the activation or development of additional meaningful self-aspects. For example, the need for positive self-evaluation or self-esteem may motivate a member of a stigmatized ethnic minority to downplay her group membership and may thus increase her readiness to emphasize additional self-aspects unrelated to her minority group membership, such as her academic achievements, political affiliation or role as mother. Of course, successful implementation of such an individualization strategy also requires that this minority member actually has access to, or can construct, additional self-aspects which are meaningfully connected with the relevant social context. For instance, her additional self-aspect as a hard-working student should be more meaningful or fitting in a university context than in the context of a neighbourhood meeting. In the latter context, her role as mother may be better suited to serve as an additional self-aspect. Relevant research will be reviewed in subsequent chapters (see especially chapter 4).

Finally, although it may seem at first glance as if a person can have only one unique ensemble of self-aspects and thus only one individual identity, it should be noted that in new situations new self-aspects can be constructed, and that in different situations different sub-sets or combinations of self-aspects may be processed and used for self-interpretation. Consequently, a person can also have different individual identities.

False opposites

It is often assumed that individual and collective identities are constructed from quite different or even opposite types or classes of self-aspects. On the one hand, a person's sex, ethnicity, nationality, political affiliation and religion are frequently thought of as collective or 'groupy' aspects of that person and thus as almost 'natural' bases for collective identities. On the other hand, physical features, psychological characteristics, tastes and abilities are often assumed to be personal or individual in nature and therefore genuine constituents or elements of individual identities (Gergen, 1971; Gordon, 1968; Triandis, 1990).

However, this opposition dissolves when scrutinized more closely. There exists no compelling reason to assume that individual and collective identities are necessarily based on inherently or essentially different types of self-aspects (see also Bodenhausen, Macrae & Sherman, 1999; Brewer & Harasty Feinstein, 1999; Simon, 1997). Although some self-aspects may appear to have more potential than others to provide a basis for a collective identity, it is important to note that such potential is highly context-specific. Religious denomination, for example, has great potential to invoke a collective identity in Northern Ireland, whereas in Germany it may be viewed more as contributing to one's individual identity. Also, most of us might be inclined to think that wearing spectacles or not is more likely to be associated with one's individual identity than with any significant collective identity. But now imagine that all people who wear spectacles are suddenly singled out for the same special treatment, perhaps because they are considered literate and therefore dangerous. No doubt, 'wearing spectacles' would then soon demonstrate great collective-identity potential (see also Tajfel, 1976).

The important point is that most, if not all, self-aspects can be experienced as socially shared or social categorical and thus serve as a basis for a collective identity under the appropriate social conditions. This view is consistent with Tajfel's (1978b, p. 28) social psychological definition of a group as a body of people who feel that they are a group, which was modelled on Emerson's (1960) definition of a nation. The fact that most, if not all, self-aspects possess a collective-identity potential, and that such potential readily manifests itself when the respective self-aspect is focused on, has long been acknowledged, or at least been capitalized on, by experimental social psychologists working in the area of group processes.

Following the minimal group paradigm (Tajfel et al., 1971), it has become a standard procedure in experimental group research to create *ad hoc* groups by informing research participants that they allegedly share a particular self-aspect with other, but not all other, participants. This procedure has proven very successful in inducing participants to act in terms of their collective identity as group members. It is especially noteworthy that this procedure has successfully been employed with a diverse variety of self-aspects such as artistic preference (e.g. preference for Klee vs. Kandinsky paintings), per-ceptual sensitivity (e.g. blue vs. green sensitivity), psychological character-istics (e.g. introverted vs. extraverted) or cognitive styles (e.g. analytical vs. holistic) (e.g. Judd & Park, 1988; Oakes & Turner, 1980; Simon & Hamilton, 1994). Evidently, the success of this procedure does not hinge so much on the specific type of self-aspect used for psychological group formation, but on the meaning which the particular social context affords the socially shared self-aspect. The social microcosm created in the minimal group paradigm affords the particular self-aspect (e.g. preference for Klee paintings) special meaning because its possession (or non-possession) is the only criterion available under such social conditions which can provide a basis for meaningful interpretation of self (and others). In short, such a microcosm facilitates focused or concentrated self-interpretation.

It follows that the same self-aspect (e.g. German) can provide the basis for a collective identity at one time ('We, the Germans'), whereas at another time it may be construed as a constituent or element of one's individual identity ('I am a psychologist, male, German, have brown eyes and so forth'). In the first case the particular self-aspect defines a social category of which oneself is one member among others, whereas in the other case it is one feature among several other features of oneself, the ensemble of which constitutes one's individual identity. In the first case the own person is allocated to the self-aspect, in the second case the self-aspect is allocated to the own person. Whether a particular self-aspect is construed as a social category or as one feature among others is thus subject to variation. A growing body of empirical work, reviewed in subsequent chapters, demonstrates that such variation is by no means random, but systematically tied to various person and social context variables.

In a similar vein, it would be misleading to construe individual and collective identity as opposites on the *social* dimension of self-interpretation. The insight that with the invocation of individual identity, intragroup similarities and obligations to fellow group members recede into the psychological background does not imply that individual identity is an 'asocial' variant of identity. It will be recalled that all self-aspects are social products in that they acquire their meaning and significance during social interaction. Self-aspects are never absolute features of an isolated monad, but relational features of interdependent human beings. This is true for self-aspects when they serve as a basis and provide the content for a collective identity, and are thus explicitly recognized as socially shared with some other (but not all other) people, but also when they are construed as elements of one's individual identity. That is, individual identity is not based on 'asocial' self-aspects, but on a unique configuration or combination of equally social self-aspects from which it then derives its content and meaning. Moreover, both individual and collective identity originate from, and are endorsed by, specific social conditions (e.g. permeable or impermeable group boundaries, respectively), and both function as mediators between these conditions and people's social perceptions and behaviours. In short, individual identity is as social 'in terms of its content, origin and function' as collective identity (Turner et al., 1987, p. 46).

The dialectic relationship between collective identity and individual identity

I have suggested that collective identity results from self-interpretation centred on a dominant self-aspect, whereas individual identity results from

self-interpretation in terms of a more complex set of self-aspects. This conceptualization implies that the psychological processes underlying collective identity and individual identity (concentration vs. de-centration) tend to be
inversely related. Also, as I will demonstrate in subsequent chapters, there
are characteristic differences in the antecedents and consequences of collective
identity and individual identity. Certain antecedents (e.g. common fate) tend
to facilitate concentration on a particular self-aspect, and hence foster collective identity with its specific consequences, whereas other antecedents (e.g.
multiple group memberships) tend to facilitate de-centration, and hence foster
individual identity with its specific consequences.

However, the relationship between individual identity and collective identity as such is not simply an antagonistic one. It will be remembered that the
same self-aspect (e.g. 'gay') can provide the basis for one's collective identity at
one time (e.g. during a Gay Pride march), whereas at another time it may
contribute, together with other self-aspects, to one's individual identity ('I am a
psychologist, male, German, gay, have brown eyes and so forth'). This dual
function of self-aspects serves as an important bridge between individual and
collective identity and allows for mutual reinforcement of both identity variants. On the one hand, individual identity imports and incorporates past
experiences with various collective identities because it also includes self-
aspects that have served as bases for collective identities on previous occasions.
Individual identity is therefore at least partly composed of the sediments or
traces of previously experienced collective identities and thus preserves these
collective identities and their potential for realization under appropriate conditions. In fact, because most self-aspects can, under the appropriate conditions,
provide the basis for a collective identity, individual identity is a reservoir for
possible, previously experienced as well as yet-to-be-experienced, collective
identities. On the other hand, collective identity, or better, collective identities
also play an important role in the maintenance of individual identity. The
multiplicity and diversity of one's collective identities reflect and endorse the
complex system of social coordinates or self-aspects within which oneself is
located and which in turn facilitates and necessitates self-interpretation as a
distinct and independent individual. This view corresponds directly to Simmel's
(1955) conception of the individual in modern society as a social being that is
positioned at the intersection of an increasing number of social groups:

> The groups with which the individual is affiliated constitute a system of coordin-
> ates, as it were, such that each new group with which he becomes affiliated
> circumscribes him more exactly and more unambiguously. To belong to any one
> of these groups leaves the individual considerable leeway. But the larger the
> number of groups to which an individual belongs, the more improbable is it that
> other persons will exhibit the same combination of group-affiliations, that these

particular groups will 'intersect' once again [in a second individual]. Concrete objects lose their individual characteristics as we subsume them under a general concept in accordance with one of their attributes. And concrete objects regain their individual characteristics as other concepts are emphasized under which their several attributes may be subsumed. To speak Platonically, each thing has a part in as many ideas as it has manifold attributes, and it achieves thereby its individual determination. There is an analogous relationship between the individual and the groups with which he is affiliated.

(Simmel, 1955, p. 140)

Furthermore, Simmel (1955) pointed out that it is the very tension, or even conflict, arising from the diversity of collective identities ('group affiliations') that contributes positively to a coherent individual identity:

it is also true that multiple group-affiliations can strengthen the individual and reenforce the integration of his personality. Conflicting and integrating tendencies are mutually reenforcing. Conflicting tendencies can arise just because the individual has a core of inner unity. The ego can become more clearly conscious of this unity, the more he is confronted with the task of reconciling within himself a diversity of group interests.

(Simmel, 1955, pp. 141–2)

In conclusion, the relationship between collective identity and individual identity is a dialectic one in that there is a continual, dynamic dialogue between the two, in the course of which they make each other possible.

Explicit and implicit identities

The dialectic relationship between individual and collective identity further implies that they serve each other as background. While one becomes explicit as the figure, the other remains implicit as the ground. However, the implicit ground still helps to shape the experience of the figure (Krech & Crutchfield, 1948). For example, although in a given situation a person may construe her various group memberships as elements of her individual identity, they still remain connected to their collective roots owing to processes of socialization and internalized (sub-)cultural routines. Conversely, when individual identity operates in the background, it can still function as an implicit interpretative frame. More specifically, it is likely to modulate, as the sediment or synthesis of a more complex ensemble of self-aspects, and to constrain, as a system of 'checks and balances', the instantiation of any specific collective identity (Simon & Mummendey, 1997; von Krockow, 1987). As Billig (1995) has shown for the case of nationality, the operation of implicit background identities might be forgotten, but they are nonetheless effectual. In fact, the process of forgetting or taking-for-granted may underlie the secret of their success.

This figure–ground relationship between collective and individual identity could also be responsible for the existence of dual or mixed attitudes (Wilson, Lindsey & Schooler, 2000). Some evaluative reactions toward an attitudinal object (e.g. a minority group) may be closely tied to one's explicit individual or collective identity, which currently acts as figure, whereas other evaluative reactions towards the same object may be connected primarily to the corresponding background or implicit identity. As taken-for-granted identities, implicit identities usually operate outside conscious awareness, whereas explicit identities are in the current focus of (self-)attention. It may therefore be tempting to align the differentiation between attitudes (and behaviours) tied to explicit identities and those tied to implicit identities with the distinction between controlled and automatic processes. Although the latter distinction seems to be an important heuristic for advancing our understanding of a variety of cognitive, affective and motivational phenomena (e.g. Dovidio, Kawakami & Beach, 2001; but see also Bargh, 1989, for important specifications), it may not be useful, and perhaps even misleading, to fully subsume the distinction between explicit and implicit identities under the distinction between controlled and automatic processes. It is not only that explicit identities can also prompt automatic attitudinal and behavioural processes and that implicit identities can also elicit controlled processes. Rather, the important point is that, for explicit identities, automatic processes (e.g. in stereotyping) are unproblematic because they typically operate in accordance with the controlled processes originating from the same explicit identities. There is simply no need to control these automatic processes. Similarly, the connection of controlled processes (e.g. school children who deliberately salute one, and only one, particular flag, namely that of their own nation) to implicit identities (e.g. national identity) is often not recognized or forgotten. That is, such 'banal' attitudes and activities are taken for granted and naturalized, but they are not necessarily automatic or uncontrollable (Billig, 1995). In any case, it is the task of any analysis of identity that aspires to be more than just an 'iceberg psychology' to dig deeper and to consider both explicit and implicit identities and their interrelated (controlled and automatic) functioning.

Identities, placeholders and essences

Researchers have suggested that 'the self may well be the largest and most rich prototype in our cognitive arsenal' (T.B. Rogers, 1981, p. 203; see also Markus & Kitayama, 1991). This view overlaps with the notion of individual identity as deriving from self-interpretation in terms of a complex configuration of self-aspects. However, the exact form of cognitive representation underlying individual identity remains debatable. In particular, it may not be necessary to assume a fixed cognitive structure in long-term memory consisting of a complex configuration of cognitively represented self-aspects. The sheer number of possible self-aspects which would need to be stored and later retrieved makes such an assumption not very plausible. Instead, it may very well be that this complex configuration is phenomenologically and cognitively condensed to a category of its own, possibly with the (meta-)self-aspects or features 'independent' and/or 'distinct' tagged to it, that then serves as a short cut or placeholder ('me') for more complex narratives, instantiations or representations of one's individual identity (as for the concept of 'placeholder', see also Medin & Ortony, 1989). The function of such a placeholder would be to reserve a cognitive place for context-dependent representations of individual identity. Instead of retrieving an invariant representation from long-term memory, context-dependent representations could be constructed in working memory, drawing both on specific information available in the concrete situation and more general knowledge retrieved from long-term memory (Barsalou, 1987; Onorato & Turner, 2001). Each time the person experiences herself as independent or distinct from other people in her social milieu, the placeholder and the respective tags would be reinforced. Such reinforcement would also provide people with a sense of unity, coherence and self-continuity, or more generally, a sense of individual essence (Medin, 1989; Medin & Ortony, 1989).

Similarly, people may also hold cognitive placeholders for their collective identities ('we') (Perdue et al., 1990). Again, such placeholders would allow for context-dependent narratives, instantiations or representations of a person's collective identities (e.g. 'We Germans'), and it is very likely that they would be associated with essentialistic beliefs implying that all ingroup members share some essence (Rothbart & Taylor, 1992). Placeholders for collective identities may then be tagged with the (meta-)feature 'essentially the same' (or 'essentially homogeneous').

As with the belief in the essence of categories in other domains, people need not know exactly what the individual or collective essence is to hold essentialistic beliefs concerning their individual or collective identities. It is sufficient to believe that the particular essence is in principle knowable (Medin, 1989; Medin & Ortony, 1989). For example, it would be sufficient to believe that there are other people, experts (e.g. psychologists or biologists), who really know or at least will know some day what that essence is. For the time being, people may quite happily take the experienced individual independence or distinctiveness, on the one hand, or the perceived ingroup homogeneity, on the other, as a 'surface' indicator of an underlying, 'deeper' individual or collective essence (e.g. genetic make-up). Moreover, it is the very fact that placeholders are rather content-free that allows for context-dependent flexibility or variability in the content of individual and collective identities. For example, the concrete instantiation of the collective identity as Germans can vary with the presence of a particular outgroup. In the presence of an American outgroup the feature 'formal' may be viewed as characteristic of German identity, whereas in the presence of a Russian outgroup the feature 'prosperous' may be viewed as particularly characteristic (see also Haslam et al., 1992). Similarly, the concrete instantiation of one's individual identity can vary with the presence of different individual others. At the same time, the belief that one's collective or individual identity is tied to some deeper, not necessarily known essence assures that the particular identity is still attributed sufficient coherence and continuity despite all context-dependent variation.

Finally, it might be tempting to assume that individual identity is more readily ascribed a deeper, underlying essence than collective identity because individual identity can be tied directly to one's own individual body as a natural anchor with a biological essence (G. Allport, 1968; Markus & Kitayama, 1991). However, although collective identity lacks such an immediate biological anchor or embodiment, it can build on (sub-)cultural artefacts and symbols, such as names, monuments, flags, songs or literature (Kashima et al., 2001). In addition, language use may play an important role in this context. More specifically, linguistic abstraction seems to be conducive to the induction or supposition of a collective essence (Maass et al., 1989). Therefore, self-aspects referred to by nouns may be particularly likely to serve as a basis for a collective identity. Nouns (e.g. worker, woman, psychologist) suggest that the respective self-aspects define discrete social types or categories with relatively clear boundaries. They appear to cut the social world 'at its joints' (Roger Brown, 1986, pp. 468–82) and thus imply underlying essences and hence essential similarities among people sharing the critical self-aspect as well as essential or qualitative differences between people who share the self-aspect and those who do not (Medin & Ortony, 1989; Rothbart & Taylor, 1992; Yzerbyt, Rocher & Schadron, 1997). Conversely, self-aspects referred to by less abstract linguistic terms or expressions (e.g. verbs) should be less likely to serve as a basis for a collective identity. This applies also to self-aspects referred to by adjectives, even though adjectives may be very similar to nouns with respect to many other cognitive functions (Semin & Fiedler, 1988). Yet, unlike nouns, adjectives suggest that self-aspects to which they refer (e.g. strong, short, extraverted) vary along underlying continua (e.g. from not very strong to extremely strong) (Gordon, 1968). 'Adjective self-aspects' are therefore seen more as a matter of degree or quantity than as a matter of quality. Accordingly, similarities and differences are viewed merely as quantitative in nature and are thus less likely to trigger essentialistic beliefs.

Viewed from the perspective of self-interpretation, the belief that nouns denote qualities or underlying essences allows nouns to incite us, to a greater extent than adjectives or other linguistic expressions, 'to go beyond the information given' (Bruner, 1957b), that is, to make additional inferences (Andersen, Klatzky & Murray, 1990; Hamilton et al., 1992; Rothbart & Taylor, 1992). Accordingly, self-interpretations in terms of noun self-aspects are richer and more saturated. Even a single noun self-aspect may then be able to provide an exhaustive self-interpretation and thus a collective identity (e.g. 'I am a socialist'). In the case of self-interpretations in terms of other self-aspects, however, more comprehensive sets of self-aspects would be necessary for satisfactory self-interpretation (e.g. 'I am quite friendly, not very religious, usually not very punctual, I like my work and so forth'). Taken together, single noun self-aspects are more likely to allow for essential(istic) and exhaustive self-interpretations so that self-interpretations are more likely centred on a single noun self-aspect than on a single self-aspect referred to by other linguistic expressions. In short, noun self-aspects should be particularly good candidates for the construction of essentialistic collective identities. However, this is not to postulate that there is something special in the *content* of noun self-aspects compared with other self-aspects (e.g. adjective self-aspects) that makes the former better candidates for the construction of collective identities. For example, while at times, 'being extraverted' or 'being intellectual' may just be another element of one's individual identity, it is certainly possible that at other times interpreting oneself primarily as 'an extravert' or as 'an intellectual' results in a collective identity (see also Bodenhausen et al., 1999). It is not content *per se* that matters here. Rather, as I have argued above, irrespective of content, most, if not all, self-aspects seem to have a collective-identity potential, and the linguistic form in which a self-aspect is expressed may be one important variable among others that facilitates or inhibits the realization of that potential.

Identity and (Post)Modernity

Classical sociological theories have conceptualized modernization as functional differentiation which is made possible, *inter alia*, by division of labour, industrialization, urbanization, mass communication, literacy and nation-building. Further characteristics of modern, functionally differentiated society are social permeability and mobility, formal equality, individualized interests and universalistic competition (Bell, 1973; Esser, 1988; Inglehart & Baker, 2000; Schimank, 1996). As shown by Esser (1988), such a conceptualization suggests that in the course of modernization traditional, pre-industrial collectives (e.g. family, guild, rank, tribe or village) should lose their capacity to sustain close social ties among people. For instance, Max Weber (1978) predicted that modernization erodes any kind of community:

> With the multiplication of life chances and opportunities, the individual becomes less and less content with being bound to rigid and undifferentiated forms of life prescribed by the group. Increasingly he desires to shape his life as an individual and to enjoy the fruits of his own abilities and labor as he himself wishes.
>
> *(Weber, 1978, p. 375)*

Similarly, Karl Marx and Friedrich Engels pointed out in the Manifesto of the Communist Party that economic modernization sets people progressively free from their traditional social ties:

> Constant revolutionising of production, uninterrupted disturbance of all social conditions, everlasting uncertainty and agitation distinguish the bourgeois epoch from all earlier ones. All fixed, fast frozen relations, with their train of ancient and venerable prejudices and opinions, are swept away, all new-formed ones become antiquated before they can ossify. All that is solid melts into air, all that is holy is profaned, and man is at last compelled to face with sober senses, his real conditions of life, and his relations with his kind.
>
> *(Marx & Engels, 1978, p. 476)*

At the same time that traditional collectives lose their importance in modern society (see also Beck, 1994; Fromm, 1942), the complexity of the social fabric increases. The system of social coordinates necessary to locate oneself increases in complexity. People no longer belong to a single dominant collective or social group which for a lifetime affects all or most aspects of their lives ('from the cradle to the grave'). Instead, they belong simultaneously to an increasing number of different, often mutually independent, but sometimes also conflicting social groups (e.g. professional groups, neighbourhoods, political parties, sports teams and so forth). Just as a group incorporates many individuals, so does now 'an individual incorporate[s] many groups' (F. Allport, 1962, p. 25; see also Simmel, 1955, p. 140).

From a psychological perspective, the placement of the individual within a more differentiated and thus more complex system of social coordinates implies the cognitive differentiation of additional non-redundant self-aspects. In other words, modern society offers access to additional non-redundant self-aspects. It thereby expands the basis for self-interpretation. It allows for self-interpretation in terms of an increasingly complex set of self-aspects and is thus conducive to individual identity. In fact, individual identity is increasingly required as an appropriate psychological reflection of one's own complex social positioning in modern society, because 'a complexly differentiated and organized society requires a parallel view of the self' (Stryker & Serpe, 1982, p. 206).

This conclusion is also supported by Elias' (1988, 1990) socio-historical analysis of changes in people's identities. Elias notes that, since the European Middle Ages, the balance between collective identity ('we-identity') and individual identity ('I-identity') has undergone a remarkable change towards an increasing pre-potency of individual identity. According to Elias, this process, the starting-point of which he sees symbolized by Descartes' famous 'Cogito, ergo sum', is accompanied and reinforced by the civilizing process which fosters self-interpretations as self-contained individuals with private 'insides' separated from other people on the outside (Elias, 1988, p. 168). In modern society, the increasing pre-potency of individual identity is sustained especially by the decreasing permanence and increasing interchangeability of 'we-relations' and finds expression, *inter alia*, in psychological privatization, reflexive subjectivism and individual self-expression (Elias, 1988; Giddens, 1991; Inglehart & Baker, 2000; Schimank, 1985).

At this point, an important specification is in order. Whereas the converging and mutually reinforcing tendencies towards societal and psychological individualization in the course of modernization seem to operate at the expense of traditional collectives (e.g. family, guild, rank, tribe, village) and the associated collective identities, these tendencies seem quite compatible with collective identity in terms of nationality. In fact, nation-building is generally recognized as a constitutive element of modernization (Esser, 1988; Kreckel, 1989), so that national identity is viewed as a post-traditional, specific modern form of collective identity (Habermas, 1992, p. 163; Hall, 1992; Wimmer, 2002; see also chapter 1). Furthermore, scholars have argued from a socio-historical perspective that nation-building and individualization are interdependent processes that (co)operate at the expense of traditional intermediate social structures and collectives (Elias, 1990; Mayer & Müller, 1994; Wimmer, 2002). On the one hand, the modern nation-state provides its citizens with individual rights and individual opportunities (including political participation) and, in its typical form as a welfare state, also promises them at least a minimum of individual economic security. Every citizen may then pursue her own distinct career and become increasingly independent of traditional intermediate structures and collectives which thus lose their binding and integrative capacity. On the other hand, each individual citizen must in return pledge allegiance to and identify with the nation-state within the limits of which the individualization process takes place. No other allegiances or collective identities with potentially centrifugal effects must stand between the individual citizen and the nation. The individual needs the nation-state as an institutional guarantor of her individuality, while the nation-state needs the individual as a constituent element, that is, as a law-abiding taxpayer in times of peace and as a patriotic soldier in times of war. From a psychological perspective, national identity and nationalism as its integration ideology may often remain implicit in modern society, but nonetheless influential (Billig, 1995).

However, what if modern society belongs to the past? Analysts have claimed that we no longer live in modern societies, but in a postmodern world characterized by economic and cultural globalization and the loss of firm standards necessary to determine 'truth', 'progress' or even 'reality' (e.g. Lash, 1990; Lyotard, 1984; B. S. Turner, 1990; for an overview, see Billig, 1995, pp. 128–53). With regard to the postmodern psyche, it is suggested by post-modernist thinkers that collective identities are an endangered, if not already extinguished, species. This verdict applies not only to collective identities that have their roots in traditional (pre-industrial) society stratified along the lines of family, guild, rank, tribe, village and so forth, but also to collective identities that are characteristic of modern (industrial and post-industrial) society, such as class and national identities. Where those collective identities are still observed in the postmodern world, they are discounted as defensive or regressive coping strat-egies of those who have not fully arrived in the postmodern world yet, cannot afford the travel or are afraid to arrive there. Conversely, postmodern identity is construed as a de-centrated, constantly altering mixture or playful pastiche of individual styles closely related to the person's variable patterns of consumption in the global economy (Hall, 1992). Anything goes that can be negotiated and consumed (Gergen, 1991) and that is sufficiently 'depthless' to be replaced momentarily (Billig, 1995, p. 135).

However, the postmodernist perspective has not remained unchallenged. From a social philosophical perspective, it has been criticized, for example, as a neo-conservative distortion unable to grasp the nature of modernity as the unfinished and yet-to-be-completed project originally initiated in the era of the Enlightenment (Habermas, 1992). Also, drawing on sociological and social psychological analyses, Billig (1995) has shattered the critical postmodernist assumption according to which globalization makes the nation-state and national identity obsolete (see also Koopmans & Statham, 1999; Wimmer, 2002). Rather, he has shown that nation-states and national identities are alive and well, especially the powerful nation-states and the associated national identities, and he has unmasked the alleged globalization process as a devel-opment towards global hegemony of the West and its super-power(s) such as the USA.

It is beyond the scope of this book to provide a comprehensive critique of the postmodernist perspective, nor do I want to imply that such a perspec-tive has nothing to contribute to an advanced understanding of identity (see McAdams, 1997). In fact, there is some overlap between this perspective and the integrative approach to identity presented in this chapter because the assumed multiplicity, variability and flexibility of postmodern identity is not entirely incompatible with the notion of individual identity as context-dependent self-interpretation in terms of a complex set of self-aspects. Also, I concur with both modernist and postmodernist analysts who seem to converge on the conclusion that there is a steady increase in the psychological importance and cultural or ideological attractiveness of individual identity relative to collective identity.

However, it would be premature to assume that collective identity has simply been rendered obsolete in the modern or postmodern world. Classic collective identities, such as those based on rank or social class, may be less salient, not so much because they, and the underlying cleavages and deprivations, would no longer exist, but because they now have to compete for attention with a strengthened individual identity as well as with alternative collective identities based on different self-aspects, such as gender, ethnicity or sexual orientation (Kriesi et al., 1995; Sampson, 1993). With regard to such alternative collective identities, it is important to note that they are not necessarily based on 'new' self-aspects, although the current world with its multiple opportunities for variegated social experiences certainly fosters the 'discovery' of numerous additional self-aspects. It is also true that the collective-identity potential of many self-aspects, old or new, more likely manifests itself in the (post)modern world where urbanization, increased intergroup contact, rapid transportation, mass communication and information technology provide ample opportunities for the formation and recognition of socially shared similarities, including collective interests and deprivations (Esser, 1988; Neidhardt & Rucht, 1993). This reasoning is in full accordance with the self-aspect model of identity presented above, which posits that most self-aspects can be experienced as socially shared and can thus serve as a basis for a collective identity under the appropriate social conditions.

In conclusion, the complex (post)modern world gives access to a multitude of self-aspects and hence strengthens individual identity, but at the same time it also provides a rich opportunity structure for the formation of various collective identities so that the number of potential or latent collective identities increases as well. However, a strengthened individual identity as well as the pluralism or even competition among (potential) collective identities should confine the activation or instantiation of each particular collective identity to specific contexts. Accordingly, I suggest that, while individual identity may hold a relatively privileged status in the (post)modern world, collective identity as such tends to be highly context-dependent and variable, with each specific instantiation of collective identity being rather transitory and fragile.

Identity, Phenomenology and Accuracy

Even though, or actually because, it has been suggested that in modern (or postmodern) society individual identity may hold a privileged status *vis-à-vis* collective identity, it is important to highlight the descriptive or phenomenological character of this suggestion. There are good reasons to assume that in modern society individual identity is usually experienced as primary *vis-à-vis* collective identity, perhaps even as reflecting the authentic or true self (e.g. Elias 1988; Simon, 1993). However, this assumption must not be (mis)understood as an ontological or even normative postulate. The important point is that modern society appears to promote experiences, or interpretations thereof, that strengthen people's individual identities (or their placeholders). The ensuing phenomenological priority of individual identity is thus not an ontological invariant, but an outcome of specific social conditions prevalent especially in modern (Western) societies (Markus & Kitayama, 1991; Triandis, 1990). Moreover, as the following chapters will demonstrate, the relative phenomenological significance of individual identity and collective identity remains variable even in modern societies, despite the chronic advantage they may afford individual identity. Metaphorically speaking, though the general 'climate' may favour individual identity, we also have variable 'weather conditions' so that the relative phenomenological significance of individual identity and collective identity still varies with the more proximate social conditions within the immediate social context (as well as with person variables) (Turner et al., 1994).

By the same token, both individual and collective identities can have psychological or phenomenological validity to the extent to which they adequately reflect people's context-dependent social positioning and related experiences. Collective identity must not categorically be viewed as a distortion of objective reality and individual identity as a generally accurate reflection of reality (or vice versa). Similarly, perceptual and behavioural consequences of collective identity (e.g. the accentuation of intragroup similarities relative to differences) are in no way less legitimate offspring of 'normal' psychological functioning than the corresponding consequences of individual identity (e.g. the accentuation of intragroup differences relative to similarities) (for an excellent discussion of this issue, see Oakes & Turner, 1990). It would therefore be misleading at best, and ideological at worst, to view individual identity and its consequences as some kind of objective standard against which to judge the validity or accuracy of collective identity and its consequences (for a divergent viewpoint on this issue, see Judd & Park, 1993). Such an individualistic approach would be predicated on the misconception that only collective identity involves abstraction (or categorization), whereas individual identity is concrete and thus closer to reality. Yet, as discussed more thoroughly by Oakes et al. (1994, pp. 114–16), individual identity, too, involves abstraction, namely, abstraction of self-aspects across time and situations which accentuates self-continuity and self-consistency. Consequently, it hardly makes sense to regard the outcome of one abstraction process as the objective baseline against which to assess the distortion allegedly involved in another abstraction process (see also Oakes & Reynolds, 1997).

Functions and Processes of Identity

Proper appreciation of identity as an explanatory social psychological construct requires an understanding of *what* identity does for the person and *how* it achieves whatever it does for the person. In other words, we need to understand the social psychological functions and processes of identity.

Identity functions

Identity is assumed here to serve a particular function to the extent to which it provides the person with a particular psychological experience (e.g. a feeling of belongingness) that promotes her social adjustment or well-being. Thereby, identity functions contribute to the attractiveness and thus to the adoption and maintenance of identity. This is true especially for identity functions that relate to important psychological needs. The psychological literature suggests that there may be at least five such identity functions related to the needs for (1) belongingness, (2) distinctiveness, (3) respect or esteem, (4) understanding or meaning and (5) agency (Baumeister, 1986; Baumeister & Leary, 1995; Breakwell, 1986; Brewer, 1991; Fiske, 2000; Maslow, 1970; Smith & Mackie, 2000; Tajfel & Turner, 1986; Tyler & Smith, 1999). I will briefly comment on each of the five identity functions.

First, identity confirms that one has a place in and thus belongs to the social world (which extends both in space and time). This is obviously true for collective identity, which results from and reflects occupation of a collective, socially shared place symbolized by a socially shared self-aspect. Hence, collective identity may be particularly conducive to a feeling of belongingness. However, individual identity can also serve the belongingness function. Although it results from and reflects occupation of an individual and hence rather exclusive place, or more precisely occupation of a unique intersection of many different places symbolized by many different self-aspects, individual identity nevertheless anchors the person in the social world. It places her in a more comprehensive network of interdependent social beings, allows her active participation in that network and thus engenders feelings of (interpersonal or inter-individual) connectedness and belongingness (Elias, 1988; Simmel, 1955). Moreover, individual as well as collective identities can provide people with a feeling of continuity over time which reflects the temporal dimension of belongingness.

Second, identity defines not only where one belongs, but also where one does not belong. It not only reflects who one is, but also who one is not. Accordingly, collective identity ensures distinctiveness from outgroups, that is, from people who do not share the focal self-aspect, while individual identity ensures distinctiveness from other individuals, that is, from people who do not share one's own complex configuration of self-aspects. Hence, both collective identity and individual identity are functional with respect to the satisfaction of the need for distinctiveness, but they serve the distinctiveness function on different levels of abstraction involving either intergroup or intragroup comparisons, respectively.

Third, another important function of identity is to provide people with respect. A respected identity (i.e. a good and secure place in the social world) in turn makes self-respect and self-esteem possible. Although identity and positive valence seem to be closely interrelated (Turner et al., 1987, p. 59), identity is not a self-sufficient source of respect, but it is dependent on the respectful recognition of relevant others in order to serve the respect function. Collective identity seems to be particularly functional in this respect (James, 1890/1950, p. 293). It signals that one shares a collective place (or self-aspect) with, and is therefore similar to, other people, though not all other people. Because similar people are likely to respect each other and what they have in common (Byrne, 1971; Tajfel & Turner, 1986), collective identity should facilitate mutual (intragroup) respect as well as shared respect for or pride in one's collective place. In addition to this intragroup source of respect, respect can also originate in the intergroup context. More specifically, to the extent to which the ingroup as a whole is respected by relevant outgroups or other significant parties in the relevant social context (e.g. superordinate authorities), people are supplied with an even more broadly respected collective identity so that they can take particular pride in their group membership, which in turn positively affects self-respect or self-esteem (Tyler & Smith, 1999). When respected by other individuals, a person's individual identity can also become the source of pride and thus self-respect or self-esteem, although it may be harder or more laborious to tap this source because, unlike collective identity, individual identity does not grant privileged access to respect from similar others.

Fourth, identity as a place in the social world provides a perspective on the social world from which this world and one's own place in it can be interpreted and understood meaningfully. Collective identity may again enjoy an advantage relative to individual identity, because the former gives access to a perspective that is socially shared and hence strengthened through social validation processes (Festinger, 1954). However, this is not to say that perspectives derived from collective identities necessarily reflect deficient thinking, cognitive laziness or passive acceptance of group norms. On the contrary, such perspectives often reflect an active, effortful and sophisticated cognitive elaboration of collective worldviews (Oakes et al., 1994). It is also important to reiterate that the understanding function, irrespective of whether it is served by individual or collective identities, involves not only the understanding of one's social environment, but also understanding of oneself. Just as the person is always part of a more comprehensive network of social relationships and exists socially only if she fits in this network, so is identity as self-understanding always part of a more comprehensive conceptual framework or perspective which helps to interpret the more comprehensive social network. Identity is meaningful only if it fits in such a framework. At the same time, identity gives access to and serves as an anchor for the more comprehensive framework, but the latter also guides the view (back) on oneself (like in a rear-view mirror). Identity thus serves to indicate that one has found a place or fits in the social world and that one has achieved a meaningful conceptual elaboration or understanding of oneself in the social world. In short, identity is an indicator of meaningful social existence.

Fifth and finally, identity serves as a marker that allows people to recognize themselves as the origin of their thoughts and actions and to experience themselves as influential social agents (Bruner, 1994; deCharms, 1968). Collective identity typically signals that one is not alone but can count on the social support and solidarity of other ingroup members so that, as a group, one may often feel as a much more powerful and efficacious social agent ('Together we are strong!'). At other times, however, restrictions and constraints imposed by one's group (e.g. norms and obligations) may move into the psychological foreground, so that individual identity may then better serve the agency function.

Identity processes

Research has identified a number of social psychological processes that operate in the service of the identity functions just listed. These processes are spurred or made possible by identity and in turn help identity to better fulfil its functions. Many of these processes have already been discussed in the previous chapter. For example, processes of self-enhancement operate in the service of the respect function because they help people to achieve, maintain or present a respected identity.

With regard to collective identity, prejudice and discrimination processes are particularly relevant here. Prejudice, defined as dislike of the outgroup or greater liking of the ingroup relative to the outgroup (Wilder & A. F. Simon, 2001; see Brown, 1995, for a more comprehensive conceptualization), operates in the service of the respect function of collective identity because increased liking among ingroup members facilitates mutual respect, while dislike of the outgroup helps to immunize oneself against outgroup members' disrespect. Discrimination is unequal or unfair treatment of individuals owing to their group membership (for a discussion of conceptual issues, see Mummendey & Otten, 2001). Social psychological research has shown that collective identity often increases the likelihood of discrimination against an outgroup in favour of the ingroup (Brewer, 1979; Messick & Mackie, 1989; Mummendey & Otten, 2001), although the relationship is by no means deterministic and is moderated by additional variables (Turner & Reynolds, 2001). From a social psychological point of view, discrimination at the behavioural level is in many respects what prejudice is at the affective level. Like prejudice, discrimination against an outgroup carries the same (often implicit) meaning that the outgroup is essentially inferior to the ingroup and therefore does not deserve the same respect. Like prejudice, discrimination thus also operates in the service of the respect function of collective identity, but it is the overt behavioural expression of respect for the ingroup and disrespect for the outgroup.[2] In addition, discrimination suggests or even proves that one has power or control over the outgroup so that the agency function is served as well. Although prejudice and discrimination processes have been investigated mostly at the level of collective identity, there is also evidence that analogous processes of valuing and favouring 'me and mine' (e.g. self-serving attributional biases) operate in the service of the respect and agency functions of individual identity (Fiske & Taylor, 1991; Hoyle et al., 1999; Miller & Ross, 1975; Smith & Mackie, 2000; Tesser, 1988).

Moreover, social psychological research has shown that stereotyping oneself and others is a typical cognitive outcome of collective identity. Once a particular collective identity is adopted, people ascribe attributes that they consider typical of the ingroup to their fellow group members as well as to themselves and ascribe attributes that they consider typical of the outgroup to outgroup members. In addition, they accentuate intragroup similarities and intergroup differences so that both ingroup and outgroup are homogenized and simultaneously differentiated from each other (Oakes et al., 1994; Simon & Hamilton, 1994). As a result, people unmistakably locate themselves in a distinct ingroup, and both the belongingness and distinctiveness functions of collective identity are served (Brewer, 1991). Because the content of the underlying (self-)stereotypes typically reflects and endorses the social reality as perceived and understood by group members, (self-)stereotypes also readily lend themselves to the explanation and justification of social reality (e.g. 'We Germans are hard-working and foreigners lazy. That's why we are, and should be, better off'). Accordingly, the understanding function of collective identity is served as well (Tajfel, 1981).

In many respects, self-stereotyping is the cognitive mediating precursor of conformity, which is another important behavioural consequence of collective identity. Conformity means that people behave in line with the norms, rules and expectations of the group with which they identify. While conformity may sometimes be the result of the reward power or coercive power of the group or its representatives over its members (French & Raven, 1959), collective identity is often sufficient to trigger conforming behaviour. From a social psychological point of view, conformity is behaviour in terms of one's collective identity (Sherif, 1967). Once a particular collective identity is adopted, behaving in terms of this identity is 'the natural thing to do'. Just like singers sing and dancers dance, so group members behave in terms of what they are. Conforming behaviour also verifies one's collective identity. It demonstrates to oneself and others that one shares a particular collective identity (i.e. belongs to a distinct collective place in the social world). Without conformity one would lose one's entitlement to a distinct collective identity. Consequently, we do what people like us do, and we don't do what people like us don't do. Like self-stereotyping at the cognitive level, conformity at the behavioural level thus operates in the service of both the belongingness and distinctiveness functions of collective identity. In addition, conformity facilitates coordinated, joint action which in turn increases the group's chances to come forth as an efficacious social agent. Hence, conformity also operates in the service of the agency function of collective identity.

Again, analogous processes operate and similar functions are served at the level of individual identity. For example, people present themselves and behave in ways that verify and are consistent with their individual identities and thus highlight their distinctiveness *vis-à-vis* other individuals (e.g. Codol, 1984; Markus, 1977; Snyder & Fromkin, 1980; Swann, 1996). They use individual behavioural standards or self-guides so that the agency function of individual identity is supported (Higgins, 1987; Higgins & May, 2001) and also tend to exaggerate their sense of individual control and mastery which supports both the understanding and agency functions of individual identity (Fiske & Taylor, 1991; Smith & Mackie, 2000). Finally, individual identity emerges from and enables social interaction and the development of interdependencies and close relationships with other individuals which promote a sense of inter-individual connectedness and thus operate in the service of the belongingness function of individual identity.

Summary

In this chapter, I presented an integrative approach to identity which incorporates important insights derived from sociologically and psychologically oriented perspectives. It was argued that identity can be viewed as the outcome of a self-interpretation process that takes shape at the meso level of the immediate interaction situation or context. Identity articulates micro-level psychological processes with macro-level societal processes and thus connects the person with groups, with social structure and ultimately with society as a whole. The integrative approach revolves around a self-aspect model of identity (SAMI) which defines collective identity as self-interpretation that is focused on a socially shared self-aspect and individual identity as self-interpretation that is based on a more complex set of self-aspects. The relative phenomenological significance of individual identity and collective identity is a function of both person variables and social context variables. It was further argued that individual identity and collective identity are not based on inherently or essentially different types of self-aspects and that both are social variants of identity. The relationship between individual identity and collective identity was characterized as a dialectic one in that there is a continual, dynamic dialogue between the two, in the course of which they make each other possible.

Their dialectic relationship also implies that they serve each other as background. While one becomes explicit as the figure, the other remains implicit as the ground, but is not ineffectual. Both individual and collective identities may be cognitively condensed into placeholders and tend to be associated with essentialistic beliefs. In the (post)modern world, individual identity may hold a relatively privileged status, but collective identity is by no means obsolete. Instead, (explicit) collective identity as such tends to be highly context-dependent and variable, with each specific instantiation of collective identity being rather transitory and fragile. Moreover, both individual and collective identities have psychological or phenomenological validity to the extent to which they adequately reflect people's context-dependent social positioning and related experiences. Finally, five general identity functions were highlighted which relate to the needs for belongingness, distinctiveness, respect, understanding and agency, and several processes were discussed that operate in the service of these identity functions (e.g. prejudice, discrimination, self-stereotyping, conformity, valuing and favouring 'me and mine', self-verification, the use of individual behavioural standards, exaggeration of individual control and mastery, development of inter-individual interdependencies and close relationships).

NOTES

1. The notion of 'de-centrating self-interpretation' must not be confused with the 'de-centring view of identity' discussed by Hall (1992) and summarized in chapter 1. The former refers to the psychological process of interpreting oneself in terms of a complex set of non-redundant self-aspects, whereas the latter refers to a (meta-) theoretical position that questions the status of identity as the person's fixed and stable inner centre. Nevertheless, because the assumption underlying the self-aspect model that identity is the variable outcome of concentrating or de-centrating self-interpretation processes is clearly non-essentialist, it is quite compatible with the de-centring view of identity.

2. This social psychological perspective on discrimination is not meant to deny the existence of systemic or structural discrimination which is built into the social structure and operates largely apart from people's prejudices and intentions. I owe this reminder to Thomas Pettigrew.

Chapter 4

Antecedents of Individual and Collective Identity

My aim in this chapter is to explore important antecedents of individual and collective identity. Naturally, it is impossible to consider all the potential antecedents of individual and collective identity. And even if a complete 'laundry list' of antecedents could be produced, such a piecemeal approach would not rid us of the more important task of uncovering the general principles that underlie the relationship between various antecedent conditions, on the one hand, and individual or collective identity, on the other. It is this task that I take on in this chapter and that also guided the selection of antecedent conditions for systematic examination.

It will be remembered that, according to the self-aspect model of identity (SAMI) presented in Chapter 3, individual identity derives from self-interpretation in terms of a complex set or configuration of different self-aspects, whereas collective identity is expected to emerge when self-interpretation centres on a single, socially shared self-aspect. Hence, I will present a series of empirical studies in which my co-workers and I have identified a number of important person and social context variables that systematically affect the critical process of concentrating or de-centrating self-interpretation. Moreover, the influence of these variables is conceptually purified and theoretically understood in terms of fundamental psychological principles, such as the principles of fit, readiness and positive self-evaluation (e.g. Bruner, 1957a; Turner et al., 1987; see also chapter 2).

Person Variables

Although self-interpretation is a general social psychological process, people's idiosyncrasies also bear on this process. It is very unlikely that someone engages in self-interpretation as a 'tabula rasa'. Instead, people have their idiosyncratic histories of prior experiences in various social roles, relationships and situations which set the stage for subsequent self-interpretation in important respects. For example, owing to different life histories, people are likely to differ in the number of self-aspects available for self-interpretation as well as in the subjective or personal importance and valence they attach to their various self-aspects. As will be shown below, these variables critically affect people's self-interpretation and the construction of individual and collective identities.

Complexity

According to SAMI, an individual identity is constructed whenever self-interpretation is based on a complex set or configuration of self-aspects. It follows that self-complexity, defined as the number of independent (i.e. non-redundant) self-aspects (Linville, 1985, 1987), should strengthen individual identity.[1] Former tennis star Martina Navratilova provided a good illustration of this mechanism when she complained in an interview about the public's overemphasis on her being a lesbian and remarked, 'But I am also a daughter, sister, dog lover, a good skier, interested in art, literature and music, a vegetarian and so on' ('Was Macht', 1996, p. 250; my translation). She obviously rejected 'being lesbian' as a dominant self-aspect and, fortunately, also had access to a complex set of additional self-aspects so that she could emphasize her individual identity.

To more systematically test the assumption that it is the complex configuration of self-aspects that underlies individual identity, Claudia Kampmeier and I (Simon & Kampmeier, 2001) varied the self-complexity of several target persons whose individuality was then rated by different research participants. As individuality, or individual identity for that matter, is a socially desirable attribute, at least in modern (Western) societies (Codol, 1984; Markus & Kitayama, 1991; Triandis, 1989), we preferred this procedure instead of the direct measurement of low- and high-self-complexity respondents' self-interpretation in order to avoid compensatory response strategies on the part of low-self-complexity persons.

In a pilot study, we first determined the self-complexity of 51 college students. This was accomplished as follows. Participants produced free-format self-descriptions and then unitized these descriptions by dividing them into individual thought elements. Subsequently, participants were instructed to sort these thought elements into clusters or classes (i.e. self-aspects) according to which elements 'you feel belong together'. To facilitate this sorting, they first numbered all thought elements and then drew, on a separate sheet of paper, as many boxes as they needed to represent all classes. Next, they distributed elements across classes by entering the respective numbers into the appropriate boxes. It was emphasized that each class (box) should contain at least one element, but also that each element could be allocated to more than just one class. We then calculated a self-complexity index based on this classification. To control for possible overlap among classes (i.e. to control for redundancy or non-independence among self-aspects), we adopted a procedure suggested by Linville (1985, 1987). More specifically, we calculated the statistical measure H, with $H = \log_2 n - (\Sigma\, n_i \log_2 n_i)/n$, where n is the total number of thought elements, and n_i is the number of elements that appear in a particular class combination (see Linville, 1985, p. 103, for further details). This measure increases with the number of non-overlapping classes (i.e. non-redundant self-aspects). A higher score thus indicates higher self-complexity. It should be noted that, whereas Linville's (1985, 1987) original self-complexity index was derived from a trait-sort task, we preferred the free-format self-description task because it appears to be less reactive (McGuire & McGuire, 1988). Moreover, additional testing confirmed that the resulting index was still highly correlated with the index derived from a German version of Linville's original trait-sort task ($r = .64, N = 27$; Kampmeier, Simon & Hastedt, 2000).

After scoring all 51 self-descriptions for self-complexity, we selected self-descriptions from persons who had exhibited either relatively low or relatively high self-complexity. Care was taken to compose two sets of self-descriptions that were as similar as possible to each other on alternative dimensions (e.g. number of words, numerical distinctiveness of self-aspects, overall positivity or negativity). The two final sets were made up of the self-descriptions of five low-self-complexity persons and the self-descriptions of four high-self-complexity persons, respectively.

In the main study, 125 research participants were presented with these (self-)descriptions and rated each target person on overall individuality and on several auxiliary measures (e.g. likeability, complexity). None of these participants had participated in the pilot study and each participant rated all nine target persons (within-subject variable: low vs. high complexity). The descriptions were ordered such that participants first rated either all low-complexity targets or all high-complexity targets. In addition, for half the participants, the descriptions were marked to explicitly demarcate each target's different self-aspects whereas, for the remaining participants, the descriptions were unmarked. As neither of these between-subjects variables qualified the results, they are not discussed further.

For data analysis, each participant's individuality ratings (from 1 to 7) concerning the low-complexity targets were averaged, as were the individuality ratings concerning the high-complexity targets. As expected, the mean individuality score of high-complexity targets (4.5) was significantly higher than that of low-complexity targets (4.1). Moreover, we observed significant correlations between perceived complexity and individuality such that when participants attributed more complexity to a target they also attributed more individuality to that target. The coefficients were $r = .66$ for the correlation computed across targets ($N = 9$) with ratings averaged across participants and $r = .30$ for the correlation computed across participants ($N = 123$ owing to missing data) with ratings averaged across targets. Correlation coefficients for the single targets ranged from .16 to .43.

Although the study provided encouraging support for the assumption that self-complexity is conducive to individual identity, it is an obvious limitation of this study that it focused on the perception of other people and that it was not directly concerned with self-interpretation. As indicated above, the focus on the perception of other people was a deliberate manoeuvre in order to avoid additional processes coming into play (e.g. compensatory processes on the part of people with low self-complexity). We have also conducted a study in which we directly examined the role of self-complexity in self-interpretation and where we explicitly considered the operation of multiple, or even conflicting, processes. However, before turning to such complications, I will first discuss two other person variables which seem to have more straightforward effects on the construction of individual and collective identities.

Personal importance and valence of self-aspects

SAMI posits that collective identity is predicated on focused or concentrated self-interpretation and individual identity on more complex or decentrated self-interpretation. It follows that factors or variables that trigger off the concentration or de-centration process should also be conducive to collective or individual identity, respectively. One variable that is likely to play such a role is the subjective or personal importance of a self-aspect. If someone attaches high personal importance to a particular self-aspect, this self-aspect should grab the person's attention and thus move into the psychological foreground during self-interpretation. Conversely, given low personal importance of a self-aspect, it is very likely that people draw on additional self-aspects to ensure comprehensive self-interpretation.

Another variable likely to affect the concentration or de-centration process is the personal valence or attractiveness of a self-aspect. There is wide agreement among social psychologists that people usually prefer positive self-evaluation to negative self-evaluation (e.g. Hoyle et al., 1999; Tajfel & Turner, 1986; Tesser, 1988; Wicklund & Gollwitzer, 1982). Consequently, it can be expected that people are more willing to focus on a self-aspect when it has positive valence than when it has negative valence. Focusing self-interpretation on a positive self-aspect, while ignoring other self-aspects, is compatible with the preference for positive self-evaluation. However, the opposite is true for self-aspects with negative valence. Focusing on a negative self-aspect should be aversive, so that, like the tennis star cited above, people should tend to incorporate additional self-aspects into their self-interpretation to avoid or dilute negative self-evaluation implications. In sum, it can be hypothesized that both high personal importance and positive valence of a given self-aspect should facilitate the construction of a collective identity as a member of the group or category of people who share the particular self-aspect. Conversely, both low personal importance and negative valence of a self-aspect should facilitate the construction of individual identity.

These hypotheses were tested in a study with 98 undergraduates as research participants (Simon & Hastedt, 1999). Participants first produced free-format self-descriptions ('How would you describe yourself? Please write down spontaneously everything about your own person that comes to your mind'). Later, participants were instructed to select, from these self-descriptions, two different attributes or aspects of themselves according to the following criteria. Half of the participants (between-subjects variable) had to select two self-aspects that had positive valence for them, whereas the remaining participants had to select two self-aspects with negative valence. Moreover, for each participant (within-subject variable), one of the two (positive or negative) self-aspects had to be important to his or her self-image, whereas the other self-aspect had to be unimportant to his or her self-image. Next, participants were asked to list the opposite for each of the two selected self-aspects. Finally, the dependent measures were administered. The main measurements concerned perceptions of self–other similarities and differences. On five-point Likert-type scales, participants estimated the degree of similarity and difference between themselves and other people who shared the same self-aspect (i.e. self–ingroup similarities and self–ingroup differences) and the degree of similarity and difference between self and people who possessed the respective opposite aspect (i.e. self–outgroup similarities and self–outgroup differences). Separate estimates were required concerning each of the two selected self-aspects and their respective opposites. We calculated a self–ingroup assimilation index (i.e. estimates of self–ingroup similarities minus estimates of self–ingroup differences) and a self–outgroup differentiation index (i.e. estimates of self–outgroup differences minus estimates of self–outgroup similarities). In keeping with the self-categorization literature (Oakes et al., 1994; Turner et al., 1987), collective-identity construction should be indicated by an increase, and individual-identity construction by a decrease, in both self-ingroup assimilation and self-outgroup differentiation.

An analysis of variance with importance (low vs. high) and valence (positive vs. negative) as independent variables and the self–ingroup assimilation and self–outgroup differentiation indices as repeated measures confirmed our hypotheses. Although self–ingroup assimilation was generally weaker than self–outgroup differentiation, the two indices were equally affected by the independent variables. As predicted, both high importance and positive valence led to a significant increase in self–ingroup assimilation and self–outgroup differentiation compared with low importance and negative valence. Thus, it was demonstrated that two variables (personal importance and valence), which were hypothesized to affect people's readiness to either concentrate or de-centrate self-interpretation, systematically influenced the construction of collective and individual identity. High personal importance and positive valence of a self-aspect was conducive to the construction of collective identity around the critical self-aspect, whereas low personal importance and negative valence facilitated the construction of individual identity.

Two other aspects of the results are noteworthy. First, in this study, many different (personally important and/or positive) self-aspects successfully served as a basis for collective identity (e.g. intelligent, open, emotional, ambitious, sporty). The exact numbers of different self-aspects selected for the high-importance/positive-valence, high-importance/negative-valence, low-importance/positive-valence and low-importance/negative-valence combinations were 35, 33, 37 and 31, respectively. We achieved this diversity by letting each participant freely choose a self-aspect in line with his or her own subjective or personal criteria of importance and valence. Participants did not know that questions concerning collective identity would be asked afterwards so that they were not prompted to select particularly 'groupy' self-aspects, that is, self-aspects traditionally associated with psychological group formation. In fact, only two participants selected such a self-aspect, namely female, and both participants considered it a positive, but unimportant self-aspect. Nevertheless, we obtained clear evidence of group formation and collective-identity construction under conditions of high personal importance and positive valence. This supports the point made in chapter 3 that most, if not all, self-aspects possess a collective or group formation potential that materializes under appropriate conditions.

Second, the finding that self–ingroup assimilation was generally less pronounced than self–outgroup differentiation suggests that people's readiness to construct a collective identity was somewhat hampered by the motivation to retain a sense of individuality or individual identity (Codol, 1984; Simon, 1993; Snyder & Fromkin, 1980). This observation is in line with the assumption introduced in chapter 3 that, in modern society, individuality or individual identity has emerged as an ideological or cultural ideal. I will return to this issue shortly because several of the studies discussed below have dealt with it in more depth.

Self-complexity

The first study reported in this chapter provided initial evidence of the role of self-complexity in identity construction. It was found that target persons with high self-complexity were attributed more individuality than target persons with low self-complexity. However, that study focused exclusively on the perception of other people and was not concerned with self-perception or self-interpretation. We pursued this strategy because we anticipated complications due to possible compensatory processes on the part of people with low self-complexity. While this strategy helped us to secure encouraging support for the hypothesized positive relationship between self-complexity and individual identity, its limitations are obvious and need to be rectified. That is, we need to return to actual self-interpretation and examine what additional processes may come into play when people with varying degrees of self-complexity engage in self-interpretation.

How may self-complexity affect the construction of individual and collective identities? The results of the first study reported in this chapter suggest that high self-complexity fosters individual identity because high self-complexity calls for self-interpretation in terms of many different self-aspects. At the same time, high self-complexity should impede the concentration of self-interpretation on a single self-aspect and thus obstruct the critical process underlying collective identity. Given high self-complexity, there are simply too many, potentially competing, self-aspects. A person with many different self-aspects simply does not fit very well into a group or social category defined primarily in terms of one particular self-aspect.

Conversely, the advantage for individual identity should diminish when self-complexity is low. Low self-complexity should make it relatively easy to concentrate or focus self-interpretation on a single self-aspect and should thus facilitate collective identity. However, another process may come into play here that could again tip the balance to the disadvantage of collective identity. In chapter 3, it was acknowledged that, in modern society, individuality and individual identity may have acquired the status of an ideological or cultural ideal. In light of our finding that self-complexity is indeed (perceived as) indicative of individuality, it thus stands to reason that people with low self-complexity may be unwilling to further reduce their individuality by emphasizing a collective identity at the expense of their individual identity (see also Snyder & Fromkin, 1980).

In conclusion, it can be surmised that when self-complexity is high, poor fit between self and social categories is likely to impede collective-identity construction, whereas collective identity may be aversive from a normative or motivational point of view when self-complexity is low. Conversely, individual identity should emerge as the better-fitting identity variant when self-complexity is high and as the more attractive identity variant when self-complexity is low. Taken together, a medium level of self-complexity should be most conducive to collective identity and least conducive for individual identity because, at a medium level, neither social categorical fit nor the motivation or readiness for collective-identity construction is too low and neither fit considerations nor readiness factors expressly call for the construction of individual identity. This prediction accords with other theorizing and research indicating that categorization and identity construction are a joint function of fit considerations and perceiver readiness (Bruner, 1957a; Oakes et al., 1994).

Evidence for a curvilinear relation between self-complexity and identity construction was indeed found in a study by Claudia Hastedt and myself ($N = 122$) in which we first determined participants' self-complexity and then measured self–ingroup assimilation and self–outgroup differentiation as the main dependent variables (Simon, 1999; see also Hastedt, 1998). Self-complexity was again determined on the basis of the free-format self-description task described above. After completion of the self-description task, each participant selected one self-aspect and labelled it. To control for valence, half of the participants (between-subjects variable) were instructed to select a positive self-aspect, whereas the remaining participants selected a negative self-aspect. Participants also named the opposite of the selected self-aspect. Subsequently, participants estimated the degree of similarity and difference between themselves and other people who share the critical self-aspect (ingroup) as well as between themselves and people who possess the opposite aspect (outgroup). The scales were the same as in the study on the effects of personal importance and valence (Simon & Hastedt, 1999), and we calculated the same self–ingroup assimilation and self–outgroup differentiation indices.

Based on participants' self-complexity scores, we partitioned our sample into three sub-samples with low, medium and high self-complexity, respectively. An analysis of variance with self-complexity and valence as independent variables and the self–ingroup assimilation and self–outgroup differentiation indices as repeated measures replicated two findings of the previous study (Simon & Hastedt, 1999). Self–ingroup assimilation was generally weaker than self–outgroup differentiation and both indices increased when the critical self-aspect was positive as opposed to negative. In addition, and more important, we also observed a significant two-way interaction between self-complexity and valence, which was not qualified by a three-way interaction involving index. As can be seen in figure 4.1, the hypothesized curvilinear relation between self-complexity and identity construction was corroborated for positive self-aspects. Here, participants with medium self-complexity showed a significantly stronger tendency towards collective-identity construction than did either of the two other sub-samples. When the critical self-aspect was negative, individual identity seemed to be the preferred choice irrespective

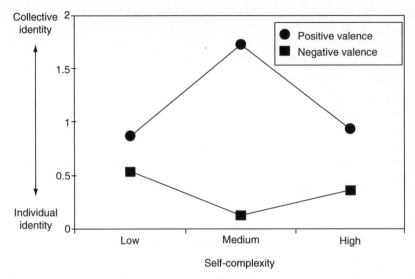

Figure 4.1 Identity construction (averaged across self–ingroup assimilation and self–outgroup differentiation) as a function of self-complexity and valence of the critical self-aspect.

of self-complexity. The three sub-samples did not differ from each other. Participants with negative self-aspects were apparently too concerned about negative self-evaluation implications so that collective-identity construction became aversive, irrespective of self-complexity. In other words, participants were generally unwilling to give up their cherished individuality for an unattractive collective identity. (Viewed from a different perspective, valence affected identity construction only for participants with medium self-complexity.) It is also noteworthy that we obtained the same interaction between self-complexity and valence for two auxiliary measures, namely perceived typicality of self as a group member and liking for ingroup members.

To summarize, a medium level of self-complexity seems to be most conducive to collective identity, at least as long as this identity is based on a positive self-aspect. The observed curvilinear relation between self-complexity and identity construction illustrates that (cognitive) fit considerations and (motivational) readiness do not necessarily cooperate harmoniously. Instead, they can also operate as opposing forces that necessitate a compromise.

Social Context Variables

The social context is another important source of variation in self-interpretation and identity construction. At the macro level, sociological analyses have suggested that, in modern society, the general social climate tends to favour individual identity relative to collective identity (see chapter 3). Yet variable 'weather' conditions at the meso level of the immediate social context or situation also influence people's relative emphasis on their individual or collective identities. Circumstances may induce people to focus on a given self-aspect so that their current self-interpretations centre on this self-aspect. Collective identity would then be fostered at the expense of individual identity. Analogous to the (micro-level) person variables discussed above, I will now report on a series of studies that investigated how social context variations concerning the valence, frequency, meaningfulness and number of self-aspects available (and/or accessible) for self-interpretation affect the construction of individual and collective identities.

Context-dependent valence of self-aspects

Different circumstances can confer differential valence on a given self-aspect. For example, being German may have positive valence at a convention of car makers, but it most likely acquires negative valence in contexts in which the Holocaust is remembered. In keeping with the principle of positive self-evaluation, the former context should be more conducive to concentrated self-interpretation as German and thus to collective-identity construction. Conversely, in the latter context, it can be expected that people of German nationality are inclined to highlight additional self-aspects in order to avoid or dilute negative implications for self-evaluation. As a consequence, their self-interpretation should move towards individual identity.

These predictions were confirmed in two experiments in which we varied the temporarily salient value connotations associated with participants' nationality (Simon, Pantaleo & Mummendey, 1995, Studies 1 and 2). The first experiment was conducted with 66 participants of an international summer school. The sample consisted of people from 10 different countries (35 from Germany, 11 from Russia, 9 from Latvia, 3 from France, 2 from Austria, 2 from Italy, 1 from the United Kingdom, 1 from Finland, 1 from Ireland and 1 from the United States). A short questionnaire was distributed that contained both the manipulation of the independent variable (valence) as well as the scales measuring the dependent variables. Half the participants were given a questionnaire in which they were first asked to list positive attributes that they thought were typical of their compatriots as well as of themselves. The other participants were asked to list negative attributes that they thought were typical of their compatriots as well as of themselves. On the next page, all participants provided estimates of self–ingroup similarities and differences on separate five-point scales. An analysis of variance revealed that, as expected, self–ingroup assimilation (i.e. estimates of self–ingroup similarities minus estimates of self–ingroup differences) decreased significantly from the positive-valence to the negative-valence condition.

We also found that German participants generally showed significantly less self–ingroup assimilation than non-German participants, but valence and nationality did not interact. There are at least two different, though not necessarily mutually exclusive, explanations for the unexpected effect of nationality. First, unlike German participants, non-German participants were abroad and thus in a numerical minority during the investigation. In other words, nationality was an infrequent and therefore a particularly 'attention-grabbing' self-aspect for non-German participants. I will deal with the role of infrequent self-aspects in identity construction in more detail shortly (see also chapter 5). Second, it is also possible that the effect of nationality was due to more stable or chronic valence differences. Indeed, survey research had uncovered similar differences before (Noelle-Neumann & Köcher, 1987), and a closer inspection of the attributes listed by our participants revealed that German participants evinced clearly less positive associations with their nationality than did non-German participants with regard to their respective nationalities. The observation that being German often has a relatively negative or less positive valence for German people is usually explained in terms of the negative connotations of German history owing to the crimes against humanity committed by Nazi Germany (see also Elias, 1992).

The second experiment was conducted in a more controlled environment. More specifically, we compared German psychology students ($N = 46$) with Italian psychology students ($N = 77$) who were all approached in their respective home countries by a native investigator. Again, participants first listed either positive or negative attributes that they associated with their own nationality before they completed the dependent measures. In addition to estimates of self–ingroup similarities and self–ingroup differences, participants also provided estimates of similarities and differences within the ingroup as a whole. The critical effect of valence was replicated. Self–ingroup assimilation (i.e. estimates of self–ingroup similarities minus estimates of self–ingroup differences) and ingroup homogeneity (i.e. estimates of intragroup similarities minus estimates of intragroup differences) decreased in the negative-valence condition compared with the positive-valence condition. And again, German participants were less willing to embrace a collective identity. They showed significantly less self–ingroup assimilation and ingroup homogeneity than Italian participants.

To summarize, both experiments demonstrate that context-dependent variations in the valence of self-aspects affect self-interpretation and identity construction. In addition to effects that were tied to the meso level of the immediate social context, we also observed effects that pointed to the influence of more stable or chronic valence differences anchored in macro-level events. More specifically, the relative reluctance of German participants to embrace a collective national identity seemed to be anchored in the historical dimension of the wider social context (i.e. the crimes against humanity committed by Nazi Germany). Finally, it is worth noting that, overall, participants seemed to be more willing to report a predominance of perceived differences among ingroup members (including themselves) than to report a predominance of perceived similarities. This finding is another indication that people's readiness to construct a collective identity may be hampered by the motivation to retain a sense of individual identity.

Frequency and meaningfulness of self-aspects

Just as, owing to different life histories, different individuals attach differential subjective or personal importance to a given self-aspect, so the immediate circumstances or social context can endow a given self-aspect with particular significance. For example, people may find themselves in a social context in which one of their self-aspects is relatively rare (e.g. a female politician during the convention of a political party with a predominantly male membership). In such a context, the rare self-aspect is likely to attract particular attention, probably because numerically distinct features are surprising and thus taken as the focus of explanation ('the effect to be explained'; Hegarty & Pratto, 2001; Kahneman & Miller, 1986) and/or because they are generally considered particularly diagnostic or informative (Fiske & Taylor, 1991; Mullen, 1991; Tversky, 1977). In any case, empirical evidence indicates that self-aspects that are shared with only a minority of other people in a given context tend to acquire a particularly strong attention-grabbing power in self-interpretation (McGuire & McGuire, 1988; Simon, 1992). One might thus expect people who share a minority self-aspect to be particularly likely to centre their self-interpretation on this self-aspect and to move towards a collective identity.

However, self-categorization theorists argue that it is not numerical distinctiveness *per se* that automatically pushes minority self-aspects into the psychological focus and thus facilitates the construction of a collective identity (Oakes et al., 1994; Oakes & Turner, 1986). Being one of two men in an otherwise all-female psychology class is unlikely to matter as to how I see myself (and others) unless the discussion shifts to relevant topics such as gender differences or affirmative action policies. That is, the social context needs to render a self-aspect not only noticeable, but also important or meaningful. While a self-aspect may become more or less noticeable as a direct function of the frequency distribution of social stimuli (i.e. people and their self-aspects) in a given context, a self-aspect acquires meaning to the extent to which it relates to the defining characteristics or relevant dimensions of the social context. In order to be meaningful, a self-aspect must find its anchor in the definition of the social context. It then fits in with this context and helps to locate the person in relation to other people. Consequently, unless there is a meaningful relation or fit between social context and self-aspect, one should not expect minority self-aspects to facilitate collective identity. Once there is such fit or meaningfulness, however, a minority self-aspect may indeed 'benefit' from its superior attention-grabbing power. Compared with a majority self-aspect, it should then facilitate the process of concentrating self-interpretation and thereby the construction of collective identity.

Evidence for the interactive influence of the frequency and meaningfulness of self-aspects on identity construction was found in an experiment by Claudia Hastedt, Birgit Aufderheide and myself (Simon, Hastedt & Aufderheide, 1997, Experiment 1, $N = 197$). We manipulated frequency (minority vs. majority self-aspect) and meaningfulness (low vs. high) as two orthogonal independent variables. Preference for either urban or rural life served as the critical self-aspect. We manipulated frequency of the critical self-aspect by giving participants false feedback about the percentage of people who shared or did not share their preference for either urban or rural life. The manipulation of meaningfulness of the critical self-aspect closely followed the notion of social contextual fit as conceptualized in self-categorization theory (Oakes, Turner & Haslam, 1991; see also Eiser & Stroebe, 1972). In the low-meaningfulness condition, it was stated that information about participants' preferences for either urban or rural life was elicited merely to serve as neutral stimulus material in the experiment, which was introduced as a study of human information processing. Moreover, we stated that previous research had clearly shown these preferences to be in no way related to personality in general or to information-processing style in particular. In the high-meaningfulness condition, we stated that we had selected these specific preferences for experimentation exactly because previous research had shown them to be related to personality in general and to information processing-style in particular. In addition, to prevent any differential status implications, we stressed that, despite clear differences in information-processing style, people with different preferences would not differ in the quality of their information processing. In short, we manipulated meaningfulness of the critical self-aspect by informing participants about the (alleged) absence or presence of a (cor)relation between the self-aspect and the information-processing task at hand. We gauged identity construction with three composite indices, namely self–ingroup assimilation (i.e. estimates of self–ingroup similarities minus estimates of self–ingroup differences), ingroup homogeneity (i.e. estimates of intragroup similarities minus estimates of intragroup differences) and prototypicality (i.e. self-ascribed typicality as a group member minus self-ascribed uniqueness as an individual).

Identity in Modern Society

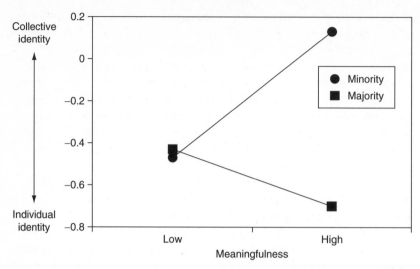

Figure 4.2 Identity construction (averaged across self–ingroup assimilation, ingroup homogeneity and prototypicality) as a function of frequency and meaningfulness of the critical self-aspect.

Source: From Simon, Hastedt & Aufderheide, 1997, Figure 1. Copyright © 1997 by the American Psychological Association. Adapted with permission.

As expected, an analysis of variance with frequency and meaningfulness as independent variables and the three indices as repeated measures yielded a significant two-way interaction between the independent variables, which was not qualified by a three-way interaction involving index. As shown in figure 4.2, participants with a minority self-aspect moved significantly more towards collective identity than participants with a majority self-aspect, but only when meaningfulness was high. Otherwise, participants with a minority self-aspect and those with a majority self-aspect did not differ from each other. Moreover, the minority–majority difference in the high-meaningfulness condition was due mainly to a significant move towards collective identity among participants with a minority self-aspect. There was no significant change in identity construction among participants with a majority self-aspect (for a conceptual replication, see Simon et al., 1997, Experiment 2).

To summarize, these results strongly suggest that infrequency and meaningfulness of a self-aspect are two important social context variables which, in conjunction, facilitate collective identity at the expense of individual identity (even though the rather low scores again point to the reluctance to completely give up one's individual identity). Owing to the superior attention-grabbing power of minority self-aspects, people with such self-aspects seem to be more inclined or ready to embrace a collective identity than people with a majority self-aspect. However, such readiness apparently translates into actual collective identity only if the minority self-aspect is meaningfully anchored in, and thus fits in with, the current social context. Because minority–majority relations are an important component of many social contexts in modern society, there is, of course, more to say about identity construction and its consequences among people with minority or majority self-aspects. I will do so in chapter 5 which is specifically concerned with minority and majority identity.

Number of self-aspects

According to SAMI, the number of (non-redundant) self-aspects involved in self-interpretation is a critical determinant of identity construction. As demonstrated earlier in this chapter, the number of self-aspects involved in self-interpretation can vary among individual persons because different life histories are likely to result in the availability and/or accessibility of a differential number of self-aspects. Another source of the variation in the number of self-aspects involved in self-interpretation is the social context. The complex social fabric of modern society provides a rich basis for the development of a great variety of self-aspects which, under the appropriate circumstances, may gain entry into self-interpretation and affect identity construction.

A first demonstration of the relative ease with which social contextual demands can prompt people to use a variable number of self-aspects for self-interpretation and to shift to either individual identity or collective identity involved 65 high school students (see Simon & Hastedt, 1997, Pretest). At first, we directed research participants' attention to one specific self-aspect by asking them to indicate their preference for either urban or rural life and to list three reasons for their preference. Subsequently, all participants completed the same free-format self-description task described above and also provided two ratings (on seven-point scales) – one concerning the extent to which they saw themselves as a typical member of the group of people who shared their preference for either urban or rural life and another concerning the degree of their own individuality. However, whereas about half of the participants first completed the self-description task and then provided the typicality and individuality ratings, the order was reversed for the remaining participants. Completion of the self-description task was expected to bring additional self-aspects to mind and thus to foster individual identity at the expense of collective identity. Consequently, when the self-description task preceded the ratings, participants were expected to (further) accentuate their individuality relative to their typicality as a group member. The prediction was confirmed. The critical index (i.e. self-ascribed individuality minus self-ascribed typicality) was significantly greater when the self-description task preceded the ratings than when it followed the ratings (1.3 vs. 0.4). Moreover, only the first mean differed significantly from zero, indicating that, after self-description, participants actually saw themselves more as individuals than as group members. Aufderheide (2000, Experiment 3, pp. 73–6) observed similar results. Using the same free-format self-description task and more refined multi-item scales for identity measurement, she also found that free-format self-description fostered individual identity at the expense of collective identity.

Of course, this self-description task gives the experimenter little control over the exact number of additional self-aspects that are brought to the participants' attention, nor can the experimenter ensure that the increase in self-aspects used for self-interpretation is constant across participants. There-fore, Claudia Kampmeier and I examined the relationship between context-dependent variation in the number of self-aspects and identity construction in a more controlled social environment ($N = 46$; see also Kampmeier, 2001). This experiment was introduced as a pilot study in occupational psychology. Depending on condition, the cover story explained that prior research had identified either one or five dimensions that were particularly useful for career planning and choice of occupation (e.g. preference for teamwork or for solitary work, preference for work concerned with a particular substantive issue or for work concerned with managerial or organizing activities, prefer-ence for specialized tasks or for more broadly defined tasks). These dimensions were selected on the basis of careful pretesting to ensure equivalent clarity and importance. Moreover, care was taken to select dimensions that were unre-lated to status differentials.

Depending on condition, participants, who all worked on individual computer terminals, indicated their preference either concerning each of the five dimensions or concerning only one dimension. In the latter condition, the critical dimension was randomly selected from the entire pool of five dimen-sions for each participant and without his or her knowledge. Participants' attention was thus directed to either five self-aspects or only one self-aspect. Subsequently, participants completed the dependent measures. They provided estimates of self–ingroup similarities and self–ingroup differences, with ingroup being defined as people who shared the critical self-aspect (i.e. preference) with the participant. Participants also rated their typicality as a group member and their uniqueness as an individual (on five-point scales). In the one-self-aspect condition, the similarity, difference and typicality judge-ments were made with respect to the self-aspect (i.e. preference) that had been determined earlier. Conversely, in the five-self-aspect condition, one of the five self-aspects was randomly selected for each participant at this stage of the experiment, and participants made judgements only with respect to that self-aspect. Finally, participants were instructed to think of an acquaintance of theirs who shared the critical self-aspect with them and to provide analogous judgements concerning this ingroup acquaintance. For both targets (i.e. self and ingroup acquaintance), we calculated an assimilation index (i.e. estimates of target–ingroup similarities minus estimates of target–ingroup differences) and a prototypicality index (i.e. ascribed typicality as a group member minus ascribed uniqueness as an individual).

Our prediction was that a decrease in the number of self-aspects would result in a shift from individual identity to collective identity. A similar shift was expected for the identity ascribed to the ingroup acquaintance because a decrease in the number of self-aspects should also reduce the number of aspects or dimensions heeded in the perception of familiar others (Markus & Smith, 1981). Specifically, when the focus is on a single self-aspect, another person with whom one shares this self-aspect is likely to be categorized as an interchangeable ingroup member and therefore ascribed the same collective identity (Turner et al., 1987).

However, as shown in figure 4.3, the predicted shift was only found for the ingroup acquaintance, but not for self (irrespective of index). When the number of self-aspects decreased, there was a significant shift from individual identity to collective identity for the ingroup acquaintance, but a significant shift in the opposite direction for self. The finding for the ingroup acquaintance is in

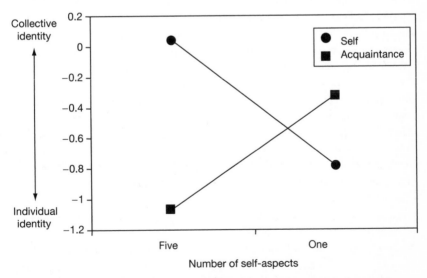

Figure 4.3 Identity construction (averaged across assimilation and prototypicality) for self and ingroup acquaintance as a function of number of self-aspects.

line with the hypothesized relationship between number of self-aspects and identity construction. It also concurs with the positive relationship, discussed earlier in this chapter, between perceived complexity of others and the degree of individuality ascribed to others. However, the finding for self strongly suggests that circumstances which set excessive limits to the number of self-aspects available for self-interpretation do not foster, but hamper collective identity. Again, it appears that people are unwilling to embrace a collective identity unless they have access to additional self-aspects which allow them to retain a sense of individuality. Viewed from this perspective, the unexpected shift to collective identity in the five-self-aspect condition concurs with our observation that a medium level of self-complexity is most conducive to collective identity (Simon, 1999). To take this reasoning one step further, it may be inadequate to portray individuality or individual identity exclusively as an opponent of collective identity. Individual and collective identity may also act as partners in a more dynamic interplay which we are just beginning to understand.

The Interplay of Individual and Collective Identities

The research discussed above suggests that a high number of self-aspects, or high self-complexity, is particularly conducive to individual identity, whereas collective identity seems to require a narrower focus on a single or only a few self-aspects. However, the available evidence also suggests that there is no simple linear relationship between the number of different self-aspects involved in self-interpretation and identity construction. Evidence for such simple relationships was found only for the construction of the identity of other people. When self was directly involved, matters were more complicated. We still observed systematic relationships between number of self-aspects and identity construction. However, access to additional self-aspects, besides the critical focal self-aspect, did not necessarily obstruct collective identity, but actually seemed to play a facilitative role. I suggested that such access allowed research participants to retain a sense of individuality and thus increased their readiness to adopt a collective identity. In other words, some sense of individuality or individual identity may itself be an antecedent or precondition of collective identity, especially in modern society where individuality and individual identity seem to have acquired the status of an ideological or cultural ideal. This interpretation is in line with the view that the relationship between individual identity and collective identity is not always an antagonistic one and that these two identity variants are involved in a more dynamic interplay (see chapter 3).

Independence and differentiation as sources of individual identity

To learn more about the conditions under which individual identity may facilitate or obstruct collective identity, Claudia Kampmeier and I (Kampmeier & Simon, 2001) conducted a series of studies that revolved around the two-component conception of individual identity described in chapter 3. Building on Simmel's (1908, 1984) analysis of individuality, SAMI suggests that two components of individual identity can be distinguished – identity as an independent individual and identity as a distinct individual. Prior psychological theorizing has typically been rather one-sided. Approaches emphasized either the independence component (e.g. Markus & Kitayama, 1991; Deci & Ryan, 1991) or the differentiation component (Turner et al., 1987). Our first aim was therefore to demonstrate the validity of the independence–differentiation distinction. More specifically, we conducted a questionnaire study to test whether independence from others and differentiation from others could be identified as two distinct dimensions of self-definition (Kampmeier & Simon, 2001, Questionnaire Study).

For this purpose, we generated an initial pool of 90 individuality-related items on the basis of three main sources. First, item selection was based on a pilot study with 125 research participants who provided written definitions of individuality. Second, items were adopted from individuality-related dimensions reported in the psychological literature. Third, we generated additional items on the basis of their face validity concerning the independence and differentiation dimensions. After pretesting items for clarity and redundancies, we compiled a set of 66 individuality-related statements to be rated for self-descriptiveness. In addition, 12 items directly measured individual identity (e.g. 'I see myself as an individual'; 'My close friends see me as an individual'). All ratings were made on seven-point scales. Two-hundred and forty-seven undergraduates completed a questionnaire with these items. After examining descriptive statistics, we eliminated 16 (of the 66 individuality-related) items because of low response variability or low endorsement rates. The underlying factor structure of the remaining 50 items was determined by a principal-components analysis with varimax rotation (and orthogonal factors). This analysis suggested a five-factor solution. The first two factors, which together accounted for 21% of the total variance, were readily interpretable as an independence component (e.g. 'I can decide on my own') and a differentiation component (e.g. 'I am different from others').

To create two succinct and reliable indicators of both the independence component and the differentiation component, we selected four representative items on the basis of the factor loadings for each of the first two factors. A final principal-components analysis with varimax rotation on the eight items extracted exactly two (orthogonal) factors that explained 30% and 29% of the total variance, respectively. Again, they could readily be interpreted as independence and differentiation components, respectively. Items and factor loadings from this final analysis as well as internal consistency coefficients are presented in Table 4.1.

The 12 items that directly gauged individual identity were averaged (Cronbach's $\alpha = .89$), and the resulting index was regressed simultaneously on the

Table 4.1 Internal consistency and factor loadings for the two individuality components (independence and differentiation)

Scales and items[a]	Cronbach's α	Factor loadings	
		Factor I	Factor II
Independence	.77		
'I am self-confident.'		.82	.11
'I can decide on my own.'		.78	−.04
'I am sovereign.'		.77	.14
'I am autonomous.'		.69	.19
Differentiation	.73		
'I am unusual.'		.04	.83
'I am different from others.'		.07	.77
'I am unique.'		.15	.69
'I have rare characteristics.'		.12	.68

[a] $N = 247$

Source: From Kampmeier & Simon, 2001, Table 1. Copyright © 2001 by the American Psychological Association. Adapted with permission.

Table 4.2 Simultaneous regression analysis with independence and differentiation as predictors and individual identity as criterion

	Independence	Differentiation
B	.31	.15
$SE\ B$	.04	.04
β	.40	.23
t	7.08 ***	3.98 ***

*** $p < .001$

$R^2 = .26$, $F(2, 244) = 42.39$, $p < .001$

Source: From Kampmeier & Simon, 2001, Table 2. Copyright © 2001 by the American Psychological Association. Adapted with permission.

independence and differentiation components (averaged across the four items, respectively). As expected, both components contributed significantly and uniquely to the prediction of individual identity (see table 4.2). The independence component emerged as the strongest predictor. It uniquely explained 15% of the variance, whereas the unique contribution of the differentiation component was 5% ($R^2 = .26$).

A number of additional tests corroborated these findings. First, participants' gender did not moderate the results of the factor or regression analyses. Second, although the other three factors obtained in the first principal-components analysis were not of theoretical interest to us, we also created a reliable index for each of these factors and included them as further predictors in the multiple regression analysis. Only independence and differentiation emerged as significant predictors of individual identity. Third, the same independence and differentiation components were identified in a follow-up study ($N = 255$) which was concerned with the individual identity ascribed to *other* people. Finally, a separate sample of 55 undergraduates rated themselves on the independence and differentiation scales at two different measurement points with a test–retest interval of 6 weeks. The (interpersonal) stability coefficients were significant, but only of low to moderate magnitude ($r_{tt} = .38$ and $r_{tt} = .59$, for the independence and the differentiation components, respectively). However, the critical two-factor structure reflecting the independence–differentiation distinction was replicated at both measurement points. In other words, whereas the exact self-placement on the independence and differentiation components may shift over time, the two-component representation of individual identity is obviously rather robust.

Taken together, the results clearly supported the distinction between an independence component and a differentiation component of individual identity. Moreover, the convergent findings for own identity and the identity of others as well as the test–retest results suggest that these components should not be understood as individual-differences variables, but rather as more general, socially shared representations (Farr & Moscovici, 1984) or theories (Medin, 1989) of what it means to be an individual or to have individual identity. Against the backdrop of these representations or theories, perceptions of independence and differentiation then emerge as important antecedents or sources of individual identity.

Compatibility of individual and collective identities

Building on the assumption that individual identity has acquired the status of a cultural or ideological ideal in modern society, it can be hypothesized that people's readiness to embrace a collective identity should increase if collective identity is also compatible with at least one of the two components of individual identity. To test this hypothesis, Claudia Kampmeier and I focused, as a starting-point, on the construction of collective identity among members of numerical minorities and majorities (Kampmeier & Simon, 2001).

Prior research suggested differential compatibility between the independence and differentiation components, on the one hand, and minority and majority membership, on the other. More specifically, minority groups often exert strong pressures towards conformity, or are at least perceived to do so (Festinger, 1954, pp. 136–7; Simmel, 1908, pp. 527–73). Minority members also tend to see their ingroup as more homogeneous than the respective majority outgroup, whereas the opposite is generally true for majority members (Simon, 1992). Similarly, minority groups tend to be perceived by others as more consistent, predictable and persistent than majorities (Bassili & Provencal, 1988). In short, membership in a minority group seems to put severe constraints on individual independence, whereas membership in a majority group should be quite compatible with this source of individual identity. The opposite may be true for differentiation from others. Minority membership implies possession of a rare self-aspect and thus assures differentiation from most other people. Conversely, majority membership implies similarity to most other people, who all possess the same frequent self-aspect, while it affords differentiation from only a few people (i.e. from those who possess the rare, opposite self-aspect). In sum, we expected minority membership to be compatible with the differentiation component of individual identity, but not with the independence component, while the opposite was expected regarding majority membership. We therefore predicted that collective identity among minority members would be facilitated when the differentiation component outweighed the independence component in the phenomenological definition of individual identity, whereas collective identity among majority members would be facilitated when individual identity was phenomenologically grounded primarily in the independence component.

These predictions were tested in a first laboratory experiment ($N = 79$) in which we manipulated the salience of the independence and differentiation components of individual identity as well as relative ingroup size (Kampmeier & Simon, 2001, Pilot Experiment). The salience manipulation was effected during a filler task that was presented as a different study allegedly concerned with the perception of individuality. During this task we announced that, according to psychological science, individuality was primarily defined as either independence or differentiation from other people. To further strengthen this manipulation, we asked participants to rate four different person descriptions with respect to the critical individual-identity component. Depending on condition, two of these target persons were portrayed as high on either independence or differentiation, whereas the remaining two persons were portrayed as low on the critical component. Cognitive style in information processing was introduced as a meaningful self-aspect and used as a criterion for ingroup–outgroup categorization. Relative ingroup size was manipulated by providing false feedback about the number of people with whom the participant allegedly shared the same cognitive style. As indices of collective identity, we measured identification with the ingroup and perceived ingroup cohesiveness, both with reliable multi-item scales. An analysis of variance yielded only the predicted two-way interaction between relative ingroup size and salience of individual-identity components, which was not qualified by index (i.e. identification vs. cohesiveness). Overall, minority members' collective identity was significantly stronger when differentiation was made salient as the central individual-identity component than when the independence component was made salient. For majority members, the opposite pattern was observed, but the simple effect did not reach statistical significance.

Although the results of the first experiment provided encouraging empirical support for the hypothesized interplay of individual and collective identities in minority–majority contexts, they required further conceptual purification. More specifically, our initial reasoning contained an implicit assumption that deserved more explicit consideration. Our original argument was that minority membership is compatible with the differentiation component of individual identity because it implies differentiation from most other people. More precisely, however, minority membership implies a high degree of *intergroup* differentiation. Conversely, majority membership was expected to be compatible with the independence component of individual identity because it exerts less conformity pressure. Again, more precisely, this compatibility should result because majority membership allows for a high degree of *intragroup* independence. Interestingly, a recent review of the minority–majority literature (Simon et al., 2001; see also chapter 5) further indicated that minority members generally tend more towards an intergroup orientation, focusing more on intergroup comparisons and relations, whereas majority members typically adopt an intragroup orientation, focusing more on intragroup comparisons and relations. We therefore suspected that a more general orientation towards either intergroup or intragroup comparisons and relations, typically but not necessarily associated with minority and majority membership, respectively, may underlie the moderating effect of relative ingroup size observed in the first experiment. An intergroup orientation may make collective identity particularly compatible with the differentiation component of individual identity because it gives access to socially recognized differences. Conversely, an intragroup orientation may make collective identity particularly compatible with the independence component because it gives people more leeway to explore and assert their freedom within their usual social milieu.

In a second experiment (Kampmeier & Simon, 2001, Main Experiment, $N = 140$), we disentangled the influence of relative ingroup size and orientation by manipulating both variables orthogonally in addition to manipulating salience of the individual-identity components. Relative ingroup size was manipulated on the basis of participants' alleged preferences for one of two painters, while salience of the individual-identity components was manipulated using the same procedure as in the first experiment. Subsequently, we primed orientation by inserting a task in which participants had to estimate the responses of an outside observer who made either intergroup or intragroup comparisons. We again measured identification with the ingroup and perceived ingroup cohesiveness, but the indices were later combined because the identification-cohesiveness distinction was not reproduced in a preliminary principal-components analysis.

The main result was a significant interaction between orientation and salience of individual-identity components (see figure 4.4). For participants with an intergroup orientation, collective identity was significantly stronger when the differentiation component of individual identity was made salient than when the independence component was made salient. The opposite was true for participants with an intragroup orientation. This result was not qualified further by relative ingroup size, and there was no evidence of an

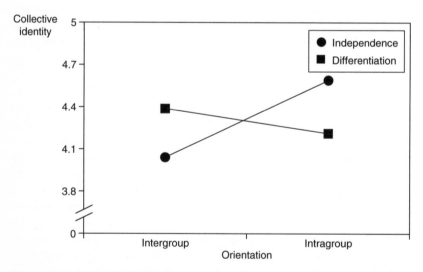

Figure 4.4 Collective identity as a function of orientation and salient individual-identity component (averaged across identification with the ingroup and perceived ingroup cohesiveness).

Source: From Kampmeier & Simon, 2001, Figure 3. Copyright © 2001 by the American Psychological Association. Adapted with permission.

interaction between relative ingroup size and salience of individual-identity components in the overall analysis. Still, we also identified a unique effect of relative ingroup size, but that effect was more circumscribed. It emerged only on a subset of collective-identity measures that directly tapped perceived intragroup similarity (e.g. 'During a group project, I would endorse a similar work ethic to other ingroup members.'). More specifically, minority members perceived a particularly high degree of intragroup similarity when the differentiation component of individual identity was made salient. However, no such effect was observed on the remaining measures, which revolved around intragroup complementariness (e.g. 'During a group project, ingroup members would complement each other well with respect to their abilities, opinions, etc.'), and the critical interaction between orientation and salience of individual-identity components was replicated in separate analyses for both similarity-based and complementariness-based measures. In conclusion, the differential orientation towards either intergroup or intragroup comparisons and relations, which may typically, but not necessarily, be associated with relative ingroup size, seems to be another important source of the dynamic interplay of individual and collective identities.

To summarize, a growing body of research testifies to the dynamic interplay of individual and collective identity, which seems to allow both antagonistic and harmonious relations between the two. It appears that people embrace a collective identity not always at the expense of individual identity but often also in cooperation with or even in the service of individual identity. Collective and individual identities can be in opposition to each other but, at other times or under other circumstances, they very well may be mutually compatible and perhaps even mutually reinforcing (see also Brewer & Roccas, 2001; Spears, 2001). One important source of this dynamism obviously lies in the dual character of individual identity, which includes identity as an independent individual and identity as a distinct individual. The dual character or the two faces of individual identity seem to be anchored in more general, socially shared representations, theories or even ideologies, but depending on social circumstances, one or the other of the two faces may be looking at us. Prior conceptualizations of individual identity typically prepared us for only one of the two faces.

Another important source of the dynamic interplay between individual and collective identities was identified through the distinction between groups with an intergroup orientation and groups with an intragroup orientation. Such consideration of the type or nature of the groups that provide the context or medium for the individual–collective interplay helps to build a bridge between two very different social psychological traditions of conceptualizing the foundations of the social group (see also Wilder & A. F. Simon, 1998). One tradition typically emphasizes intergroup relations and particularly intergroup differentiation (e.g. Brewer, 1991; Turner et al., 1987), whereas the other typically emphasizes intragroup relations and particularly intragroup cooperation for shared goals (e.g. Lewin, 1948; Rabbie & Horwitz, 1988). In many ways, minority groups seem to serve as the paradigmatic case for the first tradition, whereas majority groups better fit in with the second tradition. The parallel effects observed in our research for minority and majority groups, on the one hand, and for groups with an intergroup or intragroup orientation, on the other, support this point.

Research on the interplay between individual and collective identities thus contributes to the integration of different conceptualizations of individual identity as well as to the integration of different conceptualizations of the social group. Moreover, it promises a threefold integration by suggesting how the conceptual distinctions at the level of individual identity and at the level of the social group can be coordinated or matched such that one particular component of individual identity is compatible with one particular type or foundation of the social group (and the respective collective identity), but not with the other.

Summary

In this chapter, I discussed a number of important antecedents of individual identity and collective identity. More specifically, it was examined whether person and social context variables that are likely to affect the process of concentrating or de-centrating self-interpretation facilitate or inhibit the construction of individual and collective identities around specific self-aspects. In line with the principle of positive self-evaluation, it was found that positive valence of a self-aspect facilitated collective identity, whereas negative valence was more conducive to individual identity, irrespective of whether valence was anchored primarily in the person or in social context. High personal importance of a self-aspect also facilitated collective identity at the expense of individual identity. Moreover, high social contextual meaningfulness of a self-aspect played a critical role in identity construction. Without such meaningfulness, even rare or numerically distinct self-aspects seem unable to provide a solid basis for collective identity.

The working assumption derived from SAMI that the likelihood of collective-identity construction decreases, and the likelihood of individual-identity construction increases, with the number of different self-aspects involved in self-interpretation received only partial support, irrespective of whether the number of self-aspects was determined by the person's unique degree of self-complexity or by social context. As expected, a very high number of self-aspects tended to obstruct collective identity and to facilitate individual identity, most likely because the latter appeared as the better-fitting identity variant. However, quite unexpectedly, a very low number of self-aspects had very similar effects on identity construction. A possible explanation is that a very low number of self-aspects decreases readiness to embrace a collective identity because it does not allow people to retain a sufficient sense of individuality. This explanation was supported by the finding that a moderate number of additional self-aspects is particularly conducive to collective identity.

Acknowledging the role of individuality and individual identity as a cultural or ideological ideal in modern (Western) society, I further examined the dynamic interplay between individual and collective identities. As a first step, perceptions of independence and differentiation from other people were identified as important sources or antecedents of individual identity. Individual identity in modern society thus has (at least) two faces – identity as an independent individual and identity as a distinct individual. This distinction was then articulated with a conceptual distinction at the level of the social group, and it was shown how the differential compatibility between the different individual-identity components, on the one hand, and membership in different types of groups, on the other, can explain when individual and collective identities act either as partners or as opponents.

NOTE

1. Linville (1985, 1987) conceptualized self-complexity as a rather stable individual-differences variable and observed a relatively high test–retest correlation ($r = .70$ with a two-week interval). In our own research reported in this chapter, we used a modified self-complexity measure and also found a fair degree of stability over time with test–retest correlation coefficients exceeding .51 for three- and six-week intervals (Kampmeier et al., 2000). Nevertheless, a large proportion of variation still remains unaccounted for. It thus appears that people possess both a rather stable core of chronically accessible self-aspects and a more flexible layer or belt of self-aspects with little temporal or cross-situational stability (see also Markus & Kunda, 1986). However, the important point is that both the core and the outer layer or belt can contribute to a person's specific degree of self-complexity so that, whatever the exact sources of inter-individual variation, different people are likely to experience a given situation against a backdrop of differential self-complexity.

Chapter 5

Identity in Minority–Majority Contexts

A basic premise underlying the approach to identity presented in this book is that people and their identities do not exist in a social vacuum. Identities develop, take shape and operate in the context of social relations which, in turn, are critically structured by people's group memberships. The focus in this chapter is on identity in the context of minority–majority relations because many social contexts involve encounters between and within groups that hold either a minority or a majority position *vis-à-vis* each other (Farley, 1982; Mummendey & Simon, 1997; Tajfel, 1981). Moreover, the frequency of such encounters, or at least the potential for such encounters, should further increase in the modern, globalized world where migration processes, advanced information technology, rapid transportation and other factors fostering 'time–space compression' (Harvey, 1989, p. 240) facilitate the recognition or emergence of additional minority–majority categorizations (see also Hall, 1992).

A common definition of minority or majority membership rests on numbers or group size. Groups with fewer members are thus defined as minorities and numerically larger groups as majorities (e.g. Brewer, 1991; Moscovici & Paicheler, 1978; Simon, 1992). In addition, social status (prestige) and power are sometimes used as criteria for defining minority and majority membership (e.g. Tajfel, 1981). Such definitions assign low-status or relatively powerless groups a minority position and high-status or relatively powerful groups a majority position, even when the numerical relation is balanced or reversed. For instance, in most societies, women would then be considered a (social) minority and men a (social) majority. Similarly, during the rule of the apartheid regime in South Africa, Whites would have been considered a majority and Blacks a minority, even though the former group was numerically smaller than the latter (Tajfel, 1978c).

In this chapter, I start from a numerical definition of minority and majority membership. This approach is in line with the bulk of research on minority–majority relations conducted by experimental social psychologists (e.g. Brewer, 1998; Simon et al., 2001). Also, in real life, numerical asymmetries often, though not necessarily, co-vary with status or power asymmetries such that the numerical minority is also a low-status or relatively powerless group and the numerical majority a high-status or relatively powerful group. This appears to be the case especially in democratic societies with their ideological emphasis on majority rule (Lijphart, 1977, 1984; see also Sachdev & Bourhis, 1984; Sherif, 1966). However, this correlation also implies that the effects of relative group size and status or power are often confounded in real life. Consequently, although relative group size constitutes the central independent variable in the research discussed in this chapter, I will also explore the role of status and power asymmetries in minority–majority relations.

My main aim in this chapter is to demonstrate that membership in a minority group and membership in a majority group each constitutes a distinct social psychological situation for the particular group member and that the notion of identity helps us to better understand a variety of differential cognitive, affective and behavioural reactions which this situation elicits from minority and majority members. More specifically, I will examine the consequences of minority and majority membership for (1) self-interpretation, (2) social information processing, (3) one's well-being and (4) intergroup behaviour, especially the differential treatment of ingroup and outgroup members.

Self-Interpretation

In terms of the self-aspect model of identity (SAMI) presented in chapter 3, membership in a minority group is a rare self-aspect and membership in a majority group a relatively frequent self-aspect. In chapter 4, I have further argued that rare or minority self-aspects tend to attract particular attention and, therefore, people who share a minority self-aspect should be particularly likely to centre their self-interpretation on such a self-aspect. While the research reviewed in chapter 4 provided some preliminary evidence for this prediction, there is additional evidence for the hypothesized superior attention-grabbing power of minority self-aspects.

For example, when questioned immediately after the experimental manipulation of relative ingroup size, research participants who believed that they belonged to a numerical minority seemed to pay less attention to alternative self-aspects because they produced significantly less complex self-descriptions than research participants who believed that they belonged to a numerical majority (Simon, Aufderheide & Hastedt, 2000, Experiment 1). Interestingly, this effect was obtained despite the fact that research participants had not yet received any explicit information regarding the meaningfulness of the critical self-aspect (preference for urban or rural life). In light of the research discussed in chapter 4 which demonstrated that self-aspects need to be anchored meaningfully in the social context in order to be used for self-interpretation (Simon et al., 1997), it appears that research participants actually presupposed such meaningfulness. In fact, they may have inferred such meaningfulness on the reasonable assumption that the investigator would not dwell on meaningless self-aspects and thus violate the 'be relevant' maxim of conversational logic (Grice, 1975).[1] However, the observed difference in the complexity of minority and majority members' self-descriptions must be interpreted cautiously because it turned out to be rather fragile. It was not obtained in a condition where the self-description task was administered towards the end of the experimental session as opposed to immediately after the manipulation of relative ingroup size. Moreover, a follow-up study failed to replicate the differential (self-)complexity effect even when the self-description task was administered immediately after the manipulation of relative ingroup size (Simon, 1998a, pp. 12–14; Simon et al., 2000, Footnote 3).

Fortunately, there is also more robust (and more direct) evidence that self-interpretation is more likely to centre on minority membership than on majority membership. For example, children tend to think of themselves in terms of their gender and ethnicity especially when their respective self-aspect (e.g. being a boy or a girl) is relatively rare in their usual social milieu (McGuire & McGuire, 1988; see also Mullen, 1991). A recent laboratory experiment ($N = 61$) conducted in a more controlled social environment by Markus Lücken and myself (Lücken & Simon, 2003, Study 1; Lücken, 2002) confirmed this relationship between the rarity or numerical distinctiveness of a given self-aspect and its cognitive accessibility.

Preference for one of two different painters served as the critical self-aspect. Research participants were told either that they shared their artistic preference with only a few other people and thus belonged to a minority group, or that they shared it with most other people and thus belonged to a majority group. Group membership was kept anonymous so that there was never any knowledge about minority or majority group membership of any individual person, except for oneself. We also highlighted the meaningfulness of the critical self-aspect by stating that the minority–majority categorization was also related to important personality differences. The main dependent variables tapped research participants' current well-being and the cognitive accessibility of their group membership for self-interpretation. The results concerning well-being will be discussed in a later section of this chapter. For cognitive accessibility, a reliable multi-item scale was used that measured the extent to which research participants' thoughts centred on their group membership so that it was highly accessible for self-interpretation (e.g. 'Since I have learned that I am a member of this group, this thought enters my mind time and again' and 'Since I have learned that I am a member of this group, my thoughts are continually occupied with this fact', see also Cameron, 1999). As expected, we observed a significant minority–majority difference, indicating that group membership (i.e. the critical self-aspect) was cognitively more accessible when research participants belonged to a minority group than when they belonged to a majority group. In light of this differential capacity of minority and majority membership to take centre stage in self-interpretation, we should also expect a number of parallel minority–majority differences on related outcome variables such as collective identification and self-stereotyping.

More specifically, SAMI predicts that, because self-interpretation is more likely to centre on minority membership than on majority membership, minority members should also be more likely to adopt a collective identity based on their group membership than majority members. Supportive evidence is indeed available from several laboratory experiments (Ellemers et al., 1999; Simon & Brown, 1987; Simon & Pettigrew, 1990; Simon et al., 1997; see also chapter 4). Similarly, additional measures of collective identification administered in our experiment reported above (Lücken & Simon, 2003, Study 1) also confirmed that minority members identified more strongly with their ingroup than did majority members. And what is more, we were able to demonstrate that cognitive accessibility of one's group membership actually mediated the relationship between relative ingroup size and collective identification. Moreover, because collective identification is typically accompanied by self-stereotyping (Hogg & Turner, 1987), stronger self-stereotyping is to be expected for minority members than for majority members.

This hypothesis was tested by Simon and Hamilton (1994, Experiment 1) in a laboratory experiment which was introduced to the research participants as a study of the relationship between artistic preference and personality. Minority and majority membership was again based on participants' alleged preferences for one of two painters, with one painter allegedly being preferred by the majority of people and the other painter by only a minority of people. In order to obtain a meaningful dimension for the measurement of self-stereotyping, the cover story also stated that preference for one painter rather than the other was related to the introversion–extraversion dimension of personality. Care was taken that no differential evaluation was attached to minority and majority membership.

We used three measures of self-stereotyping. As a first measure, each participant provided self-descriptions on several rating scales referring to pretested positive and negative attributes associated with either introversion or extraversion. Self-stereotyping was thus measured in terms of endorsement of ingroup attributes and rejection of outgroup attributes. In addition, participants rated the similarity between themselves and other ingroup members as well as the homogeneity of the entire ingroup on the same attributes that were used for self-description. Analysis of variance confirmed the expected effect of relative ingroup size. Regardless of measure, minority members more strongly stereotyped themselves in terms of their group membership than did majority members. That is, minority members more strongly endorsed ingroup attributes and more strongly rejected outgroup attributes, and perceived more similarity between themselves and their ingroup as well as more homogeneity of the ingroup as a whole. This pattern was observed independent of the valence of the attribute in question, with the exception of positive outgroup attributes, on which judgements did not differ for minority and majority members.

Similarly, Brewer and Weber (1994) demonstrated that minority members aligned their self-perceptions more strongly with a portrait of another ingroup member than did majority members. And again in accordance with Simon and Hamilton's (1994, Experiment 1) findings, this minority–majority difference was observed even when it implied the incorporation of negative ingroup characteristics into self-perception on the part of minority members.

The role of status

As indicated at the beginning of the chapter, a numerical asymmetry between groups may often co-vary with a status asymmetry such that the numerical minority is also a low-status group and the numerical majority also a high-status group. However, the existence of many high-status numerical minorities or elites (e.g. the aristocracy in England, Brahmins in India or – at least for many decades – Whites in South Africa) proves that this is not necessarily so.

Markus Lücken and I (2003, Study 2) experimentally disentangled relative ingroup size (minority vs. majority) and ingroup status (low vs. high) by creating low- and high-status minority and majority groups in the laboratory. Except for the modifications that were necessary to manipulate group status, we used essentially the same procedure as in our first experiment reported above (Lücken & Simon, 2003, Study 1). Again, the alleged preference for one of two painters served as the critical self-aspect on which ingroup–outgroup categorization was based, and relative ingroup size was manipulated by false feedback about the numerical distinctiveness of the critical self-aspect. In addition to relative ingroup size, and orthogonally to that variable, we also varied (relative) ingroup status. This was accomplished by providing research participants ($N = 76$) with contrived information concerning the prestige of the two relevant painters as well as the quality of participants' artistic taste. In the low-(ingroup-)status condition, participants were told that, compared with the outgroup, members of their group obviously had a less refined artistic taste, for the painter they preferred was not regarded very highly by art experts. Conversely, in the high-(ingroup-)status condition, the ingroup was attributed a more refined artistic taste relative to the outgroup, for it was explained that the ingroup painter was regarded very highly by art experts.

The dependent variables of interest were again the cognitive accessibility of group membership and collective identification (for results on additional measures, see section on well-being). For cognitive accessibility, we replicated the finding that group membership figured more prominently in minority members' thoughts than in majority members' thoughts. This finding was not qualified by ingroup status, nor did we observe a significant main effect of that variable. However, the measures of collective identification (i.e. measures of the extent to which group members actually adopted or accepted a collective identity) revealed an interactive effect of relative ingroup size and ingroup status. Members of the high-status minority identified more strongly with their ingroup than did members of the low-status minority, whereas ingroup status did not affect majority members' (relatively low) collective identification.

Similar results were obtained by Simon and Hamilton (1994, Experiment 2) concerning self-stereotyping on ingroup attributes. Minority members were more willing to self-stereotype on ingroup attributes when ingroup status was high as opposed to low, whereas ingroup status did not affect majority members' self-stereotyping on ingroup attributes.[2]

Although high ingroup status may typically foster collective identification, probably owing to its positive implications for self-evaluation (Tajfel & Turner, 1986), it appears that minority members are usually more sensitive to differential ingroup status than are majority members (Ellemers et al., 1992). This finding clearly supports the self-aspect model of identity (SAMI) according to which (numerical) minority members' self-interpretation is much more focused or centred on their respective group membership than that of majority members, so that ingroup status is much more likely to 'hit the heart' of minority members' self-interpretation. SAMI thus explains why ingroup status had a much more powerful impact on minority members' than on majority members' self-interpretation. However, the interactive effects of relative ingroup size and ingroup status are also compatible with a 'scarcity principle' (Ditto & Jemmott, 1989) according to which the attractiveness of positively valenced and negatively valenced characteristics (e.g. high and low ingroup status) is more polarized when the frequency of these characteristics is low rather than high (e.g. when the ingroup is a numerical minority rather than a numerical majority). Although it is impossible at this point to rule out the scarcity account completely, a mediation analysis with our data (Lücken & Simon, 2003, Study 2) provided further support for the centrality account based on SAMI. This analysis strongly suggested that the increased centrality or cognitive accessibility of minority membership compared with majority membership indeed underlay the increased collective identification among members of the high-status minority.

Evidence for the reluctance of members of low-status minorities to accept a collective identity, while at the same time clearly being aware of their group membership, is not confined to groups created in the laboratory. For example, Simon, Glässner-Bayerl and Stratenwerth (1991) observed that, although gay men showed greater awareness of their group membership than did heterosexual men, the former gave lower ratings of perceived self–ingroup similarities than did the latter. Similarly, Simon et al. (1995, Study 3) found that, unlike heterosexual men, gay men were reluctant to acknowledge self–ingroup similarities compared with self–ingroup differences. Despite (or possibly because of) clear awareness of their group membership, gay men seem to downplay their collective identity in order to escape, or at least to reduce, the risk of being stereotyped or stigmatized as a member of a low-status minority.

However, we also know from numerous real-life examples that even members of low-status or stigmatized minorities (e.g. Jews, Blacks, gays) may adopt a collective identity. In analysing the conditions under which this is likely to happen, Tajfel (1981) suggested that 'a common identity is thrust upon a category of people because they are at the receiving end of certain attitudes and treatment from the "outside" ' (p. 315). In other words, members of low-status minorities may come to see each other as one because they are treated as one. Empirical support for this reasoning was found in another study with gay men as research participants in which we experimentally manipulated their awareness of special treatment of gays by the outside world (Simon et al., 1995, Study 4). In two treatment conditions, participants were instructed to recall episodes of either hostile or friendly treatment of gays, whereas participants in a control condition simply answered some irrelevant filler questions. Subsequent measurement of perceived self–ingroup and within-ingroup similarities and differences indicated stronger collective identification in each of the two treatment conditions than in the control condition. Interestingly, the quality of the treatment (hostile vs. friendly) did not influence participants' collective identification. There was no additional 'solidarity effect' in the hostile-treatment condition. Further inspection of the data suggested that the failure to find such a solidarity effect may have been due to reduced personal involvement in the hostile-treatment condition. Only a minority of the participants in that condition reported that they had experienced the recalled hostile incident personally, whereas in the friendly-treatment condition all participants except one had recalled a personal experience.

In this connection, the dual or dialectical role of stereotypes and stereotyping deserves further discussion. Although the fear of being stereotyped may often impede acceptance of a collective identity among members of low-status minorities, the actual fact of being stereotyped and treated accordingly can promote the adoption of a collective identity. Accordingly, Gordon Allport (1954/1979) noted that 'One's reputation, whether false or true, cannot be hammered, hammered, hammered, into one's head without doing something to one's character' (p. 142). Unless members of low-status minorities avoid interactions with the outside world, they are unable *not* to participate psychologically in the network of socially prevalent stereotypes, which typically reflect the view of the high-status majority. Indeed, research demonstrates that stereotypes concerning low-status minorities are often shared across group boundaries so that members of low-status minorities may eventually accept such stereotypes as self-stereotypes (Crocker, Major & Steele, 1998, p. 510) and even build a collective identity around them (Simon et al., 1991; Tajfel, 1981). This is not to say that the self-stereotypes and collective identities of members of low-status minorities are necessarily based on a distorted view of social reality. The known tendency of (self-)stereotypes to function as self-fulfilling prophecies (G. Allport, 1954/1979; Jussim, 1991; Merton, 1948; Snyder, 1984) may in part be responsible for their factual validity. More importantly, stereotypes about low-status minorities as well as the corresponding self-stereotypes possess more than just a kernel of truth because they reflect, to a significant degree, social reality as it is defined and structured by high-status majorities or other dominant groups. For example, the (self-) stereotypes of gay men as unstable and complicated (Simon et al., 1991) point to the stressful reality of discrimination and oppression which many gay men suffer and which is conducive to the development of these very characteristics. Living in constant fear of rejection or worse is very likely to foster coping or survival strategies (e.g. hyper-sensitivity and secretiveness) that make the person appear unstable and complicated.

In conclusion, the experience of being collectively stereotyped may lead members of low-status minorities to recognize, accept and develop similarities with other ingroup members which then become part and parcel of their self-stereotypes and thus provide a basis for collective identity. It is important to note the 'Janus face' or *dialectics* of this process with respect to its implications for social stability and social change (Simon, 1992, p. 26). On the one hand, this kind of self-stereotyping or collective-identity construction is likely to confirm the socially prevailing stereotypes about the low-status minority (e.g. via stereotype-consistent self-presentation) and thus to contribute to the acceptance and reproduction of the status quo. On the other hand, however, it also provides a social psychological platform or rallying point from which members of low-status minorities may eventually launch their battle for acceptance (see chapter 7). The following excerpt taken from the play *Andorra* by Max Frisch (1964) nicely illustrates both 'faces' or sides of this dialectic relation – acceptance of the socially prevailing stereotype (of Jews) and the request for acceptance (as a Jew).

> Ever since I have been able to hear, people have told me I'm different, and I watched to see if what they said was true. And it is true, Father. I am different. People told me my kind have a certain way of moving, and I looked at myself in the mirror almost every evening. They were right. I do have a certain way of moving. I can't help it. And I watched to see whether it was true that I'm always thinking of money, when the Andorrans watched me and thought: now he's thinking of money – and they were right again. I am always thinking of money. It's true. And I have no backbone. I've tried, it's no use. I have no backbone, only fear. And people told me that my kind are cowards. I watched out for this too. Many of them are cowards, but I know when I'm being a coward. I didn't want to admit what they told me, but it's true. They kicked me with their boots, and it's true what they say. I don't feel like they do. And I have no country. You told me, Father, that one must accept that, and I have accepted it. Now it's up to you, Father, to accept your Jew.
>
> **(Andri to Priest in Frisch, 1964, p. 60)**

The role of power

In the preceding sub-section, I drew on Tajfel's (1981) observation that collective identities are often thrust upon certain groups because they are at the receiving end of certain attitudes and treatment from other groups. Such attitudes and treatment often impose low status or low social prestige on the target groups, and this devaluation or stigmatization is typically reflected in, and at least partially reproduced and maintained by, the imposed collective identities and associated (self-)stereotypes. This mechanism points to the role of power in intergroup relations. In order to be able to thrust a collective identity upon some outgroup, the other group needs to possess the power to enact its intergroup attitudes and to treat the outgroup accordingly. More precisely, there must be a power differential such that one group is more powerful than the other so that the latter cannot escape from being at the receiving end of the (more powerful) outgroup's attitudes and treatment.

Unlike group status (for a review, see Ellemers & Barreto, 2001), power relations between groups have for a long time received only sporadic attention from social psychologists (Ng, 1982; Sachdev & Bourhis, 1985, 1991), although more recent work seems to indicate an increasing interest in the role of group power (e.g. Dépret & Fiske, 1999; Guinote, Judd & Brauer, 2002). The neglect in the past may have been due, at least in part, to an implicit equation of power with (high) group status and/or (majority) group size among lay persons as well as many group researchers. Indeed, as indicated above, powerful groups should in general be in a better position to disseminate the idea that they have and deserve superior social prestige or high status because 'the ideas of the ruling class are in every epoch the ruling ideas' (Marx & Engels, 1978, p. 172). Consequently, high status often reflects superior power so that people are likely to use status as a (valid) indicator of power. What is more, owing to its strong empirical association with power, status may even be perceived, and thus come to function, as a (secondary) source or basis of power (French & Raven, 1959). It can further be assumed that, especially in democratic societies with their ideological emphasis on majority rule (Lijphart, 1977, 1984), numerical superiority or majority group size is regarded or construed as another important source of power (Lücken, 2002). Moreover, such constructions or inferences seem to work in both directions (and with respect to both group status and group size) because Sachdev and Bourhis (1985) found that powerful groups were ascribed both higher status and majority size relative to powerless groups.

However, although 'Every relationship of power puts into operation differentiations which are at the same time its conditions and its results' (Foucault, 1982, p. 223), differentiations of which differential group status and differential group size may be prime examples, such differentiations do not exhaust the phenomenon of power, nor do they render power a redundant variable. Accordingly, scholars have repeatedly criticized the neglect of power in social psychological research and have proposed a variety of definitions of power as a distinct social psychological variable (e.g. Cartwright, 1959a; Dépret & Fiske, 1993, 1999). For example, Lewin (1951, p. 336) and Cartwright (1959b, p. 193) define an agent's power in terms of the maximum directional force that this agent can induce on another agent relative to the maximum counter-force or resistance of the latter. More recently, following Jones (1972), Sachdev and Bourhis (1985, 1991) defined a group's power as the degree of control that the group has over its own fate and that of outgroups. Similarly, Dépret and Fiske (1993) suggested defining a social entity's power in terms of the control that this entity has over another entity's outcomes. Reviewing different approaches to power, Haslam (2001, p. 210) noted that 'Most definitions . . . embrace the view that power is embedded in a social relationship where one party (an individual or group) has (or is perceived to have) the ability to impose its will on another by virtue of the resources at its disposal'.[3]

Up to now, research on the effect of group power on self-interpretation in intergroup contexts has failed to produce consistent results. For example, Sachdev and Bourhis (1985) found some, but very limited, evidence that group power increases collective identification, whereas in another experiment the same authors (Sachdev & Bourhis, 1991) found no effect of group power. Conversely, Dépret and Fiske (1999) observed a weak increase in research participants' identification with their ingroup when the participants expected a confrontation with a very powerful outgroup as opposed to an outgroup that was not so powerful. Unfortunately, these results are not directly comparable with those of Sachdev and Bourhis (1985, 1991) because the Dépret and Fiske (1999) experiment did not include a condition where the ingroup was clearly more powerful than the outgroup. Finally, the failure to find reliable and consistent effects may also be due in part to the rather unrefined measures of collective identification used in prior work.

More recently, Markus Lücken and I (Lücken & Simon, 2003; Study 3) examined the effect of group power on self-interpretation among members of numerical minority and majority groups. Except for the modifications that were necessary to manipulate group power, we used essentially the same procedure as in our other experiments reported above (Lücken & Simon, 2003, Studies 1 and 2), including the same reliable dependent measures. Again, the alleged preference for one of two painters served as the critical self-aspect on which ingroup–outgroup categorization was based, and relative ingroup size was manipulated by false feedback about the numerical distinct-iveness of the critical self-aspect. In addition to relative ingroup size, and orthogonally to that variable, we also varied relative ingroup power in terms of the ability of the ingroup to impose its will on the outgroup or vice versa. This was accomplished by informing research participants ($N = 73$) that, in the next stage of the experiment, each group had to work on one of two different artistic tasks (i.e. either to paint a picture or to shape a sculpture in clay). Furthermore, after participants had rated the attractiveness of both tasks, it was announced – depending on experimental condition – either that the ingroup or that the outgroup (i.e. either people with the same or people with the opposite painter preference to the participant) could freely choose one task whereas the remaining task had to be completed by the other group. This proceeding had allegedly been determined by lot at the beginning of the entire research project. The effectiveness of this power manipulation was established through pilot testing. In order not to confound the power variable with task preference, all participants in the main study eventually learned that, as a result of the (alleged) choice of either the ingroup or the outgroup, they would be able to work on the task that they personally preferred. Again, the dependent variables of interest were the cognitive accessibility of group mem-bership and collective identification (for results on additional measures, see section on well-being).

Whereas relative ingroup power was expected not to interfere with the increased cognitive accessibility of minority membership, we anticipated an interactive effect on collective identification of relative ingroup power and ingroup size. We suspected that, owing to the likely association, if not equa-tion, of numerical inferiority with low group power, minority members might be less willing to accept their collective identity when relative ingroup power was further reduced. Conversely, given their numerical superiority as well as their typically low collective identification, we reasoned that majority members may be less sensitive to variations in relative ingroup power.

For cognitive accessibility, we replicated the main effect of relative ingroup size found in our previous experiments (Lücken & Simon, 2003, Studies 1 and 2). Unexpectedly, however, we also observed a marginally significant interaction between relative ingroup size and relative ingroup power. Closer inspection revealed increased cognitive accessibility of minority membership relative to majority membership only for research participants whose (minority or majority) ingroup was less powerful than the outgroup. There was no difference in the cognitive accessibility of minority and majority membership for research participants whose ingroup was more powerful than the outgroup. Viewed from a different perspective, relative ingroup power seemed to decrease cognitive accessibility of ingroup membership for minority members, but to increase cognitive accessibility of ingroup membership for majority members. For minority members, who may generally (and justifiably) be concerned about possible disadvantages resulting from their numerical inferiority, relative ingroup power may serve as an 'all clear' signal which allows them to redirect attention away from their group membership. Conversely, for majority members, the explicit allocation of power to them *as a group* seems to move their group membership, which usually remains implicit, into the psychological foreground. It should be noted, however, that the simple effects of relative ingroup power failed to reach statistical significance and therefore this interpretation requires further empirical substantiation in future research.

For collective identification, a main effect of relative ingroup size indicated that minority members identified more strongly with their ingroup than did majority members. Although we also observed a marginally significant interaction effect, the actual means did not conform to the pattern suggested above. Whereas minority members' collective identification did not vary as a function of relative ingroup power, majority members' collective identification increased significantly when the ingroup was more powerful than the outgroup – a pattern of results that was very similar to that concerning the cognitive accessibility of majority membership. As a consequence, majority members' collective identification no longer differed from minority members' collective identification. In other words, it was the majority and not the minority group that was more sensitive to variations in relative ingroup power.

In conclusion, although a power advantage may relieve minority members of the hyper-accessibility of their group membership, it does not lead them to give up their relatively strong collective identity, which is probably wise because a strong collective identity may still prove useful in confrontations with a numerically superior outgroup (see chapter 7). Conversely, an explicit power advantage seems to awaken group consciousness among majority members and to transform them into a psychological group with an explicit and strong collective identity. This pattern suggests a unique role of group power as a determinant of collective identification in minority–majority contexts, a role quite distinct from that of group status discussed above. While the latter primarily affects minority members' collective identity, group power seems particularly important for majority members' collective identity. When low in group status, minority members seem eager to shed their collective identity, possibly because affiliation with other 'bad guys' invites further stigmatization. However, even when they lack group power, minority members stick to their collective identity, possibly because a few additional comrades are still better than being all alone in confrontations with a powerful majority outgroup. In contrast, majority members seem relatively immune against negative effects of low group status, most likely because their generally weak collective identification prevents low group status from hitting their hearts. Power over the minority outgroup, however, appears to awaken majority members' collective identity so that the majority group emerges as a self-conscious and probably also assertive collective protagonist in intergroup contexts.

Social Information Processing

Several social psychological approaches to social cognition distinguish between two major types or levels of social information processing, namely between individual-level (or person-based) processing and group-level (or category-based) processing (Brewer, 1988, 1998; Fiske & Neuberg, 1990; Turner et al., 1987). Group-level processing is characterized, among other things, by the accentuation of perceived interchangeability of all members belonging to the same group, whereas accentuation of interpersonal differences is characteristic of individual-level processing. Moreover, self-interpretation and social information processing are typically closely interrelated such that individual identity underlies, and is itself reinforced by, individual-level processing, whereas collective identity underlies, and is reinforced by, group-level processing (Turner et al., 1987; Oakes et al., 1994). Consequently, variations in the level of minority and majority members' social information processing can be expected to parallel the minority–majority differences in self-interpretation discussed in the preceding section.

Taking perceived ingroup and outgroup homogeneity as an indicator of group-level information processing, it appears that there are indeed such minority–majority differences in social information processing. Whereas members of (numerical) majority groups tend to perceive more homogeneity in the outgroup than in the ingroup, members of (numerical) minority groups often show the opposite tendency (e.g. Simon & Brown, 1987; Simon & Pettigrew, 1990). Thus, majority members seem to engage in group-level processing primarily with respect to information that concerns the outgroup and its members, whereas minority members tend to engage in group-level processing also, and perhaps even more so, with respect to information that concerns the ingroup and other fellow group members (for an overview, see Simon, 1992). These differences nicely correspond to the minority–majority differences in self-interpretation (i.e. increased collective identification among members of numerical minorities) discussed in the preceding section. However, this correspondence may not be too surprising given that measures of perceived ingroup homogeneity tend to overlap with measures of self-interpretation, or for that matter collective identification, as both are often based on direct ratings of perceived or estimated similarities and differences within the ingroup (e.g. Simon & Hamilton, 1994; see also chapter 4).

A more sophisticated experimental paradigm which is also often employed to examine group-level relative to individual-level information processing is the recognition-confusion task developed by Taylor and her colleagues, in which research participants have to remember who of a number of alleged ingroup and outgroup members made which statement (Taylor et al., 1978; for a critical review, see Klauer & Wegener, 1998). In the initial presentation stage, participants are presented with a number of statements each of which is identified as being made by either an ingroup member or an outgroup member. Statements are carefully pretested to avoid confounding variables (e.g. differential likeability of ingroup and outgroup statements), and their total number usually varies between 6 and 16 across studies. Statements are presented on audio- or videotape or simply as written sentences on a computer screen, and each alleged speaker is identified by written information (i.e. names) or photographs. In the subsequent recognition stage, participants are presented with each statement once again. But this time, information as to who the speaker was is left out. Instead, participants are provided with lists of the names or photographs of all former speakers and are instructed to remember 'who said what' and to match statements and names or faces accordingly.

Three types of confusion errors can be distinguished: (1) within-ingroup errors resulting from attributing a statement allegedly made by a particular ingroup member erroneously to another ingroup member; (2) within-outgroup errors resulting from attributing a statement allegedly made by a particular outgroup member erroneously to another outgroup member; (3) intergroup errors resulting from attributing a statement allegedly made by an ingroup member erroneously to an outgroup member or vice versa. To anticipate a general result, the latter error type appears to be rather insensitive to experimental variations of relative ingroup size. Therefore, the following discussion focuses on intragroup errors (i.e. within-ingroup errors and within-outgroup errors). High numbers of such errors indicate the degree to which group members are seen or remembered as interchangeable exemplars of their respective groups or, in other words, the degree to which the perceiver engages in group-level as opposed to individual-level information processing.

Research on minority–majority differences in social information processing using the recognition-confusion task yielded mixed results, however. Thus Brewer, Weber and Carini (1995, Experiment 3) found no differences between members of (numerical) minority and majority groups in the processing of information about outgroup members, but observed that, compared with majority members, minority members tended towards less group-level processing, or at least additional individual-level processing, when information about ingroup members was concerned (see also Klauer, Wegener & Ehrenberg, 2002[4]). The latter finding is particularly surprising in light of the preceding discussions of minority–majority differences in self-interpretation and perceived group homogeneity which suggested that minority members are particularly likely to engage in group-level, but not individual-level processing.

One promising way to reconcile this apparent contradiction is to look for possible moderator variables. Our own research indeed points to the existence of such variables. As a first step, we (Simon et al., 2000, Experiment 1) experimentally designed a standard (numerical) minority–majority context in which group membership was highlighted at the expense of participants' individuality. The recognition-confusion task was administered, and confusion errors served as the main dependent variable. As expected, minority members showed more group-level information processing than did majority members. This standard minority–majority context was then contrasted with another minority–majority context which differed from the first in only one respect. In the new context, we administered an individualizing self-description task before measuring the dependent variables. We predicted and found that this individualization process undermined the minority–majority difference in group-level information processing observed earlier. It should be noted that, as in the research by Brewer et al. (1995, Experiment 3), effects were observed only for within-ingroup errors, whereas within-outgroup errors were again insensitive to the experimental manipulations.

However, the critical interaction effect was replicated in a second experiment with different measures of information processing (e.g. participants' use of abstract vs. concrete information) (Simon et al., 2000, Experiment 2), and this time the effect was obtained for processing of both ingroup and outgroup information (although the effect was somewhat weaker for the latter). More importantly, in the second experiment, the interaction involved a significant reversal. When individualization (of self) was fostered, group-level information processing decreased for minority members, but increased for majority members. The latter then showed more group-level information processing than did minority members.

Our tentative explanation was that individualization of self is compatible with majority membership because, unlike minorities, majorities are typically construed as aggregates of individuals (Mullen, 1991). In a seemingly para-doxical fashion, individualized self-interpretation, or in other words individual identity, may thus reinforce majority members' group membership and their group-level perspective. This reasoning was supported by the results on an auxiliary measure that gauged the extent to which participants thought they would fit in their ingroup. In the standard minority–majority context, minor-ity members perceived greater self-ingroup fit than did majority members. However, the opposite was true in the individualized minority–majority con-text. Majority members now thought they would fit better in their respective ingroup than minority members thought they would fit in theirs.

Although the pattern of information-processing results obtained in our individualized minority–majority context closely resembled that observed by Brewer et al. (1995, Experiment 3), it remains an open question whether or exactly how individual identity may have been operating as a moderator variable in Brewer et al.'s experiment. One possibility is that individualization processes were inadvertently set in motion in that experiment through the assignment of individual ID numbers, even though the assignment was appar-ently arbitrary (Brewer et al., 1995, p. 36; see also Brewer, Manzi & Shaw, 1993). It is a well-established social psychological phenomenon that arbitrary category labels trigger processes of group formation (Tajfel, 1982). By the same token, arbitrary individual ID numbers may foster individualization processes.

More generally, this line of research also points to a possible articulation of minority–majority differences in social information processing (and in the underlying self-interpretation) with a classic distinction encountered in both sociology and social psychology. In both fields, scholars have contrasted community (Gemeinschaft) with society (Gesellschaft; Tönnies, 1887/1957), mechanical solidarity with organic solidarity (Durkheim, 1893/1960), or similarity-based with interdependence-based (or complementariness-based) group formation (Turner et al., 1987; Wilder & A. F. Simon, 1998). Essen-tially, the distinction is between groups that are held together primarily by the similarity between their members and groups that are held together primarily by their members' individual, but interdependent and complementary roles. Also, the first type of group is usually assumed to define itself in a context of intergroup relations and especially intergroup differentiation (e.g. Brewer, 1991; Turner et al., 1987), whereas the second type is expected to emphasize intragroup relations and especially intragroup cooperation for shared goals (e.g. Lewin, 1948; Rabbie & Horwitz, 1988). As suggested in chapter 4, minority members may cognitively construe their ingroup more in terms of the first type of group, whereas majority members seem to draw on a cognitive representation of their ingroup that corresponds more to the latter type. Moreover, collective identity derived from membership in groups of the first type appears to be quite compatible with identity as a distinct individual, while collective identity derived from membership in groups of the second type tends to be reinforced by identity as an independent individual. It is therefore very likely that the seemingly paradoxical effect of individualization on major- ity members' social information processing (Simon et al., 2000) – as well as its inhibitory effect on group-level information processing among minority members – was due primarily to the independence component of individuality (as opposed to its differentiation component). Although these two components had not been differentiated in the Simon et al. (2000) research, later work revealed that individualization of self-interpretation is particularly closely connected with feelings of independence (Kampmeier & Simon, 2001; see also chapter 4, table 4.2).

In conclusion, individualization processes, especially those that foster self- interpretation as an independent individual that is able to flexibly engage in exchanges with many different ingroup members, may serve an important social integrative function in majority groups (as well as in other interdepend- ence-based groups) and thus strengthen collective identity and group-level information processing among their members. However, collective identity may then take on a somewhat different meaning because, under such circum- stances, it may not necessarily be majority members' mutual interchange- ability that is highlighted, as is usually the case for minority members (or members of other similarity-based groups). Instead, the shared goal or common purpose is likely to move into the psychological foreground.

The role of status

In this section, I have so far focused on minority and majority groups that were defined in purely numerical terms. I now turn to intergroup contexts in which ingroup and outgroup differ not only in size, but also in status. For example, Lorenzi-Cioldi (1998, Study 7) manipulated relative ingroup size and ingroup status as orthogonal experimental variables and examined their effects on information processing using the recognition-confusion task. He found that relative ingroup size did not influence information processing. Instead, there was only a general effect of relative group status. Participants showed more group-level processing (i.e. more within-group errors) for infor- mation concerning low-status groups than for information concerning high-status groups, irrespective of whether these groups were (minority or majority) ingroups or outgroups. Lorenzi-Cioldi (1998) interpreted these processing differences in terms of socially shared, stable and generalized conceptions about low-status and high-status groups which, for various cognitive (e.g. attributional) and social (e.g. normative and ideological) reasons, should involve more differentiated mental representations of high-status groups relative to low-status groups (see also Sedikides, 1997).

However, such a static view may underestimate the role of motivated and strategic cognition in social information processing (Fiske & Taylor, 1991; Kunda, 1990). For example, research by Doosje, Ellemers and Spears (1995) as well as by Simon and Hastedt (1997, Experiment 1) suggests that members of low-status or otherwise unattractive groups prefer group-level information processing as part of a group-level strategy to cope with their collective predicament, whereas they tend more towards individual-level information processing when individual escape seems possible or acceptable. We (Simon & Hastedt, 1997, Experiment 2) also uncovered such a motivated or strategic use of social information processing in an experiment with members of laboratory-created minority and majority groups.

In addition to relative ingroup size, the experiment comprised two other independent variables. As an analogue of ingroup status, we varied ingroup attractiveness by highlighting either positive or negative ingroup characteristics. Although this manipulation differs from the standard manipulation of (relative) ingroup status (e.g. Simon & Hamilton, 1994; Lorenzi-Cioldi, 1998), it still captures the central social psychological component of the concept of ingroup status, namely its (positive or negative) implications for group members' self-evaluations (Tajfel & Turner, 1986). Individualization of self was manipulated as a third independent variable because it was directly relevant to testing the role of motivated or strategic cognition in social information processing. Whereas half of the participants worked on the dependent measures immediately after the manipulation of relative ingroup size and ingroup attractiveness, the remaining participants were additionally given an individualizing self-description task between the manipulation of the two other independent variables and the measurement of the dependent variables. Within-ingroup errors derived from the recognition-confusion task served again as the main dependent variable. (There were no effects on within-outgroup errors in this experiment.)

It was predicted and found that our third independent variable served as an important moderator of the combined influence of relative ingroup size and ingroup attractiveness. When individualization of self was difficult (i.e. in the standard intergroup context without the individualizing self-description task), ingroup attractiveness had opposite effects on minority and majority members: Minority members showed more group-level information processing when the ingroup was attractive as opposed to unattractive, whereas majority members showed more group-level information processing when the ingroup was unattractive. However, when individualization of self was facilitated by way of a self-description task, ingroup attractiveness had identical effects on minority and majority members: Irrespective of relative ingroup size, group-level information processing was stronger when the ingroup was attractive as opposed to unattractive.

Taken together, these results suggest that high ingroup status generally motivates minority members to engage in group-level information processing, whereas low ingroup status motivates them to engage in individual-level information processing. This is probably so because, depending on ingroup status, a group-level perspective and an individual-level perspective are differentially conducive to the achievement or maintenance of positive self-evaluation (Tajfel & Turner, 1986). More specifically, when ingroup status is high, group-level information processing endorses one's positive collective identity and thus contributes to positive self-evaluation. Conversely, when ingroup status is low, individual-level information processing helps to distance oneself from, and thus softens the impact on self-evaluation of, one's negative collective identity and paves the way for a compensatory influence of one's individual identity.

For majority members, however, the relationship between ingroup status and information processing seems to depend on an additional strategic consideration. As indicated above, group-level information processing can be part of a group-level strategy to cope collectively with a shared predicament such as low ingroup status (Doosje et al., 1995; Simon, 1998b). Moreover, large ingroup size can be an important resource in the collective struggle for social change (Klandermans, 1997). In light of their numerical superiority, members of low-status majority groups may therefore consider a group-level strategy including group-level information processing a viable option, but only until they are offered an easier individual way out of the predicament, such as distancing oneself from the ingroup and one's collective identity through individualization. Conversely, for minority members, who do not have superior group size as an additional resource at their disposal, a group-level strategy to cope with low ingroup status is certainly much riskier and therefore less likely (though not impossible as will be shown in chapter 7).

The role of power

To my knowledge, the effect of group power on minority and majority members' social information processing has not yet systematically been investigated by social psychologists. However, there seems to be an increasing interest in power relations and the associated consequences for social information processing among social psychologists (for reviews, see Dépret & Fiske, 1993; Fiske, 1993; Fiske, Morling & Stevens, 1996; also Guinote et al., 2002). Though not directly concerned with power relations in the context of (numerical) minority and majority groups, this work may nevertheless be informative. For example, building on the observation that powerful individuals generally pay little attention to powerless individuals, most likely because the former can afford such ignorance (Fiske, 1993), one may hypothesize that members of powerful groups, irrespective of relative ingroup size, generally tend towards group-level as opposed to individual-level processing of information concerning powerless outgroups. Moreover, the tendency towards group-level information processing may also extend to the ingroup. In the section on self-interpretation, I discussed the finding that superior group power increased collective identification among majority members, whereas there was no change for the generally strong collective identification of minority members (Lücken & Simon, 2003, Study 3). Given equivalent levels of collective identification in powerful minority groups and powerful majority groups, together with the facilitating effect of a strong collective identity on group-level processing of information concerning the ingroup (Turner et al., 1987), one may then expect a similar preference for group-level processing of information concerning the ingroup among members of both powerful minority and majority groups.

Turning to people with a power disadvantage, research by Fiske and colleagues (Fiske, 1993; Fiske et al., 1996) demonstrates that individuals pay particular attention to powerful others and their individual attributes, possibly in order to regain some control. In other words, they tend towards pronounced individual-level social information processing with respect to the powerful. However, while this research focused on interpersonal contexts, more recent work by Dépret and Fiske (1999) suggests that things may be quite different in salient intergroup contexts. In such contexts, group-level processing seems to be the dominant cognitive strategy to deal with information about more powerful outgroups, possibly because this strategy facilitates collective action aimed at changing the power structure (Reynolds et al., 2000). It is an open question, however, whether this tendency towards group-level information processing will hold true both for members of powerless minority groups and for members of powerless majority groups, for the research by Dépret and Fiske (1999) also suggests that individual-level information processing may again come into play when one is confronted with a powerful heterogeneous aggregate. As it is not unlikely that majority groups are construed as such (Simon, 1992), group-level processing of information concerning the powerful may indeed be undermined among members of powerless minority groups. Finally, systematic research is also outstanding when it comes to possible effects of inferior group power on minority and majority members' processing of information concerning their own group. Little can be said at this point except that the stronger collective identification observed in our research among members of powerless minorities compared with members of powerless majorities (Lücken & Simon, 2003, Study 3) certainly makes the former stronger candidates for group-level information processing with regard to the ingroup.[5]

Well-being

Who we are, or who we (and other people) think we are, is not without consequences for our emotions or feelings (G. Allport, 1954/1979; Lewin, 1948; Turner et al., 1987). Accordingly, I examine in this section whether there are systematic differences in minority and majority members' well-being. As neither the quantity nor the quality of the research available for this purpose allows a more fine-grained differentiation, I look at well-being in a rather broad sense, including a variety of temporary emotional or affective states (e.g. happiness, depression or insecurity) as well as more stable positive or negative feelings about oneself and one's place or identity in the social world (e.g. self-respect or self-esteem).

From a theoretical point of view, there is good reason to assume that membership in a (numerical) minority group may be associated with a less satisfactory collective identity and thus less positive feelings or well-being than membership in a (numerical) majority group. At least in Western societies, with their ideological emphasis on majority rule (Lijphart, 1977, 1984), numerical inferiority is likely to be associated with error and deviance as well as weakness or powerlessness (Gerard, 1985, p. 174; Lücken, 2002; Sachdev & Bourhis, 1984; Sherif, 1966, p. 111: 'There is safety in numbers'). As a consequence, members of minorities should feel less good about themselves and less secure than members of majorities. The minority–majority difference in well-being may be further accentuated because members of relatively small groups are typically at a disadvantage, compared with members of larger groups, when it comes to soliciting consensual validation from many similar others concerning characteristics related to their group membership (Festinger, 1954). In fact, such a deficit should be particularly painful for minority members, for whom their group membership is generally a central self-aspect (Lücken & Simon, 2003, Study 1; McGuire & McGuire, 1988; see section on self-interpretation).

Although empirical research into the well-being of members of minority and majority groups that are defined in purely numerical terms is still sparse, evidence for the hypothesized minority–majority difference is gradually accumulating. For example, although they found no overall difference between minority and majority members on a mood adjective checklist, Bettencourt, Charlton and Kernahan (1997, Study 1) observed that minority members felt less relaxed than majority members. Similarly, using an indirect scenario methodology, Bettencourt, Miller and Hume (1999, Study 2) found that research participants, who were themselves not assigned to any group, but simply served as judges of hypothetical minority and majority members, expected minority members to experience more anxiety than majority members. More direct and robust evidence was found by Markus Lücken and myself in the laboratory experiment already mentioned in the section on self-interpretation (Lücken & Simon, 2003, Study 1). In addition to the measures of cognitive accessibility of one's group membership and acceptance of one's collective identity, we also administered a reliable multi-item measure of affect, including feelings of elation, anger and depression in our experiment. As expected, this measure revealed that research participants' feelings were significantly less positive after assignment to a minority group than after assignment to a majority group.

However, it should also be noted that other researchers have argued that minority members should be more satisfied with their group membership than majority members because minority groups provide both sufficient inclusiveness within the ingroup and sufficient differentiation between ingroup and outgroup (Brewer, 1991; Leonardelli & Brewer, 2001). Unlike majority identities, minority identities would therefore be optimally distinct.

Leonardelli and Brewer (2001, Experiments 2 and 3) indeed found higher satisfaction among minority members than among majority members. However, those authors compared minority and majority members only after members of both groups had experimentally been induced to identify strongly with their respective ingroup. Hence, we cannot be sure that the differential satisfaction with minority and majority memberships observed by those authors also holds true for more typical minority—majority contexts, in which minority members' collective identification is not additionally bolstered and in which majority members' collective identification is usually rather weak.

The role of status and power

To the best of my knowledge, only very few researchers have tried systematically to disentangle the influence that relative ingroup size, on the one hand, and relative ingroup status or ingroup power, on the other, has on well-being. For example, with respect to feelings of group pride, Ellemers et al. (1992) found that relative ingroup size and ingroup status interacted such that members of high-status minority groups took most pride in their group membership, while members of low-status minority and low- and high-status majority groups did not differ from each other.[6] However, this pattern could not be replicated by Ellemers et al. (1999), who used a more general measure of group esteem. Instead, Ellemers et al. (1999) only found a status main effect showing that group esteem was higher for members of high-status groups than for members of low-status groups, irrespective of relative ingroup size. The second experiment by Markus Lücken and myself, already described in the section on self-interpretation (Lücken & Simon, 2003, Study 2), is also of relevance in this context. In the experiment, we manipulated both relative ingroup size and ingroup status and again measured affect – in addition to cognitive accessibility of group membership and acceptance of collective identify. We observed only a significant main effect of relative ingroup size, whereas all other effects were non-significant. Minority members reported less positive affect than did majority members, irrespective of relative ingroup status.

Evidence for a positive relationship between relative ingroup size and well-being also emerged in experiments in which relative ingroup power was considered as an additional independent variable. In our third experiment already described above, Markus Lücken and I also measured research participants' affect as a function of relative ingroup size and ingroup power (Lücken & Simon, 2003, Study 3). We found that research participants assigned to a minority group reported significantly less positive affect than did research participants assigned to a majority group, but only when the respective ingroup was less powerful than the outgroup. When the ingroup was more powerful, affect did not vary as a function of relative ingroup size.

Finally, Sachdev and Bourhis (1991) manipulated all three variables – relative ingroup size, ingroup status and ingroup power. They found that well-being was influenced by relative ingroup size irrespective of relative ingroup status and ingroup power. Minority members felt less comfortable, less satisfied and less happy about their group membership than did majority members. Obviously, more systematic research is needed to ascertain whether relative ingroup size affects group members' well-being alone or in interaction with other variables, such as relative ingroup status or ingroup power, as well as to specify precisely what aspects of well-being are most likely affected. Nevertheless, the available experimental work strongly suggests that members of numerically inferior groups are more at risk of suffering emotionally for who (they and others think) they are than members of numerically superior groups.

Contrary to the paucity of work conducted in more controlled experimental environments, a much larger body of research is available with respect to well-being in real-life minority–majority contexts, in which numerical asymmetries are typically confounded with status and/or power asymmetries. In line with the preceding discussion, the bulk of the research was guided by the theoretical assumption that members of disadvantaged (low-status and/or powerless) minority groups should have lower self-esteem than members of advantaged (high-status or powerful) majority groups (Crocker & Major, 1989). However, several reviews of pertinent empirical work came to the conclusion that self-esteem deficits among members of disadvantaged minority groups are not very common, especially if self-esteem is conceptualized as a stable trait of the person (Crocker & Major, 1989; Crocker et al., 1998; Crocker & Quinn, 2001). These reviews prompted many efforts to account for the apparent discrepancy between theory and data. As a result, research provided valuable insights into several psychological mechanisms by which members of disadvantaged minority groups may protect their self-esteem (e.g. attributional externalization, selective social comparisons), but it also identified possible harmful effects of such mechanisms (Crocker et al., 1998; Crocker & Quinn, 2001; Major & Crocker, 1993; Schmitt & Branscombe, 2002).

At the same time, however, new evidence is accumulating which confirms that, at least under some conditions, members of disadvantaged minority groups differ in well-being from members of advantaged majority groups as originally expected. For example, in Bangladesh, Hewstone, Islam and Judd (1993, Experiment 2) found lower self-esteem among Hindus (a disadvantaged minority) than among Muslims (an advantaged majority). Research conducted by Islam and Hewstone (1993) in a similar context further indicated that, in direct intergroup encounters, members of disadvantaged minority groups may suffer from increased intergroup anxiety. In addition, Frable, Platt and Hoey (1998) found that members of disadvantaged minority groups whose group membership (or stigma) was concealable as opposed to visible experienced lower self-esteem and more negative affect than members of advantaged majority groups. Frable et al.'s (1998) observation that the well-being of members of disadvantaged minority groups was negatively affected only when their group membership could be concealed is in line with other research that points to the positive or compensatory role of intragroup support and collective identification in the well-being of members of disadvantaged groups (Branscombe, Schmitt & Harvey, 1999; Schmitt & Branscombe, 2002; Phinney, 1990; Verkuyten, 1995). These compensatory resources should be less easily available when it is not immediately clear (or visible) who is one of 'us'. Similarly, Simon et al. (1991) observed that members of a disadvantaged minority group who could conceal their membership (gay men) tended to be less happy with their group membership than members of the corresponding advantaged majority group (heterosexual men).

Finally, a recent field study conducted by Markus Lücken and myself (Lücken & Simon, 2003, Study 4) suggests that even if members of disadvantaged minority groups may escape permanent damage to their (trait) self-esteem, they are still likely to suffer from feelings of insecurity. Research participants ($N = 197$) were students at the University of Kiel who belonged either to a disadvantaged minority or to an advantaged majority group on the basis of mostly visible categorization criteria such as age, gender, body size, physical (dis)ability or nationality/ethnicity. Collapsing across the different disadvantaged minority groups as well as the corresponding advantaged majority groups, we found that minority members felt significantly more insecure when their respective group membership was made salient than did majority members, but minority and majority members did not differ in (trait) self-esteem. Further analyses indicated that minority members' insecurity was due to a large extent to perceptions or fears of being disadvantaged, while majority members' security was positively related to perceptions or feelings of being powerful. In addition, perceptions or expectations of intragroup respect seemed to mitigate minority members' insecurity at least to some extent.

In conclusion, members of minority groups may be able partly to mitigate the negative affective implications of their group membership and ward off permanent damage to their self-esteem by drawing, *inter alia*, on resources that their collective identity affords them, such as intragroup respect. Nevertheless, this review also strongly suggests that their membership constitutes a permanent challenge to their well-being. When minority membership cannot be concealed, this challenge is likely to materialize, and to take its toll, in numerous social encounters. By definition, there are more majority members than minority members, so that it is usually difficult for minority members to avoid contact with people who quickly notice that they are different and remind them of it by word and deed. However, as our research in which group membership was kept anonymous suggests (Lücken & Simon, 2003, Studies 1, 2, and 3), minority members are likely to experience heightened awareness of their group membership even when group membership is concealable. Our research also demonstrated that this heightened awareness is often accompanied by negative affect, especially when minority membership is factually or psychologically associated with a power disadvantage. Minority members thus find themselves in a *cognitive–affective crossfire*. On the one hand, it is difficult for minority members to forget or ignore their group membership, while, on the other, their membership entails stressful emotional experiences. In other words, compared with majority members, there are stronger cognitive forces pushing minority members towards their group (or keeping them in it), while at the same time there seem to be also stronger affective forces pulling them away from it (or keeping them out of it).

As a consequence, minority members should develop strategies to escape from, or at least to cope with, this cognitive–affective crossfire. Depending on the perceived affordances or opportunity structure of the social context, they

may seek individual exit from their group or at least psychological dis-
identification (Crocker et al., 1998), look for relief or strength within their
group (e.g. Lücken & Simon, 2003, Study 4; Schmitt & Branscombe, 2002) or
opt for assertive intergroup behaviour and collective action (see next section as
well as chapter 7). Yet, whatever strategy they may opt for, it is difficult for
minority members to ignore the intergroup dimension of their life space. They
need to be mindful of it, be it in order to adjust to the intergroup context of their
existence individually (e.g. by exit from their group, by mimicry or by assimilation to the majority group) or collectively (e.g. by mutual intragroup support) or
be it in order to collectively restructure that context (e.g. by assertive collective
action). Conversely, majority members, who interact most of the time with their
own kind and who are usually not in the line of an unfriendly cognitive–affective
crossfire, can be more mindless in this respect.

Note that their mindfulness, in and of itself, is likely to create a distinct
identity problem for minority members. They tend to be constantly on guard
to justify or at least to explain their existence to themselves and others, usually
with the majority group as the (implicit) point of reference (Hegarty & Pratto,
2001; Kahneman & Miller, 1986; Moscovici & Paicheler, 1978). This way,
identity easily loses its lightness or 'naturalness'. Unlike majority members,
who can take their collective identity for granted and may actually forget it
(without losing it) and experience themselves as 'happy individuals', minority
members may exhaust, and possibly also caricature, themselves in the course
of a Sisyphean effort of collective-identity construction (see also Taylor, 1997)
– a mechanism that perpetuates and further aggravates their condition as
'unhappy group members'.

Intergroup Behaviour

The socially undesirable phenomenon of intergroup discrimination (i.e. inappropriate preferential treatment of ingroup members relative to outgroup
members) is widely regarded as the paradigmatic case of intergroup behaviour (Sumner, 1906; G. Allport, 1954/1979; Tajfel, 1982). This discussion
of minority–majority differences in intergroup behaviour therefore focuses
primarily on minority–majority differences in intergroup discrimination.

Currently, the most prominent social psychological explanation of intergroup discrimination is provided by social identity theory (Tajfel & Turner,
1986). It holds that, from a social psychological perspective, intergroup discrimination can be understood as an attempt to establish a positively valued
distinctiveness for one's ingroup in order to achieve or maintain a positive
collective (social) identity. Although there are still many open questions concerning this phenomenon and its adequate explanation, and even definition

(Mummendey & Otten, 2001), there is nevertheless wide consensus among social psychologists that social identity theory provides a very helpful framework for a better understanding of intergroup discrimination in general (Smith & Mackie, 2000) and in minority–majority contexts in particular (e.g. Mullen, Brown & Smith, 1992).

Most researchers who examined the effect of relative ingroup size on intergroup discrimination started with the expectation that members of (numerical) minorities should show stronger intergroup discrimination than members of (numerical) majorities (for a notable exception, see Moscovici & Paicheler, 1978). There are two typical accounts as to why this should be the case. For one, it is argued that, owing to its numerical distinctiveness or salience, minority group membership engenders a 'heightened sense of kindredness' (Gerard & Hoyt, 1974) or, in other words, is more 'identifying' than majority group membership (see also Leonardelli & Brewer, 2001; Mullen et al., 1992). As a consequence, minority group membership arouses stronger collective-identity concerns (i.e. a stronger motivation to achieve, maintain or simply express a positive collective identity) which then translate into more discriminatory behaviour. Note that this account is in full accordance with the centrality hypothesis derived from SAMI, according to which minority members' self-interpretation is much more focused or centred on their respective group membership than that of majority members (Lücken & Simon, 2003, Study 1).

The second account centres on possible threatening implications of being in the numerically inferior group. As reviewed in the preceding section on well-being, there is good theoretical reason as well as a growing body of empirical evidence that suggests that members of minority groups experience more negative affect and feel more insecure than members of majority groups (e.g. Lücken & Simon, 2003). In order to cope with their affective predicament and insecurity, minority members may therefore strive to strengthen their collective identity (i.e. make it more positively distinct) by discriminating against the majority outgroup, when given the opportunity (Sachdev & Bourhis, 1984). I will now review the empirical evidence for the hypothesized minority–majority difference in intergroup discrimination and examine the explanatory power of the salience (or centrality) and threat accounts.

In a meta-analysis of research findings secured over a time span of 15 years, Mullen et al. (1992) found that their index of intergroup discrimination decreased as a function of the proportionate size of the ingroup (i.e. the size of the ingroup divided by the sum of the size of the ingroup and the size of the outgroup). However, their index of intergroup discrimination was derived primarily from ingroup and outgroup ratings on evaluative attribute dimensions which are at best indirect or remote indicators of actual intergroup behaviour (Brewer & Silver, 1978; Jackson, 1999; Struch & Schwartz, 1989).

Fortunately, other research has employed more direct measures of intergroup behaviour. Following Tajfel et al. (1971), researchers have used various types of resource-allocation tasks in which research participants are requested to distribute meaningful resources between ingroup and outgroup members (e.g. money or course credit with students as research participants). Using such a task with laboratory-created minority and majority groups, Sachdev and Bourhis (1984) obtained a complex pattern of results. They found some indication that, unlike majority members, minority members were more concerned about their ingroup's absolute outcome than about intergroup fairness. But majority members also showed discriminatory tendencies. Although they did not appear particularly interested in maximizing their ingroup's absolute outcome, majority members seemed concerned about maintaining or establishing outcome differentials between ingroup and out-group that favoured their ingroup.

More recent experimental research with similar allocation tasks yielded results more in line with the expected minority–majority difference in inter-group discrimination, but produced at best inconsistent findings concerning the explanatory power of the salience and threat accounts (Bettencourt et al., 1997, 1999; Leonardelli & Brewer, 2001). In the context of forced intergroup cooperation, Bettencourt et al. (1997, Study 1) found that when participants' attention was not experimentally focused on particular aspects of the coopera-tive setting (control condition), members of minority groups showed more intergroup discrimination against the outgroup than did members of majority groups. The latter even tended towards reversed discrimination in favour of the minority outgroup.

In two additional experimental conditions, participants were instructed by the experimenter to focus their attention either on interpersonal aspects of the cooperation (individual-focus condition) or on each group's contribution to the overall task (task-focus condition). While the interpersonal focus did not eliminate the minority–majority difference in intergroup discrimination, the task focus did. In fact, there was even a slight reversal in the task-focus condition such that majority members now seemed to show more intergroup discrimination than minority members. Note that Bettencourt et al.'s (1997, Study 1) results do not support the salience account of increased intergroup discrimination on the part of minority members compared with majority members, because such a minority–majority difference was observed even when minority members' attention was experimentally redirected away from their group membership to interpersonal aspects. However, the reversal towards more intergroup discrimination on the part of majority members in the task-focus condition may be interpreted as support for the threat account of intergroup discrimination. As suggested by Bettencourt et al. (1997, p. 653), the task-focus instructions which requested all participants to acknowledge each group's contribution to the cooperative endeavour could have strengthened especially the minority group who would have received less recognition otherwise. Thus rendered on more equal footing with majority members, minority members may have felt less threatened and therefore less motivated to discriminate against the majority outgroup. In contrast, for majority members, this equal footing could have lessened their presumed superiority and may thus have spurred their motivation to discriminate against the minority outgroup.

Bettencourt et al. (1999, Study 1) found evidence of more intergroup discrimination among minority members compared with majority members in a condition that was designed to increase the salience of participants' group membership, but not in a low(er)-salience condition. Unfortunately, their salience manipulation was perfectly confounded with a threat variation so that their results are inconclusive with regard to the differential explanatory power of the salience and threat accounts.

Conversely, Leonardelli and Brewer (2001, Experiment 1) found more intergroup discrimination among minority members relative to majority members when minority and majority members' collective identification was experimentally weakened, but not when it was strengthened. This interaction was due to the fact that minority members' tendency to discriminate remained strong irrespective of experimentally manipulated collective identification, whereas intergroup discrimination on the part of majority members increased with collective identification. This pattern of results is consistent with the assumption that collective identification is a necessary condition for intergroup discrimination and that it is spontaneously aroused in minority members. To the extent to which collective identification is reflective of high salience of one's group membership, Leonardelli and Brewer's (2001, Experiment 1) findings support the salience account of minority–majority differences in intergroup discrimination. However, because high collective identification may also be associated with perceived or experienced intergroup threat (Schmitt & Branscombe, 2002), it would be premature to reject the threat account.

Interestingly, Leonardelli and Brewer (2001) also endorse a threat account, but reserve it for the explanation of intergroup discrimination on the part of majority members. While they seem to suggest that minority members show some kind of gratuitous intergroup discrimination, simply to celebrate their (generally satisfactory) collective identity, these authors further argue that majority members, once they identify with their group, feel threatened by its insufficient distinctiveness which in turn motivates them to discriminate against the minority outgroup. In light of the likely negative implications of (even purely numerically defined) minority membership for one's well-being (see preceding section), I fear that Leonardelli and Brewer (2001) endorse too narrow a view on the meaning of discrimination in minority—majority contexts.

Instead, I suggest that intergroup discrimination by minority members is, at least to some degree, an affirmation or better assertion of their existence in an environment that is usually structured in such a way that it ignores minority members' needs and routinely discriminates against them in and through daily practice. Minority members' assertiveness in turn is likely to awaken majority members' collective identification and thereby also their willingness to engage actively and self-consciously in discrimination against the minority group. Then, 'the empire strikes back' – apparently in self-defence. Thus, in light of the fact or perception that the status quo is unfavourable to their ingroup and its members, the 'assertive' intergroup discrimination by minority members will naturally aim at the achievement of absolute improvements. In contrast, majority members usually only need to show 'defensive' intergroup discrimination in order to put minority members back in their place and (re-)establish the ingroup's privileges *vis-à-vis* the minority outgroup. Such patterns of intergroup discrimination were indeed observed by Leonardelli and Brewer (2001, Experiment 3) as well as by Sachdev and Bourhis (1984) (see also Azzi, 1992, 1993).

The role of status and power

Intergroup discrimination has also been examined in laboratory contexts in which, in addition to relative ingroup size, relative ingroup status and/or ingroup power were manipulated as well. For example, Mummendey et al. (1992, Experiment 2) varied both relative ingroup size and ingroup status and found main effects of both variables, but no interaction effect. Members of (numerical) minority groups showed more intergroup discrimination than members of (numerical) majority groups, and members of low-status groups showed more intergroup discrimination than members of high-status groups. As a result of the additive effects of relative ingroup size and ingroup status, members of low-status minority groups were most discriminatory. Similar findings have been obtained in other work (Espinoza & Garza, 1985; Jackson, 1999; Otten, Mummendey & Blanz, 1996), but researchers have also observed that relative ingroup size failed to affect intergroup discrimination, both alone as well as in interaction with relative ingroup status (Ellemers et al., 1992, 1999).

Sachdev and Bourhis (1991) also manipulated relative ingroup size and ingroup status and even added relative ingroup power as a third independent variable. Unfortunately, they used the same criterion (i.e. creativity) for both the status manipulation and the resource-allocation task. This confound renders the status effects inconclusive because it is impossible to decide whether allocation decisions in favour of the high-status ingroup are to be considered a true effect (i.e. intergroup discrimination) or simply a manipulation check (i.e. a reproduction of the experimentally induced status differential). I therefore limit the discussion here to the effects of relative ingroup size and ingroup power, including their interactive effects. Sachdev and Bourhis (1991) again found a complex pattern of results. More specifically, their results indicated that members of minority groups were generally less fair than members of majority groups, although the latter again appeared to be concerned about maintaining or establishing some intergroup differentials in favour of the ingroup (Sachdev & Bourhis, 1984; Leonardelli & Brewer, 2001). Moreover, members of powerful minority groups tended to be more discriminatory than members of powerful majority groups, while the opposite tendency was observed for members of relatively powerless minority and majority groups.

This interactive effect of relative ingroup size and ingroup power points to an interesting explanation as to why the evidence of increased intergroup discrimination on the part of minority members compared with majority members is often weak or inconsistent. Owing to their numerical inferiority, minority members may often suffer from insufficient self-confidence or insufficient trust in their collective efficacy which then prevents them from engaging in assertive intergroup behaviour. Threat may thus play a dual, and perhaps contradictory, role in minority–majority relations (see also Ng & Cram, 1988). On the one hand, the threatening implications of the numerical inferiority of one's ingroup may lead to feelings of insecurity and an increased need for a positive collective identity which in turn increases the willingness to discriminate against outgroups. On the other hand, numerical inferiority likely threatens minority members' self-confidence or feelings of collective efficacy which are necessary preconditions for assertive intergroup behaviour (Klandermans, 1997). In other words, minority members may often feel the need for discriminatory behaviour in favour of the ingroup, but at the same time they may lack the necessary power or confidence to put this desire into action.

Summary

The focus in this chapter was on identity in the context of minority–majority relations. I examined how minority and majority memberships shape people's identities and thereby elicit from them a number of distinct cognitive, affective and behavioural responses. Although I started from a numerical definition of minority and majority membership, I also explored the role of status and power in minority–majority relations.

I first demonstrated that, as suggested by the self-aspect model of identity (SAMI), (numerical) minority membership can be viewed as a rare socially shared self-aspect that is cognitively particularly accessible and thus fosters self-interpretation in terms of a collective identity to a greater extent than does (numerical) majority membership. Minority members also show greater sensitivity to differential ingroup status than majority members, which further supports SAMI, according to which ingroup status is more likely to hit the heart of minority members' self-interpretation. However, although members of low-status minority groups may thus often hesitate to accept their collective identity, the experience of being collectively stereotyped can lead them to recognize or develop similarities with other ingroup members, which may eventually result in the acceptance of one's collective identity. Conversely, it seems that relative ingroup power does not affect minority members' willingness to adopt a collective identity, whereas superior ingroup power is likely to awaken such identity among majority members.

I then reviewed research on social information processing in minority–majority contexts. Although there is some indication in the literature that, in line with their greater emphasis on collective identity, minority members tend towards more group-level and less individual-level information processing than do majority members, individualization processes can undermine or even reverse this tendency. In addition, research points to the role of motivated or strategic cognition, especially when status or power differentials come into play as well. For example, when ingroup status is relatively low, both minority and majority members are likely to engage in more individual-level information processing at the expense of group-level information processing, at least as long as they can hope for individual escape from such unfavourable circumstances. When individual escape is difficult, however, group-level information processing tends to increase as part of a collective coping strategy, at least among majority members, who can draw on large ingroup size as a valuable resource in their collective struggle.

Turning to a third domain, I examined the effects of minority and majority membership on well-being. Both theory and empirical work suggest that minority membership, even when defined in purely numerical terms, is associated with less positive feelings or well-being than membership in a majority group. Members of minority groups may be able partly to mitigate the negative affective implications of their group membership and ward off permanent damage to their self-esteem by drawing on resources that their collective identity affords them (e.g. intragroup respect). But their membership constitutes a permanent challenge, if not threat, to their well-being – a challenge that appears to be particularly serious when minority membership also entails a power disadvantage. Together with the heightened cognitive accessibility of minority membership, this challenge creates an unfriendly cognitive–affective crossfire for minority members in which they find themselves as mindful and unhappy group members, whereas majority members can often enjoy the privilege of living rather mindlessly as happy individuals.

Finally, turning to intergroup behaviour, I discussed evidence and possible explanations of intergroup discrimination in minority–majority contexts. Although the literature is not entirely consistent, an increasing body of (experimental) research suggests that minority members more readily discriminate against outgroups and/or favour their ingroups than do majority members. Explanations typically revolve either around the increased salience of minority membership (or minority identity) or around its threatening implications. Although the salience account must not be ruled out prematurely, the threat account offers the intriguing interpretation of intergroup discrimination on the part of minority members as an act of self-assertion which may in turn evoke defensive intergroup discrimination from majority members. It may only be because in real life minority members often do not have the opportunity or the means to act on their intentions that we do not see such intergroup behaviours more often or regularly. That is, minority members often simply do not possess the power necessary for assertive intergroup discrimination, while, for the same reason, majority members usually do not need to have recourse to defensive intergroup discrimination.

NOTES

1. Such presuppositions or inferences may routinely be made unless the meaningfulness of the self-aspect in question is explicitly revoked by the investigator (Simon et al., 1997).
2. It should be noted, however, that majority members rejected outgroup attributes in their self-descriptions to a greater extent when ingroup status was high rather than low. That is, although ingroup status did not affect majority members' tendency to (directly) self-stereotype in terms of ingroup attributes, members of the high-status majority were obviously anxious to deny any commonality with the low-status minority outgroup ('I am not like them').
3. Analytically, it may also prove helpful to distinguish between the *possession* of power, which refers to the repertoire of potential acts that one party can perform in order to induce forces on another (Cartwright, 1959b, p. 202), and the *exercise* of power, which is 'an action upon action' (Foucault, 1982, p. 220). Nor should the exercise of power be equated with controlling another party's behaviour, because the power exercised by one party is usually only one of many forces impinging on the target (Cartwright, 1959b, pp. 194–6; Dépret & Fiske, 1993, p. 184). In fact, Foucault (1982) suggested that total behavioural control and exercise of power are mutually exclusive because 'Power is exercised only over free subjects, and only insofar as they are free . . . ; slavery is not a power relationship when man is in chains' (p. 221). The following discussion in the main text is primarily concerned with the actual or at least anticipated exercise of power rather than the mere possession of it (for additional analytical distinctions, see Foucault, 1982, pp. 222–4).

4. Interestingly, Klauer et al. (2002) observed both increased group-level processing and increased individual-level processing of information about targets that were numerically distinct in the experimental context, irrespective of whether the targets were ingroup or outgroup members. With regard to the present discussion of minority and majority members' information processing, the relevance of their results is questionable, however, because those authors did not vary relative ingroup size as such (i.e. relative size of research participants' ingroup in the wider inter-group context), but only the relative frequency of (gender-based) ingroup and outgroup targets in the experimental stimulus material. Other research suffers from similar limitations (e.g. Biernat & Vescio, 1993; Taylor et al., 1978; Van Twuyver & Van Knippenberg, 1999).

5. Of course, the level of information processing may also be affected by the extent to which members of the target group actually display either uniform or more idiosyncratic characteristics and behaviours (e.g. as a result of self-stereotyping or conformity processes), which may in turn depend again on relative group power (Guinote et al., 2002).

6. Jackson (1999) observed similar interaction effects of relative ingroup size and ingroup status, albeit in more complex intergroup contexts that comprised three groups – one ingroup and two outgroups. While one outgroup was always larger and of higher status than the ingroup and the second outgroup, ingroup size and ingroup status were manipulated relative to the second outgroup. In other words, in addition to a high-status majority outgroup, there were two minority groups with lower status – one ingroup and one outgroup – the relative (small) size and (low) status of which were further manipulated. Thus, Jackson's (1999) research did not involve true (low- or high-status) majority ingroups, nor did it involve truly high-status minority ingroups, which undermines its relevance with regard to the present discussion.

Chapter 6

Identity in Intercultural Contact

Most, if not all, modern societies are currently experiencing an increase in the opportunities for intercultural contact. What has always been quite common for classic countries of immigration, such as the USA or Canada, is now also becoming a daily experience for natives of many Western European countries who, for a long time, believed that different cultures only existed 'out there' and that contact with them was basically a tourist experience.

This certainly applies to the country in which the author of this book lives and which is the biggest country in the European Union. However, despite regular political declarations to the contrary and collective denial, even Germany has *de facto* long been a country of immigration. At least since the recruitment of foreign 'guest workers' for the labour force in West Germany in the period between the economic boom in the 1950s and the economic crisis in the early 1970s and a similar admission of foreign workers to the former German Democratic Republic (GDR), it is a fact that Germany comprises a variety of different national or ethnic groups. This situation has been re-inforced by processes of family reunion whereby family members from the country of origin were also admitted to Germany. Moreover, it is now being intensified by the rising second and third generation of non-German descent.

Notwithstanding national or regional specificity, politically and economic-ally motivated migration has become a worldwide phenomenon, especially since the collapse of the Soviet Union and the disappearance of the iron curtain. This tendency is further accelerated by rapid processes of globaliza-tion and the emergence of supranational political and economic entities such as the European Union. Although there is no shortage of political attempts to implement repressive counter-measures against large-scale immigration, na-tional boundaries are becoming increasingly permeable, with the inevitable result that intercultural contacts have increased and will continue to do so.

Although intercultural contacts have many positive effects on both the collective and the individual level and can thus enrich social life (e.g. by way of international cooperation, import of innovative ideas or intercultural friendships), they also have a potential for social conflict, like any other intergroup contact. They tend to foster social comparison processes across national or ethnic boundaries and can thus lead to competition between national or ethnic groups for material resources, such as housing or jobs, as well as to intergroup competition for less tangible resources, such as prestige or social status, which confer a positive collective identity upon group members (Sherif, 1967; Tajfel & Turner, 1986).

The social psychological literature on intergroup relations has long acknowledged the positive effects but also the potential dangers of such contacts (G. Allport, 1954/1979; Gaertner & Dovidio, 2000; Hewstone & Brown, 1986; Nemeth, 1997; Pettigrew, 1998). Quite a number of models have been advanced to explain when and how intergroup or intercultural contacts have positive or negative effects on social life. In particular, social psychologists have analysed the conditions under which, and how, contact helps counteract negative stereotyping, prejudice and discrimination against outgroups and may thus contribute to harmonious intergroup relations. In the remainder of the chapter, I will therefore first present an overview of the most influential models of intergroup or intercultural contact and examine what role they ascribe to identity. I will then proceed to issues of contact and identity in the context of immigration and outline some under-researched avenues to social integration and the participation of immigrants in the society of settlement. Subsequently, I will turn to the social psychology of the political struggle against multiculturalism and a respectful integration of immigrants. The focus will be on right-wing extremism and the role of national identity. Finally, I will conclude this chapter with a comment on the discourse upon cultural differences and racism.

Models of Intergroup Contact

Gordon Allport's (1954/1979) intergroup contact hypothesis – formulated shortly after the Second World War – undoubtedly laid the foundation for a voluminous body of social scientific work on the effects of intergroup contact on intergroup relations (Pettigrew, 1971, 1998). According to G. Allport (1954/1979), intergroup contact reduces negative stereotyping, prejudice and intergroup discrimination and thus improves intergroup relations when four key conditions are met. First, the groups making contact must have equal status within the contact situation. Second, the groups must strive for a common goal. Third, attainment of common goals must involve a cooperative effort across group boundaries and without intergroup competition. Finally, authorities, the law or custom must sanction intergroup contact. Building on

G. Allport's intergroup contact hypothesis, researchers have suggested a number of different social psychological processes that should mediate the positive effects of intergroup contact on intergroup relations.

Decategorization and personalization

According to Brewer and Miller (1984), intergroup contact as prescribed by G. Allport (1954/1979) has positive effects on intergroup relations if such contact undermines the salience of group or category memberships. Members of different groups should come to see themselves and each other not as representatives of their respective groups, but as separate individuals or persons with unique characteristics. Group memberships and collective identities then lose their meaning, and undifferentiated favouritism towards ingroup members and undifferentiated mistreatment of outgroup members are replaced with greater perceptual and behavioural variability as a function of the individuality of the interaction partners. For example, when I no longer see myself as a German being confronted with 'one of those Turks', but appreciate a personalized contact with Mustafer, the psychological basis for stereotypic perception and group-based (mis)treatment no longer exists. Repeated personalized contacts with many different outgroup members will eventually lead to a permanent reduction in the salience and meaning of group memberships and collective identities and will thus make generalized contact effects possible (Brewer & Gaertner, 2001). Research by Pettigrew (1997, 1998) indeed demonstrates that intimate personalized contacts across group boundaries have positive effects on intergroup relations, and such effects seem to be stronger than the reverse effects (e.g. the negative effect of prejudice on friendships with outgroup members).[1] Interestingly, this mechanism also seems to operate indirectly or vicariously, because even mere knowledge that a fellow ingroup member is in friendly contact with an outgroup member can improve intergroup attitudes (Wright et al., 1997).

Recategorization and common ingroup identity

In line with self-categorization theory (Turner et al., 1987), Gaertner and Dovidio (2000) suggest that recategorization at a higher level of social inclusiveness is the key to positive effects of intergroup contact. Intergroup contact should be structured in such a way that the original ingroup–outgroup categorization is dissolved, or more precisely, transcended and transformed into a common, superordinate or more inclusive collective identity. Ideally, the transformation of the original 'us' and 'them' into a more inclusive 'we' elevates former outgroup members to the level of more favourable perception and treatment as ingroup members and thus removes the original problem (Gaertner et al., 1989).

In keeping with this perspective, research demonstrates that G. Allport's key conditions or antecedents of successful intergroup contact unfold their positive effects on intergroup relations – at least partially – by way of the formation of more inclusive collective identities. For example, a survey study conducted by Gaertner et al. (1994) revealed that the more students attending a multi-ethnic high school felt like one group, the less negative their affective reactions to ethnic outgroups relative to ingroups. In addition, the relationship between the optimal conditions for contact and the affective reactions to ethnic outgroups relative to ingroups was significantly, though not fully, mediated by students' sense of belonging to a common, more inclusive ingroup. Despite such promising and encouraging results, a possible danger or at least potential drawback of the recategorization strategy should be noted. While it may ensure harmony on one level of intergroup relations, it cannot guarantee all-round harmony because there remains the possibility that the original intergroup conflict is later replaced with a conflict on a higher level of inclusiveness between the common ingroup and some new outgroup (Kessler & Mummendey, 2001).

Mutual intergroup differentiation

Contrary to the personalization and common ingroup identity models, Hewstone and Brown (1986) argue that the original group boundaries should not completely be ignored in intergroup contact (see also Vivian, Hewstone & Brown, 1997). Group memberships and the respective collective identities are often an integral part of people's sense of who they are and serve a variety of important psychological functions (see chapter 3). It might therefore be both an unrealistic and unwise prescription for designers of and participants in intergroup contact to swim against the tide and to try to suppress any awareness of group membership and collective identity. On the contrary, such awareness may even further facilitate positive effects of intergroup contact as along as people's collective identities are not threatened in the contact situation. More specifically, Hewstone and Brown (1986) recommend that the contact situation be structured so that group members can recognize and value mutual superiorities and inferiorities. This process of mutual intergroup differentiation helps to achieve and maintain a satisfactory and mutually respected collective identity on both sides of the group divide. Respect received from the outgroup adds to the positive contact experience, and awareness of the *intergroup* nature of the experience facilitates generalization beyond the immediate contact situation (Brown,

Vivian & Hewstone, 1999; González & Brown, 2003; Van Oudenhoven, Groenewoud & Hewstone, 1996).

Finally, it should be noted that mutual intergroup differentiation is not necessarily incompatible with the formation or recognition of a more inclusive common collective identity. On the contrary, Stephan and Stephan (1984; also Stephan, 1987) recommend that, in addition to involving a focus on valued (real) intergroup differences, intergroup contact should also contribute to the explosion of myths about (false) intergroup differences and direct group members' attention to fundamental intergroup similarities (e.g. their shared human identity). Similarly, other researchers have acknowledged the useful- ness of a dual-identity strategy that combines the maintenance of the original ingroup–outgroup distinction and respect for the corresponding collective identities with the benefit of recognizing that one shares a more inclusive group membership or collective identity with the original outgroup (Brewer & Gaertner, 2001; González & Brown, 2003; Hornsey & Hogg, 2000).

Longitudinal intergroup contact

Based on a comprehensive review of both theory and empirical research on intergroup contact, Pettigrew (1998) proposed an integrative model of optimal intergroup contact with a long-term perspective. The model specifies five essential conditions for successful intergroup contact and a sequence of three main contact stages, with each stage promoting one of the social psychological mediating processes discussed above. In addition to G. Allport's (1954/1979) four key conditions for intergroup contact (equal status, common goal, cooperation and authority sanction), Pettigrew (1998, p. 76) suggests that 'friendship potential' is another essential condition. There must be sufficient opportunities for extensive and repeated contact in a variety of social contexts so that close interaction, self-disclosure and eventually friendships across group boundaries are made possible.

Once the contact situation has been prepared in accordance with the five essential conditions (and possibly other facilitating factors), the initial stage of the contact process should promote decategorization and personalization in line with Brewer and Miller's (1984) model. This stage also facilitates interper- sonal liking across group boundaries and thus contributes to the reduction of intergroup anxiety (Stephan & Stephan, 1985). After personalized contact has successfully been established, the focus should shift to participants' group memberships and their collective identities. According to Hewstone and Brown (1986), this would be the stage in which mutual intergroup differenti- ation and respect should be promoted and which facilitates the generalization of positive contact effects to other encounters with the same outgroup and possibly also to encounters with entirely different outgroups (Hewstone, 1996; Pettigrew, 1997). In the final stage, the emphasis should be on recategorization processes so that the benefits of a common collective identity are then also extended to former outgroup members.

In addition to processes of personalization, mutual intergroup differentiation and recategorization at a higher level of social inclusiveness, Pettigrew (1998) identifies four other interrelated processes that are likely to operate at all stages of optimal intergroup contact and that contribute to its success. First, through contact, people learn new information about the outgroup that helps to disconfirm negative stereotypes. Second, in addition to cognitive learning effects, contact with high friendship potential generates affective ties across group boundaries and thus builds affective bridges between ingroup and outgroup for the flow of positive emotions such as empathy, sympathy or even admiration. Third, contact with outgroup members often requires behavioural adaptation which in turn can lead to improvement in intergroup attitudes (e.g. towards integrated neighbourhoods) as a way to resolve dissonance between new behaviour and old attitudes. Finally, optimal intergroup contact enriches group members' views of the social world and puts ingroup norms and customs into perspective. The ingroup can no longer be seen as the centre of the world and its norms and customs must be reappraised. As a consequence, the outgroup is judged more respectfully against less ingroup-centric and more pluralistic standards. Pettigrew (1998, p. 72) refers to this process as 'deprovincialization'.

Identity in models of intergroup contact

All major social psychological models of intergroup contact ascribe a critical role to identity processes (Brewer & Gaertner, 2001). According to the personalization model (Brewer & Miller, 1984), it is the shift from collective identity to individual identity that reduces conflict and facilitates harmony between members of different groups. Conversely, the common ingroup identity model (Gaertner & Dovidio, 2000) and the mutual differentiation model (Hewstone & Brown, 1986) suggest intriguing ways in which collective identity, at various levels of social inclusiveness, can be enlisted in the pursuit of intergroup harmony. The personalization model and the common ingroup identity model revolve around identity variants that are very different from each other on the dimension of social inclusiveness and sometimes even represent opposite extremes on it (i.e. individual identity vs. human identity).[2] Yet the proponents of both models share a scepticism regarding the positive role that collective identity at the level of the original ingroup–outgroup categorization may play according to the mutual differentiation model. The former therefore also share a preference for psychological interventions that shift group members' self-interpretations away from the original intermediate-level collective identity.

However, such endeavours may often be too idealistic in view of the social macro structure. As long as the real world outside the immediate contact situation sustains the original group boundaries, it is unlikely that such identity shifts will be sufficiently stable to ensure long-term harmony between groups. Alternatively, the mutual differentiation model builds on the social psychological insight derived from social identity theory (Tajfel & Turner, 1986) that intergroup conflict is also always a collective-identity struggle. The model does not deny or downplay the material bases of intergroup conflict and cooperation (Sherif, 1967), but acknowledges and targets the social psychological dimension of intergroup conflict, namely the fact that intergroup conflicts are fought *for and with collective identities*. Group memberships that are meaningfully anchored in social (and) psychological reality provide group members with important collective identities that are inextricably implicated in intergroup conflicts, both as goals because people strive for positive and respected collective identities and as means because collective identities are instrumental in mobilizing one's troops (see also chapter 7). Without large-scale changes in the social macro structure, it would be unrealistic to hope that one could simply do away with the critical collective identities and thereby completely remove the social psychological basis for the conflict. However, it should be possible to skilfully arrange extensive and repeated intergroup contacts, in accordance with Pettigrew's (1998) integrative model, that provide group members with robust experiences of mutual respect for their collective identities. Such contacts may not result in complete conflict resolution, but in the long run promise significant conflict reduction through a better management of the social psychological components of the conflict.

Immigration, Identity and Social Integration

As indicated at the beginning of the chapter, processes of globalization and mass (im)migration provide more and more opportunities for intercultural contact in modern society. More often than not, such contacts take place under circumstances that do not fulfil the criteria of optimal intergroup contact (G. Allport, 1954/1979; Dovidio & Esses, 2001; Pettigrew, 1998). Hence, it is hardly surprising that their positive potential (e.g. for innovation and cultural enrichment) often fails to manifest itself, whereas their problematic aspects (e.g. their potential for intergroup conflict) move into the foreground – also because they are often highlighted for various political reasons.

The social psychological models of intergroup contact reviewed above have provided valuable insights into the psychological challenges of intercultural encounters as well as into the possibilities of successful management of these challenges. In addition, research on contact in the context of immigration has been informed in important ways by cross-cultural psychology (Berry, 2001). More specifically, much research in cross-cultural psychology has focused on acculturation, which is 'a process that entails contact between two cultural groups, which results in numerous cultural changes in both parties' (Berry, 2001, p. 616). Accordingly, psychological acculturation refers to the various psychological changes that members of a cultural group experience when they come into continuous first-hand contact with members of another cultural group, with cultural groups being defined, *inter alia*, in terms of language, religion or ethnicity. As a result of immigration, many, if not most, modern (but not only modern) societies are culturally plural or heterogeneous. In culturally heterogeneous societies, people are confronted with the issue of how to acculturate. According to Berry (1997, 2001), people adopt or work out acculturation strategies that revolve around two major issues or questions.

One issue concerns cultural maintenance, the other contact and participation. The critical questions that people are confronted with are, respectively, 'to what extent are cultural identity and characteristics considered to be important, and [should] their maintenance [be] strived for' and 'to what extent should they become involved in other cultural groups, or remain primarily among themselves' (Berry, 1997, p. 9). With regard to members of (non-dominant) immigrant groups, Berry (1997, 2001) suggests four major ideal-typical acculturation strategies that result from the combination of positive or negative responses to these issues or questions. These are the strategies of assimilation (no maintenance of one's own cultural or collective identity, but contact with the indigenous group and participation in larger society), separation (identity maintenance, but no contact/participation), integration (both identity maintenance and contact/participation) and marginalization (neither identity maintenance nor contact/participation). The corresponding ideologies or expectations of the larger society or members of the (dominant) indigenous group as to how members of immigrant groups should acculturate are termed 'melting pot' (or even 'pressure cooker'), segregation, multiculturalism and exclusion (Berry, 2001, p. 618).

According to Berry (1997), empirical evidence suggests that integration is usually the most successful strategy with regard to positive or good adaptation of immigrants. Marginalization is the least successful strategy, while assimilation and separation strategies are intermediate. The successful pursuit of the integration strategy predicts both good psychological adaptation, which involves psychological and physical well-being, and good sociocultural adaptation, which refers to how well the person manages daily life in the new cultural context. However, integration is not a one-way street to be walked only by members of immigrant groups. Instead, mutual accommodation is required. For integration to be attained, immigrants need 'to *adopt* the basic values of the receiving society, and at the same time the receiving society must be prepared to *adapt* national institutions (e.g., education, health, justice, labor) to better meet the needs of all groups now living together in the larger plural society' (Berry, 2001, p. 619, emphases in the original). Obviously, in a negative social psychological climate, characterized by negative stereotyping, prejudice and intergroup discrimination, such mutual accommodation is difficult to attain. How can immigrants be expected to adopt the core values of a society that receives them with negative intergroup attitudes and behaviours and that immigrants in turn perceive and to which they react in similarly negative terms? By the same token, willingness to adapt may initially be low on the part of the larger society and members of the indigenous group. Intercultural encounters carefully arranged in accordance with the models of (optimal) intergroup contact discussed above may therefore help remove critical obstacles and set in motion processes of mutual accommodation, thus paving the way for successful integration.

Evidence for the positive role of such encounters was obtained in a questionnaire study with German and Turkish members of various intercultural organizations in the German state of Schleswig-Holstein that provide their members with specifically arranged opportunities for intercultural contact and exchange (Simon & Kampmeier, 2002). Twenty-two respondents were German and of German descent, while 34 participants were Turkish or of Turkish descent with German citizenship. Respondents in both the indigenous group and the immigrant group were predominantly female. They completed a questionnaire, composed in either the German or Turkish language, in which we measured indicators of the five essential conditions (equal status, common goal, cooperation, authority sanction and friendship potential) and the three processes characteristic of the main contact stages (personalization, mutual intergroup differentiation and recategorization at a higher level of inclusiveness) specified in Pettigrew's (1998) integrative model of optimal intergroup contact. In addition, the questionnaire included several other measures. Prejudice was measured with Pettigrew and Meertens's (1995) positive-emotions scale of subtle prejudice which gauges (the absence of) feelings of sympathy and admiration for the outgroup. We also administered measures of acculturation strategies and expectations revolving around the adoption of mainstream culture (or identity), the maintenance of immigrant culture and the value of immigrants and their culture for the larger society as well as measures of national or ethnic identification, identification with the intercultural organization and respect experienced in the organization.

Preliminary analyses confirmed that, overall, intercultural encounters in the organizations approximated the essential conditions for optimal intergroup contact and also provided many experiences indicative of the three main contact processes. However, respondents' reports on the temporal order of these experiences did not conform to the optimal sequence suggested in Pettigrew's (1998) model. The reports indicated that Turkish respondents generally made the relevant experiences at a later point in time compared with German respondents, but there was no clear temporal order within groups. Instead, it seemed that, within each group of respondents, the three kinds of experiences coincided with each other. The high intercorrelations of (the amount of) these experiences also suggests that the three main contact processes or stages were hardly distinguishable from each other in these organizational contexts ($.62 < r < .80$ and $.61 < r < .81$, for German and Turkish respondents, respectively). Consequently, the three indicators were combined (averaged) to form an overall measure of contact process (Cronbach's $\alpha = .88$, for both German and Turkish respondents). Similarly, the indicators of the five essential conditions for optimal intergroup contact were combined to form an overall measure of contact condition (Cronbach's $\alpha = .65$ and $.84$, for German and Turkish respondents, respectively).

We then conducted hierarchical multiple regression analyses with the condition and process measures as predictor variables and the measures of prejudice and acculturation strategies and expectations as criterion variables. The condition measure was entered into the equation in the first step, and then the process measure was added in the second step. All analyses were performed separately for German and Turkish respondents. A number of interesting statistically significant relationships were observed (which should be interpreted with appropriate caution given their correlational nature). For German respondents, prejudice was related to the process measure, but not to the condition measure, neither in the first nor in the second step of the regression analysis. The more experiences German respondents had in ac- cordance with the three contact processes, the weaker their prejudice against Turks living in Germany. A similar relationship was observed when the same respondents indicated the extent to which they thought that the presence of Turks in Germany was 'a good thing'. The more pronounced the contact processes, the more German respondents valued the presence of Turks in Germany. The condition measure was also positively related to this dependent variable in the first step of the regression analysis, but it lost its predictive value when the process measure was added in the second step. This pattern of relationships – together with the positive correlation between the condition and process measures ($r = .58$) – strongly suggests that contact processes played a critical mediating role between the essential contact conditions and the positive value ascribed to Turkish immigrants for the larger society.

For Turkish respondents, intercultural contacts seemed to have positive effects especially on willingness to adopt the German mainstream culture and

identity. More specifically, their willingness to 'live here in Germany in accordance with the rules and values of the German culture' was positively related to
the process measure, but unrelated to the condition measure. A similar relationship was observed between the process measure and identification with
Germany (e.g. 'I identify with Germany'). Interestingly, the condition measure
made a positive contribution to the prediction of identification with Germany in
the first step, but lost its predictive value in the second step. Together with the
positive correlation between the condition and process measures ($r = .65$), this
pattern again points to a mediating role of contact processes.

It thus appears that the right intercultural contacts can promote accommodation among members of both the indigenous group and the immigrant
group. On the one hand, they can help indigenous people to lose their
(negative) prejudices and to see that immigration may even be a good thing
that enriches the larger society. Such an emphasis on the gains rather than the
losses should be particularly important if the goal is the genuine integration of
immigrants into a multicultural society, which usually requires concessions
and willingness to change also on the part of the indigenous group (Berry,
2001). On the other hand, the right intercultural contacts can familiarize
immigrants with, and initiate them into, the culture of the receiving society,
thus making its rules and values as well as identification with that society in
general more acceptable.

Our results also support the assertion that the contact processes specified in
various social psychological models are the active ingredients in successful
intercultural encounters. Conversely, the various contact conditions, once they
are realized to a sufficient degree, may make no further contribution to
contact success, but even when they do, their contribution seems to depend
critically on the operation of the right contact processes (see also Gaertner &
Dovidio, 2000). Interestingly, in our study, we were unable to empirically
differentiate the three contact processes – personalization, mutual intergroup
differentiation and recategorization. This may be due largely to the fact that
the intercultural encounters examined in our study were not specifically
designed to separate the different contact stages as specified in Pettigrew's
(1998) model. However, the observed interrelationships may also be due at
least in part to inherent overlap (or sub-processes shared) among the three
processes. For example, both personalization and recategorization likely entail
the perception of shared characteristics (see also note 2), while both recategorization and mutual intergroup differentiation likely involve the recognition of
shared values (Turner et al., 1987).

Finally, two other observations are noteworthy because they point to hitherto under-researched social psychological avenues or mechanisms through
which immigrants may find their respected place in the society of settlement.
First, we observed that, among German respondents, respect experienced

within the intercultural organization was negatively related to prejudice and positively to the appreciation of the presence of Turks in Germany as 'a good thing'. Similarly, among Turkish respondents, identification with the intercultural organization was negatively associated with prejudice and positively with identification with Germany and willingness to live 'in accordance with the rules and values of the German culture'. These relationships are suggestive of a positive role of intercultural organizations in integration processes. That is, intercultural organizations may serve as effective germ-cells of mutual accommodation to the extent to which they provide their members with mutual respect and/or a sense of collective identification. In particular, the relationship between organizational identification and identification with Germany observed for Turkish respondents ($r = .41$) suggests that intercultural organizations could be important vehicles that – through some kind of piggy-back mechanism – accelerate the psychological arrival of members of immigrant groups at the society of settlement.

The second mechanism concerns the politicization of immigrant identity. One item in our questionnaire gauged the strength of the Turkish respondents' call for more rights for Turks living in Germany. This political claim was positively related to ethnic identification as a Turk ($r = .32$), which points to a politicization of immigrant identity. However, because politicized collective identity usually 'presupposes identification with the more inclusive social entity that provides the context for . . . power struggles for social change' (Simon & Klandermans, 2001, p. 326), we also examined the relationship between Turkish respondents' political claim and their ethnic identification at different levels of their identification with Germany (for the role of the national frame in immigrant claims-making, see also Koopmans & Statham, 1999). As anticipated, the political claim was unrelated to ethnic identification when identification with Germany was low according to a median split ($r = -.04$), but there was a substantial correlation when identification with Germany was high ($r = .58$). It thus seems that a politicized immigrant identity is predicated on a specific variant of dual identity, namely a strong ethnic identity combined with strong identification with the society of settlement (e.g. identity as a 'German Turk'). To the extent that the participation of immigrants in the political arena is another indicator, and possibly also additional reinforcement, of their integration into the society of settlement, the politicization of immigrant identity may be another, although controversial and conflict-laden, integration mechanism that deserves more attention in future social psychological research. However, the (collective) identity of indigenous people too can politicize in the context of intercultural contact, and this process often works against the integration of immigrants and strategies of multiculturalism. It is this counter-force that I examine in the next section.

Right-Wing Extremism and National Identity

In the 1980s, Western Europe witnessed the emergence (or revival) of extreme right-wing parties and a corresponding change in the established political party system (Ignazi, 1992; 1997; Klandermans & Mayer, 2003). Writing at this date, in the early 2000s, it seems that we are again witnessing an increase in support for extreme right-wing ('populist') movements in Western Europe and beyond, with similar consequences for the political landscape. Although the strength of extreme right-wing parties is not necessarily a positive predictor of violent resistance against immigration (Koopmans, 1996), 'an exhaltation of natural community and a hostility towards foreigners' are among the core ideological components of right-wing extremism, together with 'a refusal of modernity, a hate of divisions and a search for harmony, . . . a faith in hierarchical structures and a distrust of parliamentary debate' (Ignazi, 1992, p. 12). In fact, immigration control seems to be the leading issue for all right-wing parties, even for less extreme ones (Ignazi, 1992).

A recent interview study that Ludger Klein and I conducted in the context of a collaborative research project on right-wing extremism in Europe (Klandermans & Mayer, 2003) illustrates that the conflict around the issue of immigration is also *a power struggle for and by means of collective identity* (Simon & Klein, 2003; see also Klein, 2003). In this struggle, right-wing extremist collective identity (RWE identity) figures as the politicized collective identity of (some) members of the indigenous group. For our semi-structured interviews, which lasted between 50 and 200 minutes, we recruited 19 male and six female persons from the extreme right-wing political spectrum in Germany, with ages ranging from 22 to 78 years. The majority of interviewees were members of the political party 'Die Republikaner' (The Republicans). In the remainder of this section, I will first demonstrate the social psychological reality of RWE identity by citing evidence for its functioning, including the operation of supporting processes. I will then proceed to the discussion of RWE identity as a form of politicized collective identity and its relation to national identity.

RWE identity: functions and processes

The interviews demonstrated that, like other variants or forms of identity, RWE identity serves important social psychological functions for the person, such as providing her with feelings or experiences of belongingness, distinctiveness, respect, understanding and agency (for a more detailed explication of these concepts, see chapter 3). For example, with respect to belongingness, one interviewee remarked: 'And of course, there is such a feeling of togetherness [in the party]. Although I wouldn't be friends with everyone, you know. But I . . . simply feel close ties with them, without seeing each other a lot.' The distinctiveness function becomes visible in statements such as 'The party differs – that really matters – it differs from other parties in that it approves of the nation; the nation as historical reality' or 'Well, I would call it patriotic idealism, that exists among Republicans, about which one does not need to talk much, but it is simply and naturally there . . . I have not experienced it like this anywhere else.' The interviewees also reported experiences in accordance with the respect function. For example, it was stressed that 'through the appreciation of others, especially others in the party, I started to develop a certain self-esteem'. The understanding function was nicely captured by an interviewee who claimed that his ingroup (i.e. party) provided him with important insights regarding 'the relationship between family, woman, children, and state, that everything is connected in a certain way'. Similarly, another interviewee was grateful to his ingroup for making it possible that 'one increasingly saw the problem of asylum seekers in Germany'. The agency function is served as well because the adoption of RWE identity 'means at the moment to get something done together with people with whom I get along well, with people from whom I can learn something, to get something off the ground together'. And as another interviewee remarked: 'Perhaps overall our party can move something some day. One does not know that yet, that is not clear yet. But I don't feel so powerless.'

There was also evidence in the interviews that these identity functions were supported by a number of social psychological processes, such as (self-)stereotyping, conformity, prejudice and discrimination (see also chapter 3). For example, the interviewees stereotypically ascribed idealism and patriotism, respect for traditional values (e.g. order, punctuality, diligence and discipline) and a 'national-conservative' orientation to the ingroup and themselves, while outgroups outside the extreme right-wing spectrum were portrayed as those who 'have almost entirely sacrificed German interests . . . betrayed their own nation'. As a consequence, the self is unmistakably located in a distinct ingroup, and both the belongingness and distinctiveness functions are served. At the same time, RWE identity seemed to prescribe behavioural conformity in line with its ideological content, demanding that 'this central theme in this entire acting, in the entire work is Germany' and that fellow group members 'go with me in this direction'. By specifying what is appropriate behaviour and what is inappropriate behaviour for people 'like us' and by promising social support (in the case of appropriate behaviour), identity-specific conformity reinforces feelings of belongingness, distinctiveness and agency, respectively.

Although the interviewees seemed generally anxious to avoid expressions of blatant prejudice, there were clear indications of more subtle forms of prejudice such as a special liking for ingroup members and a firm belief in ingroup superiority (Pettigrew & Meertens, 1995). Most relevant to the issues of intercultural contact and immigration, interviewees expressed a clear affective preference for their own nation or culture relative to other nations or cultures. For example, notice the subtle, but revealing differentiation in the statement that 'the German culture I love, the other cultures I respect'. Another interviewee declared along similar lines that 'I am really proud of my home country . . . especially in light of everything that we have achieved so far, things that the people in this country have achieved so far . . . Other nations have simply not achieved this.' The latter quotation also nicely illustrates the contribution of (subtle) prejudice to the fulfilment of the respect function.

Finally, the interviews revealed tendencies towards discrimination, which also serves the respect function, but is the overt behavioural expression of respect for the ingroup and disrespect for the outgroup. In short, discrimination is prejudice in action, and because it suggests or even proves that one has power or control over the outgroup, discrimination also serves the agency function. Most notably, discrimination (or at least the intention to discriminate) was directed against national, ethnic or cultural minorities in Germany, especially Turks and asylum-seekers. It was requested that 'we must do somewhat more for our fellow citizens than for asylum-seekers or false asylum seekers' because, as another interviewee declared, 'I just want that Germany remains the home for Germans, predominantly at least.' Similarly, other interviewees demanded that 'we must not let in all and everyone, especially because we also import criminality' or declared that 'I am also strictly against Germany being an immigration country' because 'our culture must by no means perish or be diluted'.

In conclusion, the analysis of the functions and processes of RWE identity clearly substantiated the social psychological reality of this variant of collective identity. However, it also soon became apparent that an adequate understanding of RWE identity, at least in the German context, is impossible without recognition of its relation to the more inclusive national identity and the interpenetration of the two identity discourses, to which I now turn.

RWE identity as politicized national identity

The national perspective emerged as a consistent theme in our interviews with German right-wing extremists (Simon & Klein, 2003). Except for one interviewee (who had already publicly turned away from right-wing extremism), all other interviewees highlighted their 'German standpoint' in one way or another. As already evident from several of the quotations listed above, this theme penetrated the functions and processes of RWE identity, providing them with content and direction. In fact, national identity as a German served as the most important frame for self-interpretation and political action. One interviewee succinctly summarized this point as follows: 'The most important goals and ideas is first of all, I say, to represent and to defend my fatherland; to defend in so far, well, to be allowed as a German to show my nationality, my national consciousness, my patriotism, and also to be allowed to live it. – This is number one for me.' Overall, RWE identity was construed as a more exclusive form of collective identity, but one that was clearly nested within national identity. Although it was considered the ideal representative or prototype of national identity, RWE identity was presented as secondary relative to national identity in the sense that it would be enacted only in the service of national identity. Accordingly, it was claimed that membership of the party 'Die Republikaner' 'is really a tool for something'. 'Because otherwise you can't do anything, you are totally helpless. You can do it only through a party in a democratic system. The party is like a tool for me, to form something and to exert influence.' In short, RWE identity may be understood as the politicized form, or one of the politicized forms, of national identity, at least in the German context.

Recently, Bert Klandermans and I suggested that politicized collective identity (PCI) is a form of collective identity that underlies group members' intention to 'engage, as a mindful and self-conscious collective (or as representatives thereof), in . . . a power struggle knowing that it is the wider, more inclusive societal context in which this struggle takes place and needs to be orchestrated accordingly' (Simon & Klandermans, 2001, p. 323). This definition rests on three critical pillars – collective identity, the struggle for power between groups and recognition of the societal context of this power struggle.

The interview study on right-wing extremism (in Germany) showed that RWE identity too rests on such pillars (Simon & Klein, 2003). First, right-wing extremists do not understand themselves or act as single, isolated individuals in the political arena. Instead, they are aware that they share important social and political attitudes (e.g. concerning immigration) with other people, but not everyone. Second, they want to exert influence in order to propagate their positions, but they also anticipate the resistance of other groups and hence consciously engage in a power struggle with their opponents. Collective identity and power are closely intertwined in this struggle. As evidenced by the prominence of the immigration issue in extreme right-wing propaganda, it is to a large extent a struggle for (or against) the hegemony or dominance of a specific collective identity. Right-wing extremists fight for the dominance of the national identity of the indigenous group. (More precisely, they fight for the dominance of a specific kind of national identity – one defined on their own terms.) Accordingly, they strive for cultural homogeneity and demand assimilation from immigrants, if they accept any immigration at all. Their struggle for a dominant national identity forbids multiculturalism because the latter would undermine cultural hegemony and ultimately entail power sharing with immigrant groups. It should be noted that such power concerns are not restricted to right-wing extremists. In fact, research conducted outside the context of right-wing extremism indicates that indigenous people or cultural majority groups in general tend to prefer the melting-pot approach, requiring assimilation on the part of immigrants or minority members, whereas immigrants or cultural minority groups tend to prefer integration strategies and multiculturalism (Gaertner & Dovidio, 2000, p. 163). It stands to reason that fear of power loss and hope of power gain underlie these differential preferences, respectively.[3]

However, right-wing extremists not only engage in a power struggle for collective-identity purposes, they also struggle by means of collective identity. Such an instrumental role of collective identity is not restricted to the mobilization of members of the immediate ingroup (e.g. other 'Republikaner' in Germany). It also extends to the wider societal context, which brings me to the third pillar of PCI. Right-wing extremists know that the power struggle takes place in a wider societal context so that additional groups or segments of the larger society are likely to get involved (e.g. other political parties, the government, the police, the general public or the media), which need to be taken into account and, if possible, enlisted for one's own political purposes. Here more inclusive collective identities come into play. For example, by invoking national identity and stressing that they are doing it for the fatherland, German right-wing extremists attempt to legitimize their struggle against immigration and to mobilize additional supporters (Klein, 2003; see also Wimmer, 2002).

In our triangular model of PCI, Bert Klandermans and I (Simon & Klandermans, 2001) further proposed that PCI, defined by the conceptual triad of collective identity, power struggle and societal context, unfolds through a politicization process which can be summarized as an (idealized) sequence of three steps – awareness of social grievances, adversarial attributions to blame opponents and involvement of society by triangulation.

Evidence for these steps was also found in the German interview study (Simon & Klein, 2003), and the national theme was again pervasive. For instance, the construal of shared grievances revolved to a large extent around the alleged exploitation of the German welfare state by immigrants or asylum seekers at the expense of indigenous people. Interviewees complained: 'I don't see that this can work at all, when you are a welfare state, when you have a social security system, that this is then used by people – I refrain from saying abused now – but used, who come here and have never contributed a penny' or 'I was a social welfare recipient, had to sell everything. And then I saw the hallways full of social welfare recipients who had no command of the German language. For them, everything worked out much better.' As regards adversarial attributions, immigrants or other aliens were blamed because they were perceived as the immediate problem, while 'those who are in the government for years', the media and the political left were clearly seen as the opponents or even enemies, who were blamed for doing nothing or too little to protect the interests, culture and identity of Germans. Finally, in accordance with their self-understanding as the active carriers of the national torch, the interviewees hoped to be able to triangulate the struggle against their political opponents and for the alleviation of (national) grievances particularly by involving the hitherto silent majority of the people so that 'some day the bill will be presented, that the people wake up after all'. If only they were adequately informed and forced to take a stand, the people would eventually take sides with them against their political opponents and against immigration.

In conclusion, during the entire politicization process, right-wing extremists appear eager to emphasize the interconnectedness of RWE identity and national identity. On the one hand, national identity thus gives RWE identity meaning, while RWE identity gives national identity a concrete politicized form. On the other hand, the (alleged) interconnectedness of RWE identity and national identity also helps right-wing extremists to propagate a conception of national identity modelled on RWE identity. In this sense, RWE identity gives national identity not just form, but also content. Anti-immigration and anti-multiculturalism attitudes seem to lie in the centre of such interconnectedness or interpenetration of RWE identity and national identity, which allows right-wing extremists to exploit both identities as well as their connection as transmission belts for political mobilization against immigration and multiculturalism.

Cultural Differences and Racism: A Comment

In the preceding sections, I have argued that intercultural contact, such as contact between immigrant and indigenous groups, has considerable potential for social conflict and that intercultural conflicts are, to a significant degree, power struggles for and by means of collective or cultural identity.[4] The issue of cultural differences figures prominently in such struggles as cultural differences between indigenous people and immigrants are usually highlighted by protagonists on either side of the group or cultural divide, although they draw on different discourses and use somewhat different rhetoric in order to support their specific claims. Indigenous groups that fight for the (national) dominance of their collective identity argue that the differences undermine the cultural homogeneity of the nation or society and demand assimilation from immigrants and immigration control by the government. Immigrant groups that fight for the recognition of their collective identity build on the notion of the (positive) value of cultural heritage – a notion that is often popular among the majority of indigenous people as well – and demand respect for their cultural distinctiveness. In other words, indigenous groups often use the cultural-differences argument to justify rejection of immigrants, whereas immigrant groups use another variant of the cultural-differences argument to claim respect. Cultural differences easily take on an essentialistic meaning in the sense that they are construed as indicators of immutable and insurmountable differences between indigenous people and immigrants with respect to a deeper, underlying psychological, if not biological, make-up or essence (Medin & Ortony, 1989; Rothbart & Taylor, 1992). Accordingly, the first variant of the cultural-differences argument is regularly countered with the accusation of racism, by immigrants as well as by indigenous people that support multiculturalism.

A similar debate is going on among social scientists. For example, Pettigrew and Meertens (1995) suggest that the exaggeration of perceived cultural differences between indigenous people and immigrants by indigenous people is an indicator of their (subtle) prejudice against immigrants. By way of contrast, Coenders et al. (2001, p. 288) argue that a high score on the cultural-differences scale may simply mean that 'the respondent is acknowledging a social reality, not necessarily expressing a subtle prejudice . . . [because] the items on cultural differences register predominantly perceptions but not necessarily exaggerations nor evaluations'. However, the problem with Coenders et al.'s (2001) argument is that there is no immaculate perception in the social domain. Social perception is neither pure in its origin nor innocent in its consequences. Similarities and differences in general, and between people or groups of people in particular, are not simply given and passively perceived. Instead, the perceiver, with her particular identity, motives and interests, plays an active role (Medin, Goldstone & Gentner, 1993; Oakes et al., 1994; Simon, 1992, 1998a; see also chapter 4 in this book). Popper (1982, p. 375) put forward a similar argument concerning the role of position and interest in the perception of similarities and differences.

Moreover, the perception of cultural differences has important consequences for social attitudes and social behaviour. For example, researchers observed significantly positive relationships between respondents' scores on Pettigrew and Meertens's (1995) cultural-differences scale and their scores on (commonly accepted) measures tapping various other aspects of prejudice (for an overview, see Pettigrew & Meertens, 2001). Similarly, the interviewees in our study on right-wing extremism in Germany (Simon & Klein, 2003) drew on the (first variant of the) cultural-differences argument to demand discrimination against immigrants and/or more favourable treatment of indigenous people. From the interviewees' perspective, equal treatment of what they consider to be fundamentally unequal cultural groups would amount to social injustice. Incidentally, resistance against equal rights for gays and lesbians compared to heterosexuals is often justified along similar lines – and not just by right-wing extremists. Once homosexuals and heterosexuals (and their respective intimate relationships) are perceived or portrayed as fundamentally different, it seems that equal rights for gays and lesbians, such as the right to marry one's same-sex partner, can be refused as steps towards *illegitimate equality*.

However, it must also be acknowledged that, in the final analysis, accusations of exaggerating (or neglecting) cultural differences as well as accusations of racism (or xenophilia) are value judgements regularly used as weapons in the power struggle for and by means of cultural identity. The same logic also applies to struggles involving other collective identities, such as sexual-orientation identity or gender identity. This is not to succumb to relativism and to let racists off the hook, but to acknowledge the political dimension of racism (or any other 'ism') and pertinent research. I am still convinced that we (!) have good scientific reasons to call certain people, their attitudes and behaviours, racist[5] – though I don't believe that it makes much sense to differentiate between people who 'really are' racists and those who 'only' act as racists. At the same time, I am aware that when I concern myself as a social scientist with the issue of racism I not only enter the political arena, but I also occupy a particular value-laden position (or collective identity) in it (Pettigrew, 1996, p. 17). Together with people that hold the same position, I argue with and against people holding different positions. As long as the accusation of racism is a sharp sword and my opponents are anxious to escape or repudiate such accusations, there is indication of agreement about basic values associated with a more inclusive collective identity and therefore hope that political as well as scientific reason, argument and controversy (i.e. social influence) can combat racism and lead to progress (see also the excellent discussion of relativity and relativism in stereotyping by Oakes et al., 1994, pp. 199–211). However, once the accusation of racism becomes a blunt sword because there is no longer any common ground or fundamental value consensus that connects us with our opponents, the latter turn into enemies and the political struggle is likely to develop into, or be replaced by, a war fought with much more dangerous weaponry (i.e. coercion or open violence).

Summary

Globalization, the emergence of supranational political and economic entities and mass migration lead to an increase in the opportunities for intercultural contact in modern society. Despite its many desirable aspects, such contact also has a considerable potential for social conflict. In this chapter, I concerned myself with the role of identity in intercultural contact and the contributions of identity to harmony and conflict between cultural groups. The first major section presented an overview of the most influential social psychological models of intergroup or intercultural contact and the roles they ascribe to identity. I discussed the personalization model (Brewer & Miller, 1984), the common ingroup identity model (Gaertner & Dovidio, 2000), the mutual differentiation model (Hewstone & Brown, 1986) and Pettigrew's (1998) integrative model of longitudinal intergroup contact.

I then turned to identity and intercultural contact in the context of immigration and articulated the social psychological perspective on intergroup contact with research on acculturation conducted within the framework of cross-cultural psychology (Berry, 2001). I presented some preliminary evidence that intercultural encounters, arranged in line with social psychological models of optimal intergroup contact, facilitate mutual accommodation among indigenous people and immigrants and thereby the respectful integration of the latter into a multicultural society. I also outlined two under-researched avenues to such integration and the participation of immigrants in the society of settlement. First, I pointed out the role of intercultural organizations as vehicles that can accelerate the psychological arrival of members of immigrant groups at the society of settlement through some kind of piggyback mechanism. Second, the politicization of immigrant identity was suggested as another – though more controversial – integration mechanism. The latter mechanism is in line with the observation that intercultural conflicts are – to a significant degree – power struggles for and by means of collective or cultural identities.

This theme was corroborated and further explored in a section on right-wing extremism and national identity where I discussed the functions and processes of right-wing extremist identity (RWE identity) and its relation to national identity. In particular, I suggested that RWE identity is a politicized form of national identity on the part of (some) indigenous people that emerges from and underlies intercultural conflicts and power struggles in contexts of immigration. Finally, I commented on the discourses upon cultural differences and racism and argued that, as social scientists, we must acknowledge the political dimension of research on racism and can do so without falling prey to naive empiricism or relativism.

NOTES

1. Germany seems to be a notable exception in this respect. Pettigrew (1997, p. 180) reports that, for the German sample, the path from higher prejudice to fewer outgroup friends was stronger than the opposite path from more outgroup friends to lower prejudice.

2. However, with respect to individual identity and human identity, one may also have to take into consideration a possible equivalence of the extremes because, in the final analysis, individuality, especially individuality in terms of independence, implies fundamental similarity or equality among humans (see chapter 3).

3. In this connection, I venture the hypothesis that indigenous people are wary of language maintenance among immigrants not only because it may interfere with the acquisition of the main language spoken in the country of settlement, but also because they may fear that a 'secret language' – one that they find too bothersome to learn – gives immigrants an undue power advantage.

4. Issues of power and collective identity are closely intertwined, if not inseparable, in such struggles because collective identity can be a source of power as much as power can ensure recognition of one's collective identity. We may therefore deal here with a whole family of struggles involving power and identity as either means or ends or even both (i.e. struggles for collective identity and/or power by means of collective identity and/or power).

5. Wimmer (2002, pp. 201–2) identifies five themes that can serve as guidelines for the definition of racism (and racists): (1) 'fear of being "inundated" by foreigners and estranged from one's own culture', (2) 'the idea that mixing different cultural or biological entities is harmful', (3) 'the idea that the marks of certain biological and cultural characteristics are so "profound" that they cannot be changed during the lifetime of an individual or the history of a group', (4) 'hierarchisation of the different entities in which one's own group comes first', (5) 'the perception of a zero-sum game between foreigners and "ourselves" '.

Chapter 7

Identity, Mobilization and Participation

A basic premise underlying the approach to identity developed in this book is that identity not only results from interaction in the social world, but in turn also guides (inter)action in the social world. In chapters 5 and 6, I discussed discriminatory behaviour as a likely outcome of collective identity in the context of minority–majority relations and in (other) intercultural contexts. In this chapter, the specific emphasis is on the role of identity in social behaviour that is typically performed together, and often in explicit coordination, with many other people. This is not to imply that the discriminatory behaviour reviewed in the preceding chapters is typically performed in isolation and never in coordination with other people's behaviour. In fact, much of the behaviour considered in this chapter is in many ways closely related to discriminatory behaviour. More specifically, a large part of this chapter revolves around rather controversial forms of social behaviour, such as social movement participation and collective protest which may be construed, depending on one's value-laden point of view, as either legitimate reactions to systematic discriminatory treatment by others or as illegitimate discriminatory actions themselves. However, I also consider other forms of social behaviour, such as intragroup cooperation and volunteerism, for which there seems to exist a broad social consensus that they are highly desirable and thus pro-social.

Identity and Social Movement Participation

The focus of this section is on people who by virtue of their membership in some social category or group find themselves in a disadvantaged (low-status, subordinated or dominated) segment within the wider social context. Membership in such groups can lead – in addition to objective or material disadvantages – to a psychological predicament because it is usually incompatible with positive self-evaluation and can thus pose a threat to one's self-esteem or self-respect (Tajfel & Turner, 1986). Consequently, members of disadvantaged groups who do not want passively to accept their lot have to find ways to improve their (material and/or psychological) situation. To do so, they can adopt a variety of strategies ranging from individual strategies of social mobility to collective strategies of social change. The former rest on the belief that one's own situation can be improved by moving from one social position to another as an individual (Tajfel, 1981). Individual strategies thus involve leaving a disadvantaged group physically or at least psychologically. Conversely, collective strategies are adopted if a person believes that 'the only way for him to change these [disadvantageous] conditions . . . is together with his group as a whole' (Tajfel, 1981, p. 247). Collective strategies include militant forms of intergroup behaviour or collective action such as revolts and strikes, but also more moderate forms such as signing a petition or attending a group meeting.

Research indicates that individual social mobility strategies are often preferred over collective social change strategies, especially when group boundaries are (or seem to be) permeable at least to some degree (Ellemers, van Knippenberg & Wilke, 1990; Lalonde & Silverman, 1994; Wright, 2001b). However, individual social mobility is not always the preferred choice. Under certain circumstances, members of disadvantaged groups do in fact engage in collective action in order to improve their situation (for reviews, see Tyler & Smith, 1998; Wright, 2001a). Social movements are a case in point.

According to a classic social psychological definition, '[A] social movement represents an effort by a large number of people to solve collectively a problem that they feel they have in common' (Toch, 1965, p. 5). Similarly, more recent approaches define social movements as 'collective challenges by people with common purposes and solidarity in sustained interaction with elites, opponents and authorities' (Tarrow, 1995, pp. 3–4; also Klandermans, 1997, p. 2). Social movements are complex social phenomena, and the articulation of different levels of analysis is required to provide comprehensive answers to the questions of when and how people come to join social movements or form them in the first place (Klandermans, 1997; McAdam, McCarthy & Zald, 1988). On the one hand, macro-level analyses focus on the social structural antecedents of social movements. Traditionally, this is the domain of sociology, political science and economics. For example, an important aim of macro-level analyses is to identify the frictions and contradictions inherent in the larger society and thereby the critical social structural cleavages or fault lines, involving asymmetries in wealth, status or power, along which social movements emerge and mobilize their supporters. Accordingly, the origin of the labour movement has been traced back to the frictions and contradictions of a society structured by social class, whereas the roots of the feminist movement are seen in the integrative problems arising for women in modern, functionally differentiated societies (Neidhardt & Rucht, 1993). Further, macro-level analyses are also concerned with the role of opportunities and opportunity structures in the emergence and mobilization of social movements. For example, it is examined whether and how the availability of, or access to, specific resources, such as money, people, modern technology (e.g. mass communication and rapid transport) or alliances within the institutionalized political system, facilitates a social movement (Esser, 1988; Kriesi et al., 1995; McCarthy & Zald, 1973, 1977).

On the other hand, micro-level analyses are also required because it is always individuals, and not groups or movements as such, that have psychological experiences, develop motives and eventually act. Important aspects of the social (macro) structure must be experienced psychologically, and these experiences must be converted into motives and eventually actions. For example, social structural inequalities or asymmetries in wealth, status or power must be experienced as grievances, lead to feelings of discontent, engender motives to improve one's situation and prompt appropriate action. Similarly, opportunities at the social structural level must lead to feelings of hope and self-efficacy before people seize these opportunities and act accordingly. Experiences, motives and actions of individuals, as well as the relationships among experiences, motives and actions, are the focus of micro-level analyses, and this level of analysis is usually viewed as the domain of psychology.

However, people rarely, if ever, experience social structure directly and they also rarely act directly on the social structure. Instead, the social structure needs to be *translated* into psychological experiences, motives and actions before these experiences, motives and actions can further be *translated* into social movement activities which aim at, and may eventually result in, social structural change. In order to understand these macro–micro and micro–macro translations (i.e. how the social structure gets into the individual and how the individual is able eventually to act on social structure), a meso level of analysis is required that specifies the critical mediating processes (Pettigrew, 1996). This level of analysis is the true domain of social psychology. It focuses on the situation or immediate context of social interaction because it is in socially structured interaction situations that 'macro meets micro', or more precisely, where 'macro is connected with micro' and the critical social psychological mediating processes take shape. As argued in chapter 3, identity is such a (meso-level) mediating process that connects (macro-level) social structure with (micro-level) psychological experiences, motives and actions of individuals and makes bi-directional influences possible. It is therefore reasonable to assume that identity plays an important role in social movement participation and collective protest. Moreover, because it is not single, isolated individuals, but individuals united as groups that form social movements and engage in collective protest, collective identity should be particularly relevant. In fact, Tajfel (1981, p. 244) specified Toch's (1965) original definition of a social movement accordingly and suggested that social movements should be understood as 'efforts by large numbers of people, *who define themselves and are also often defined by others as a group*, to solve collectively a problem they feel they have in common, and which is perceived to arise from their relations with other groups' (my emphasis).

In accordance with Klandermans (1997; also Klandermans & Oegema, 1987), participation in social movements or collective protest can be understood as the result of a complex process involving several stages or steps at which different facilitative and inhibitory factors come into play. More specifically, with regard to the potential participant, Klandermans (1997) identifies four critical steps: (1) becoming part of the mobilization potential, (2) becoming a target of mobilization attempts, (3) becoming motivated to participate and (4) overcoming barriers to participation. I will now specify each step in more detail and discuss the role of identity and especially, but not exclusively, the role of collective identity at each step. However, the emphasis will be on the third step (i.e. becoming motivated to participate) because most of the research that my co-workers and I have conducted to examine the role of collective identity in social movement participation actually concerns this step.

Becoming part of the mobilization potential

According to Klandermans (1997), someone can be considered part of the mobilization potential to the extent to which she sympathizes with or has a positive attitude towards the movement. More specifically, the mobilization potential of a movement consists of people who share a 'collective action frame' *vis-à-vis* the movement's cause. Collective action frames consist of shared sets of beliefs that serve to interpret and explain social issues and to suggest appropriate collective (re)actions (Gamson, 1992a). Three specific components can be distinguished according to Gamson (1992a; see also Klandermans, 1997). First, collective action frames have an injustice component because they provide people with interpretations and explanations of personal grievances in terms of injustice (e.g. interpretation of lower salary for women compared with men as discrimination against women) which, in turn, are likely to engender feelings of moral indignation and anger (Guimond & Dubé-Simard, 1983). Second, they possess an identity component in that they foster interpretations of self and others in terms of an 'us versus them' antagonism (e.g. 'They, the men, discriminate against us women'). Third, collective action frames have an agency component in that they facilitate beliefs that social change is possible and that the movement is actually capable of bringing about the desired change.

The generation and adoption of collective action frames is a function of a multifaceted social influence process operating against the background of individual dispositions and cultural themes and counter-themes. Notwithstanding these complexities, research has shown that social influence is more readily accepted if the target shares a relevant collective identity with the source (Kelly, 1993; Mackie & Cooper, 1984; Turner, 1991). Hence, social movements that can build on (pre)existing categorizations and collective identities (e.g. the women's movement, which can build on the male–female categorization) should be particularly successful in disseminating collective action frames and thus in 'consensus mobilization' (Klandermans, 1997). In other words, people should be more willing to construct and adopt collective action frames if such frames relate to existing or chronically accessible collective identities. This facilitative effect is most obvious with regard to the identity component of collective action frames. If an existing or chronically accessible collective identity is related to the movement's cause, the identity basis, on which the social movement and its entrepreneurs can build, is already in place.

However, collective identity can also play an important facilitating role with regard to the injustice and agency components. Research suggests that disadvantaged people experience stronger deprivation and more injustice when their shared group membership is highlighted as opposed to their individual personalities (Smith, Spears & Oyen, 1994; see also Dubé & Guimond, 1986; Gurin & Townsend, 1986; Tougas & Veilleux, 1988). Disadvantages and grievances are thus very likely to be interpreted as injustices if they systematically affect 'people like us' (Smith et al., 1994). Moreover, people with a strong collective identity tend to perceive increased ingroup homogeneity and to construe such homogeneity as a collective asset which strengthens people's belief in the ingroup as an efficacious collective agent ('United we stand, divided we fall') (Simon, 1992, 1998b; see also Mummendey et al., 1999).

Although necessary, the adoption of collective action frames – with their injustice, identity and agency components – is not a sufficient condition for movement participation. Further steps need to be taken to turn sympathizers into participants.

Becoming a target of mobilization attempts

Sympathy with a social movement and its cause is not enough. People must be reached in order to inform them about specific actions (e.g. sit-ins or demonstrations) and to influence their willingness to take part in these actions. The mass media and direct mailing, including electronic mailing using modern information technology such as the internet, are possible routes through which people can be reached. In addition, research has shown that recruitment networks based on friendship ties and ties with organizations play a critical role in this process (for an overview, see Klandermans & Oegema, 1987). Targeting organizations or friendship networks, instead of single individuals, is particularly efficient because it makes '*en bloc* recruitment' possible. Collective identity comes into play here in at least two ways. First, if a social movement is rooted in a social group which provides group members with an important collective identity, the social movement can more easily gain access to the organizations of that group and its friendship networks by stressing that 'we are all one'. The civil rights movement, which drew heavily on church organizations in the African-American community, is a case in point (Friedman & McAdam, 1992). Second, targeted organizations (e.g. churches) or friendship networks (e.g. peer groups) may themselves constitute important bases for collective identities. Consequently, as soon as representatives of organizations or central figures (leaders or prototypes) of friendship networks show interest in the social movement's cause, such interest is likely to become normative within the respective circles (Haslam, 2001). This should in turn lead to a better flow of relevant information as well as increased information-seeking behaviour within the targeted circles.

To be sure, social movement entrepreneurs or activists strive to provide targets with information that increases targets' willingness to participate in social movement activities. However one-sided that information may be, being informed about specific actions is not tantamount to being motivated to participate. This brings me to the third step.

Becoming motivated to participate

Research on people's motivation or willingness to participate in social move-ment activities has been influenced in important ways by expectancy-value or rational-choice models of social behaviour (Ajzen & Fishbein, 1980; Opp, 1989). Accordingly, willingness to participate in social movement activities is typically viewed as a function of the expected costs and benefits of participa-tion. More specifically, Klandermans (1984, 1997) suggests considering three different motives or incentives, with each of them originating from a different type or class of expected costs or benefits. First, the collective incentive derives from the value of the social movement's collective goals (e.g. reduction of group-based discrimination) for the potential participant, weighted by the perceived likelihood that these goals will be reached. More formally, the collective incentive is conceptualized as the multiplicative function of the subjective (positive or negative) value of the goals of the social movement and the subjective expectation that these goals will be reached through collective action.

Second, the normative incentive derives from the expected reactions of others, weighted by the personal importance of these others' reactions to the potential participant.[1] More formally, it is conceptualized as the multiplicative function of the subjective (positive or negative) quality of the expected reactions of others and the subjective importance of these reactions. The normative incentive thus corresponds to Ajzen and Fishbein's (1980) notion of a subjective norm which they conceptualized as the multiplicative function of normative beliefs and the motivation to comply.

Finally, the reward incentive concerns more personal or idiosyncratic gains or losses, such as losing money or time, making new friends or risking one's health. More formally, it is conceptualized as a multiplicative function of the subjective (positive or negative) value of such gains and losses and the subjective expectation that they will actually ensue.

Willingness to participate in collective action organized by the social movement should increase with (the subjective positivity of) the expected value of the collective outcome of participation (collective incentive), the expected reactions of important others (normative incentive) and the expected value of the personal outcomes of participation (reward incentive). Put in terms of Ajzen and Fishbein's (1980) theory of reasoned action, the collective incentive and the reward incentive together determine the attitude towards social movement participation, while the normative incentive corresponds directly to the subjective norm component. Attitude and subjective norm then co-determine the intention or willingness to participate.

The conceptualization of the potential participant in social movement activities as someone who weighs costs and benefits has been challenged and criticized, however, as overly atomistic and individualistic. Specifically, the neglect of the role of collective identity has been criticized (Friedman & McAdam, 1992; Gamson, 1992b; Kelly, 1993; Rucht, 1995). This criticism vindicates Tajfel's (1981) reformulation of Toch's (1965) 'classic' definition of social movements whereby Tajfel added a collective-identity component to Toch's definition (see above). More generally, this criticism is in accord with the social identity or self-categorization perspective (Tajfel & Turner, 1986; Turner et al., 1987), which has long argued for the pivotal role of collective identification processes in group processes and intergroup relations. According to this perspective, social movement participation is group-serving behaviour qua group member so that collective identification is the basic social psychological process underlying that behaviour. Unfortunately, Tajfel's (1981) (re)definition of social movements, as well as the social identity or self-categorization perspective in general, has for a long time had only very little influence on social movement research. In fact, social movement research, on the one hand, and research on group processes and intergroup relations inspired by the social identity or self-categorization perspective, on the other, have long coexisted as two rather strictly separated domains, with the former being oriented more towards sociology and the latter more towards psychology.

In a series of empirical studies, my co-workers and I pursued the task of bringing together these different research traditions and thus contributing to empirical and theoretical integration (for similar endeavours, see Kawakami & Dion, 1993, 1995; Kelly, 1993; Kelly & Breinlinger, 1996). To this end, we conducted a series of (cross-sectional) field studies in different social movement contexts (i.e. the older people's movement, the gay movement and the fat acceptance movement). In each case, we distributed questionnaires among members of the respective mobilization potential in order to measure and compare the influence of collective identification processes and collective, normative and reward incentives on willingness to participate in social movement activities. Because prior social movement research had already established the predictive value of the collective, normative and reward incentives in several social movement contexts (Klandermans, 1984, 1997), we were particularly interested in the unique contribution of collective identification to the prediction of willingness to participate in social movement activities. In addition, we also examined possible moderation or interaction effects of collective identification and the 'traditional' incentives usually considered in social movement research.[2]

Being old, gay or fat: it moves! In chapter 3, I argued that, in the (post)modern world, classic collective identities, such as those based on social class or rank, tend to be less salient, not so much because they, and the underlying cleavages and deprivations, no longer exist, but because they now have to compete for attention with the outcomes of alternative self-interpretations. More specifically, classic collective identities may have to compete not only with a strengthened individual identity, but also with a variety of collective identities based on self-aspects such as gender, age, sexual orientation or body weight (Sampson, 1993). Though not necessarily new, such self-aspects are particularly likely to unfold their collective-identity potential in modern society where functional differentiation, urbanization, increased intergroup contact, rapid transportation, mass communication and information technology provide ample opportunities for the formation and recognition of socially shared similarities, collective interests and deprivations involving these self-aspects (Esser, 1988; Neidhardt & Rucht, 1993). Moreover, the (political) opportunity structure in modern society seems highly conducive to the mobilization of social categories or groups of people who share such self-aspects and the corresponding collective identities, and modern society has in fact witnessed the emergence of many so-called 'new' social movements (Kriesi et al., 1995).

Our first study on the role of collective identity in (new) social movements was concerned with the older people's movement in Germany (Simon et al., 1998, Study 1). Ninety-five registered members of the German Senior Protection League 'Grey Panthers' (mean age = 74 years, range = 60–91 years) participated in the questionnaire study in which we measured the collective, normative and reward incentives as well as collective identification and willingness to participate in movement activities. The three incentives were operationalized in line with Klandermans's (1984) expectancy-value approach. For each incentive, the two components were measured separately and then combined multiplicatively. Consultations with leading movement activists, pretesting and additional checks in the main questionnaire ensured that the measurement of the three incentives indeed covered the relevant costs and benefits.

The collective incentive concerned collective goals such as guaranteed minimum pension and medical care or anti-age-discrimination legislation. The normative incentive involved, inter alia, the expected reactions of family, neighbours and friends, and the reward incentive covered personal gains such as social contact with other old people or meaningful leisure time activity and personal losses such as health risks or loss of time. For identification processes, we considered two levels of collective identity. The first concerned the broader social category from which the older people's movement typically recruits its members, that is, old people in general. The second level targeted the specific social movement organization (SMO), the Grey Panthers. To overcome limitations of prior work (e.g. Kelly & Breinlinger, 1995), we measured identification with old people in general and identification with the Grey Panthers with matched multi-item scales (e.g. 'I feel strong ties with other old people/Grey Panthers'; Cronbach's $\alpha \geq .71$). Willingness to participate in (future) movement activities was measured concerning four relevant actions (e.g. public demonstrations; Cronbach's $\alpha = .83$). Our general expectation was that the three incentives as well as both indicators of collective identification would be positively correlated with willingness to participate. However, we also expected identification with the Grey Panthers to be a better predictor than identification with old people in general because identification with the movement itself should be more directly tied to an activist identity, which typically has embedded within it specific implications for action (Friedman & McAdam, 1992).

As expected, the collective, normative and reward incentives, as well as identification with old people in general and identification with the Grey Panthers, were significantly and positively correlated with willingness to participate. Correlation coefficients ranged from .31 for identification with old people in general to .72 for the reward motive. A multiple regression analysis was then performed in which the three incentives and the two identification indicators served as the predictor variables. Willingness to participate in movement activities served as the criterion. As can be seen in table 7.1, the collective and reward incentives remained significant predictors, whereas the unique contribution of the normative incentive was only marginally significant. At the same time, identification with the Grey Panthers remained a significant predictor, whereas identification with old people in general lost its predictive value. In addition, using moderated regression analysis, we found no evidence that identification with the Grey Panthers qualified the relationship between any of the incentives and willingness to participate (or that the incentives qualified the relationship between identification with the Grey Panthers and willingness to participate). The only significant interaction or moderation effect that we observed involved identification with old people in general and the collective incentive such that the predictive value of the collective incentive further increased when identification with old people in general decreased. This effect is somewhat surprising, because, if anything, one might expect the importance of the collective incentive to decrease with decreasing collective identification. However, this effect was not replicated in our subsequent research (see below), so that I will refrain from further speculation.

The results of this study thus strongly suggest that collective identification processes constitute a second pathway to social movement participation, in addition to and mostly independent of cost–benefit calculations. The finding that identification with the social movement organization was a better predictor than identification with the broader recruitment category further suggests that an activist identity is particularly conducive to social movement participation. Indeed, identification with the social movement organization mediated the relationship between identification with the recruitment category and willingness to participate. It thus appears that identification

Table 7.1 Regression analysis with willingness to participate in the older people's movement as criterion

	Collective incentive	Normative incentive	Reward incentive	Identification with old people	Identification with Grey Panthers
ß	.20	.14	.47	.02	.24
t	3.05**	1.73(*)	5.30***	0.23	2.44*

(*) $p \leq .10$, *$p \leq .05$, **$p \leq .01$, ***$p \leq .001$
$R^2 = .70$, $F(5, 81) = 37.29$, $p < .001$
Source: From Simon et al., 1998, Table 2. Copyright © 1998 by the American Psychological Association. Adapted with permission.

with a broader social category increases willingness to participate in collective action on behalf of that category only if such a collective identity is transformed into a more politicized form of collective or activist identity (Simon & Klandermans, 2001).

Two limitations of this study need to be acknowledged at this point. First, the findings may be limited to the specific social movement under scrutiny. The Grey Panthers are a formal organization with a registered membership, which is not true for all (new) social movements (Klandermans, 1997; Kriesi et al., 1995). It therefore remains to be seen whether the present findings also generalize to a less formally organized social movement (and – because most respondents in the first study were female – also to male sympathizers of social movements). Second, given the correlational nature of the first study, no definite conclusions about cause–effect relationships can be drawn. As with all correlational research, the direction of causality remains unclear, and there is always the possibility that the observed correlations are spurious because of the influence of a third variable.

We therefore conducted a second study for which we recruited (male) research participants in the context of the US gay movement (Simon et al., 1998, Study 2). One hundred and seventeen gay men (mean age = 39 years, range 19–73 years) participated in this questionnaire study in which we again measured the relevant collective, normative and reward incentives for participation in movement activities as well as identification with the broader recruitment category (i.e. gay people in general) and identification with the movement itself (i.e. the gay movement) – all on reliable multi-item scales. However, unlike the respondents in Study 1, respondents in this study were not registered members of a single social movement organization, but were recruited at meetings of various gay groups or in gay coffee houses in San Diego or San Francisco. Similarly, the questionnaire did not refer to a specific gay movement organization, but more generally to 'the gay movement'. This is in accord with the notion of the gay movement as a rather loosely knit network of groups, which is nevertheless able to elicit a fair degree of collective identification (Adam, 1987; Cruikshank, 1992).

In order to move towards a causal analysis of the role of collective identification processes, we also included an experimental manipulation of the strength of identification with the gay movement. To this end, we varied the awareness or salience of the common fate of gay people as a disadvantaged group before the measurement of the other variables. In the common fate condition, respondents were asked to recall and describe 'an incident that you experienced yourself or you have heard about where gay people were threatened or treated violently by non-gay people (e.g. gay bashing)'. In the control condition, respondents were simply asked to provide a short description of 'what you did today'. Making their common fate as a disadvantaged group highly salient should strengthen respondents' identification with the gay movement which should, in turn, lead to increased willingness to participate in movement activities.

We first conducted similar correlation and multiple regression analyses as in the previous study. The collective, normative and reward incentives as well as both identification indicators were again significantly and positively correlated with willingness to participate. Correlation coefficients ranged from .27 for the collective incentive to .64 for identification with the gay movement. The multiple regression analysis also yielded very similar results to those of the previous study, with one exception. Again, the collective incentive retained a significant predictive value and the normative incentive a marginally significant predictive value. But the reward incentive made no unique contribution to the prediction of willingness to participate. More importantly, identification with the gay movement was again a significant predictor, whereas identification with gay people in general again had no unique predictive value. Additional analyses also replicated these results with frequency of previous participation as a control variable, revealed no moderation or interaction effects and demonstrated that identification with the gay movement mediated the relationship between identification with gay people in general and willingness to participate.

The experimental effects also confirmed our expectations. Both identification with the gay movement and willingness to participate increased significantly when common fate as a disadvantaged minority was made salient. No effects were observed for identification with gay people in general or for any of the three incentives. Path analysis revealed a significant indirect effect of the common fate manipulation on willingness to participate by way of identification with the gay movement, which mediated a substantial proportion of the total effect of the common fate manipulation on willingness to participate (see figure 7.1).

The results of this study thus confirm that, even in the context of a less formally organized social movement, collective identification processes emerge as another important pathway to social movement participation, in addition to and independent of various cost–benefit calculations. Again, identification with the social movement itself seems particularly important. The experimental evidence suggests that this more politicized form of collective identity may actually have a causal effect on willingness to participate in movement activities. More precisely, it seems to play an important mediating role between shared grievances or common fate, rooted in the (macro) structure of intergroup relations, but typically experienced in concrete (meso-level) interaction situations, and their willingness to act collectively on the social structure in order to change it.

Evidence for the calculation and identification pathways to social movement participation has also been found in a questionnaire study in the context

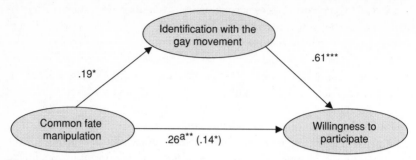

Figure 7.1 Path diagram of the role of identification with the gay movement as a mediator between the common fate manipulation and willingness to participate in movement activities. Coefficients are (standardized) regression weights.

[a]Regression weight from the analysis without the mediator; the regression weight from the analysis with the mediator is given inside parentheses. $^*p \leq .05$, $^{**}p < .01$, $^{***}p < .001$.

Source: From Simon et al., 1998, Figure 2. Copyright © 1998 by the American Psychological Association. Adapted with permission.

of the US fat acceptance movement, with 136 registered members of the National Association to Advance Fat Acceptance (NAAFA) as research participants (Stürmer et al., 2003). More specifically, the reward incentive and identification with the social movement organization NAAFA uniquely predicted willingness to participate in movement activities. Again, there were no moderation or interaction effects involving the incentives, on the one hand, and the identification indicators, on the other. In addition, this study further elaborated on the micro-level processes involved in collective identification. In line with the assumption that an activist identity typically has specific implications for action embedded within it (Friedman & McAdam, 1992), we hypothesized that the relationship between identification with NAAFA and willingness to participate would be mediated by way of an inner obligation to behave as a 'good' (i.e. active) member. Indeed, we found a complete mediation such that, with increasing identification with NAAFA, respondents felt increasingly obligated to behave in terms of the 'raison d'être' of their organization (i.e. to be active) which in turn strengthened their willingness to actually participate in the activities of NAAFA (see figure 7.2). In short, while the calculation pathway is obviously paved primarily with specific extrinsic rewards, the identification pathway seems to lead to intrinsic involvement based on the internalization of organizational or group standards (Haslam, 2001).

Taken together, the findings from the older people's movement, the gay movement and the fat acceptance movement converge to suggest a dual-

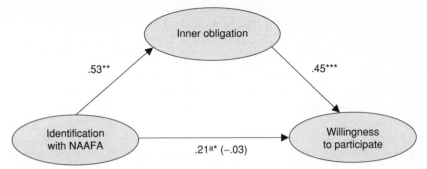

Figure 7.2 Path diagram of the role of felt inner obligation as a mediator between identification with the social movement organization NAAFA and willingness to participate in movement activities. Coefficients are (standardized) regression weights.

[a]Regression weight from the analysis without the mediator; the regression weight from the analysis with the mediator is given inside parentheses. $^*p < .05$, $^{**}p < .01$, $^{***}p < .001$.

Source: From Stürmer et al., 2003, Figure 1.

pathway model of the processes underlying people's motivation or willingness to participate in social movement activities. One pathway is calculation of the costs and benefits of participation, with the weights of specific costs and benefits varying across social movements (Klandermans, 1997). The second pathway is (collective) identification. Especially identification with the social movement itself seems to carry strong motivational implications such that adoption of the corresponding collective identity obliges one to act in terms of that identity: 'If I know who I am, then I also know what I have to do.' In Lewinian terms, an internal tension seems to arise from identification with the social movement which disrupts psychological equilibrium and motivates the person to restore it by way of appropriate action (Hornstein, 1972; see also Gollwitzer & Kirchhof, 1998). Our research further suggests that the calculation and identification pathways often operate independently, resulting in additive effects on willingness to participate, which is not to deny the theoretical plausibility and empirical possibility of interaction effects (Kelly & Breinlinger, 1996; Simon, 1998b; Terry & Hogg, 1996).

Finally, I want to highlight that the samples from the three 'new' social movements considered here varied on a number of non-trivial dimensions (e.g. nationality, gender composition, degree of formal organization). The fact that there was consistent evidence, especially for the identification pathway, across all three movement contexts thus speaks well for the validity and generalizability of the respective findings. Conversely, one might argue that the identification pathway is particularly relevant, if not confined, to the older people's movement, the gay movement and the fat acceptance movement because they all represent a type of movement that 'follow[s] a much more expressive logic in which collective action and the identities it produces become ends in themselves' (Kriesi et al. 1995, p. 84). However, a growing body of research also points to the importance of the identification pathway for social movements that are usually ascribed a more strategic or instrumental orientation, such as the labour movement (Kelly, 1993; Veenstra & Haslam, 2000), the farmer's movement (De Weerd & Klandermans, 1999; Klandermans, 2002) or right-wing political movements (Catellani, Milesi & Crescentini, 2003; Simon & Klein, 2003). It is therefore not very likely that the identification pathway is restricted to social movements with an explicit identity orientation. Let us now turn to the last step towards social movement participation.

Overcoming barriers to participation

Even if someone is highly motivated to participate in the activities of a particular social movement, obstacles beyond her control (e.g. illness or lack of transportation) can prevent her from actually participating. It is unlikely that collective identity has much direct influence on the (non-)occurrence of barriers that are not under the volitional control of the potential participant. However, because identification with the social movement strengthens one's motivation to participate, people should actually try harder to overcome barriers, and also help other potential participants to do so, when they place strong emphasis on collective identity derived from the social movement. By the same token, people may then also try harder to anticipate and prepare for potential barriers, thus increasing their (actual and perceived) 'behavioural control' (Ajzen & Madden, 1986).

Although I am not aware of any research that has explicitly investigated the role of collective identification in overcoming barriers to participation, our own research demonstrates that collective identification increases the likelihood of actual social movement participation, which suggests that collective identification has also contributed to overcoming barriers (Stürmer & Simon, in press). More specifically, we conducted a longitudinal panel study with two measurement points in the context of the German gay movement. Research participants were 199 registered male members of a large formal organization (Schwulenverband in Deutschland, SVD) within the German gay movement.[3] They first filled in a questionnaire in which we measured the collective, normative and reward incentives as well as their identification with gay men in general and SVD in particular. In a second questionnaire, administered about 12 months later, the same respondents reported their actual participation in various collective-protest activities of the gay movement during the last nine months. In line with the above-mentioned results concerning willingness to participate in various other social movements (e.g. Simon et al., 1998), a multiple regression analysis with the three incentives and the two identification indicators as predictors (all measured at Time 1) revealed that identification with SVD, but not identification with gay men, predicted frequency of actual subsequent participation (reported at Time 2). In addition, the normative incentive also received a significant and positive regression weight confirming the importance of the calculation pathway. Neither the collective incentive nor the reward incentive had a unique predictive value.

A number of additional findings are noteworthy. First, we observed no moderation or interaction effects involving the incentives, on the one hand, and the identification indicators, on the other. Second, neither group-level resentment (the affective component of experienced group-level relative deprivation) nor perceived group efficacy mediated the effect of identification with SVD on actual movement participation (cf. Kessler & Mummendey, 2001; Mummendey et al., 1999). Third, cross-lagged panel analyses suggested that the causal relationship between identification with SVD and participation in collective protest of the gay movement may be bi-directional. Reciprocal causation is indeed very plausible because, in addition to the mobilizing effect of collective identification, participation in collective protest typically involves experiences of intergroup contact, if not intergroup conflict, which increase the salience of one's collective identity. In addition, participation in collective protest is likely to engender feelings of agency and empowerment and thus likely to strengthen or even radicalize collective identity (Drury & Reicher, 1999, 2000; see also Klandermans, 2002).

Finally, the same study provided evidence that even identification with the broader recruitment category, which had so far proved ineffective as a unique predictor of (intended and actual) social movement participation, can have a direct mobilizing effect under specific circumstances. More than two years after the distribution of the first questionnaire, the German gay and lesbian movement started an initiative requesting legislation to allow same-sex marriage. As this initiative encountered fierce opposition from the conservative political parties in Germany, the movement launched a public campaign in support of same-sex marriage. We reasoned that this climate would promote a general politicization of gay identity and therefore conducted follow-up telephone interviews with former respondents and recorded their (self-reported) participation in collective action organized by the movement in support of the campaign for same-sex marriage. Interestingly, only identification with gay men in general, measured almost three years before the telephone interviews, now predicted movement participation. It thus appears that, in the highly politicized climate characterized by intergroup conflict and polarization as well as attempts on the part of the main protagonists to involve and enlist the general public (Simon & Klandermans, 2001), membership in the more inclusive social category of gay men emerged as the most meaningful self-aspect for self-interpretation and the associated collective identity as a powerful guideline for social behaviour.

In terms of self-categorization theory (Oakes et al., 1994; Turner et al., 1987), the measurement of the strength of identification with gay men several years ago most likely gauged respondents' rather stable readiness to adopt a collective identity as a gay man. This identity then lay dormant until political developments supplied a fitting social context in which it could eventually unfold its mobilizing power (and probably also provided sympathizers with the extra motivation to overcome critical barriers to participation in collective action). In times of peace, social movement organizations may routinely provide their members with mobilizing collective identities. In times of war, however, 'we are all in this together' so that membership in the more inclusive recruitment category is likely to provide the most meaningful, mobilizing and possibly also most empowering collective identity.

To conclude this section on identity and social movement participation, figure 7.3 summarizes how collective identity as a social psychological (meso-level) process plays an important mediating role in social movement participation. While collective identity itself is reflective of cleavages and

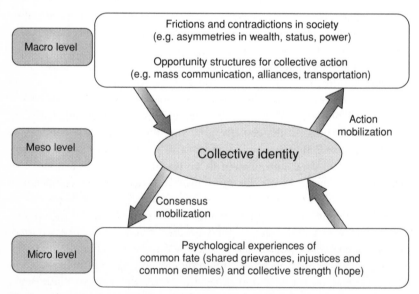

Figure 7.3 The role of collective identity as a mediating variable in social movement participation.

opportunities in the (macro-level) social structure, it facilitates consensus mobil-ization so that (macro-level) frictions and contradictions are translated into (micro-level) psychological experiences of common undesirable fate involving shared grievances, injustices and common enemies. Similarly, (macro-level) opportunities are translated into (micro-level) psychological experiences of collective strength and hope. Strengthened by this awareness of common fate and collective strength, collective identity then facilitates action mobilization so that, by way of social movement participation, people act on (macro-level) social structure and may eventually change it. Finally, though not explicitly depicted in figure 7.3, the underlying collective identity may in turn be strengthened in the process of participation due to an increase in cognitive salience of this identity and/or to increased feelings of agency and empower-ment. The strengthened collective identity then again promotes subsequent social movement participation.

Identity, Organizational Participation and Intragroup Cooperation

Social movement participation is a controversial form of social behaviour because it typically involves participation in collective action aimed at people that are perceived and treated as opponents or even enemies. However, social movement participation also comprises less controversial activities that revolve more around intragroup cooperation than intergroup conflict. Although most of the research reviewed in the preceding section focused on participation in collective-protest activities, in one study we also collected data concerning cooperation within a formal social movement organization.

More specifically, in the study of the German gay movement (Stürmer & Simon, in press), we explicitly differentiated between participation in collect-ive-protest activities directed outwards, such as public demonstrations, rallies or boycotts, and more inward-directed organizational participation, such as attending meetings, assuming office or participation in special task forces. Analyses of the effects of collective identification on organizational participa-tion yielded results that were very similar to those concerning collective protest reported above. A multiple regression analysis with the two identification indicators as well as the collective, normative and reward incentives as pre-dictors (all measured at Time 1) revealed that identification with the social movement organization SVD, but not identification with gay men in general, predicted frequency of actual subsequent organizational participation (reported at Time 2 about 12 months later). None of the three incentives emerged as a unique predictor of organizational participation (nor had they a collective predictive value when they were entered as a single block), nor did we observe any moderation or interaction effects involving the incentives, on the one hand, and the identification indicators, on the other. However, unlike the analyses concerning participation in collective protest, cross-lagged panel analyses provided little evidence for a bi-directional causal relationship between identification with SVD and organizational participation. This finding is not very surprising, though, because organizational participation rarely involves experiences of direct intergroup contact or even conflict which usually strengthen collective identification by way of increased cognitive salience of one's collective identity.

Evidence for the role of collective identification in intragroup cooperation has also been found outside social movement contexts in the more controlled environment of a laboratory experiment (Simon & Stürmer, 2003). Analogous to the experiment in which we demonstrated that collective identification plays an important mediating role between experiences of shared grievances rooted in intergroup relations and willingness to participate in collective protest (Simon et al., 1998, Study 2), this laboratory experiment examined the role of collective identification as a mediator between experiences of intragroup treatment and intragroup cooperation. It was inspired by procedural justice research that indicates that a respectful treatment (i.e. a fair, trustworthy and dignified treatment) by authorities strengthens commitment to the organization or group that the authority represents (Lind & Tyler, 1988; Tyler & Blader, 2000; Tyler & Lind, 1992; Tyler et al., 1997). Analogously, we reasoned that respectful treatment by fellow group members should be an important intragroup antecedent of collective identification which in turn should promote intragroup cooperation.

The experiment ($N = 163$) was allegedly concerned with cooperation in virtual (computer-mediated) groups. Groups of five to eight university students participated in each experimental session. Group members were seated at individual computer terminals separated by screens and all interaction among them took place via electronic mail. Their collective task was to develop suggestions about how to improve teaching and education at their university and to design a poster to present the suggestions to the university administration. Respectful versus disrespectful intragroup treatment was manipulated by way of (dis)respectful commentaries made allegedly by fellow group members concerning the participant's contribution to the group task.[4] In reality, these commentaries were pre-programmed. They had been fabricated on the basis of careful pretesting in order to convey either respect or disrespect, but as little explicit positive or negative evaluation as possible.

At the same time, positive versus negative intragroup evaluation was also manipulated as a second independent variable by providing research participants with explicit evaluative performance feedback allegedly from the same fellow group members. The order in which (respectful vs. disrespectful) intragroup treatment and (positive vs. negative) intragroup evaluation were manipulated was counterbalanced. In line with the procedural justice literature, no strong effects were expected for intragroup evaluation because this variable is primarily task-related and less reflective of the quality of the self-ingroup relationship, whereas intragroup treatment has typically been found to be more directly relevant to relational or identity concerns (Smith et al., 1998, p. 478; Tyler & Blader, 2000, pp. 89–102).

Both identification with one's virtual group and (intended) intragroup cooperation in the experimental session (i.e. willingness to take on extra tasks in the group such as structuring the discussion, writing down goal agreements or sketching the poster) were measured with reliable multi-item scales (Cronbach's $\alpha \geq .82$). The results confirmed our expectations. Respectful as opposed to disrespectful intragroup treatment significantly increased collective identification as well as (intended) intragroup cooperation, and collective identification at least partially mediated the effect of treatment on cooperation. Intragroup evaluation had no effects, nor did it qualify the main effects of intragroup treatment. No effects were found on a measure of (intended) intragroup cooperation outside the experimental session.

Moreover, path analyses using the manipulation check measure of perceived intragroup treatment as the antecedent variable (and the manipulation check measure of perceived intragroup evaluation as a control variable) actually revealed a full mediation of the effect of perceived (dis)respectful intragroup treatment on intragroup cooperation by way of collective identification (see figure 7.4). Analogous analyses with intragroup cooperation outside the experimental session as the criterion uncovered a similar, but weaker, mediation effect of collective identification, but also an unmediated negative effect of intragroup treatment. The latter finding suggests that, once achieved, intragroup respect may entice group members 'to rest on their laurels' if perceived intragroup respect is not translated into collective identification. Taken together, this experiment further illuminates the mobilizing power of collective identity. It demonstrates that, if we respect a person and treat her as one of us, she views herself as one of us and is likely to act as one of us, often irrespective of the immediate positive or negative outcomes such as explicit positive or negative performance evaluation. Thus, collective identity not only promises (intragroup) respect (see chapters 3 and 5), it also results from experiences of respect (see also chapter 6). Experienced respect pushes collective identity forward as much as promises of and hopes for respect may pull it forward. More generally, the experiment demonstrates how collective identity is shaped in the immediate (meso-level) interaction situation and how it transforms the experiences which one has in such situations into intentions to act.

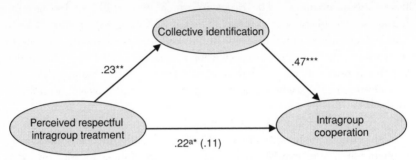

Figure 7.4 Path diagram (controlling for perceived intragroup evaluation) of the effect of perceived (dis)respectful intragroup treatment on intended intragroup cooperation by way of collective identification. Coefficients are (standardized) regression weights.

[a]Regression weight from the analysis without the mediator; the regression weight from the analysis with the mediator is given inside parentheses. $^*p < .05$, $^{**}p < .01$, $^{***}p < .001$.

Source: From Simon & Stürmer, 2003, Figure 2. Copyright © 2003 by the Society for Personality and Social Psychology, Inc. Reprinted by Permission of Sage Publications, Inc.

Identity and Volunteerism

I want to conclude this chapter with a study that illustrates the mobilizing power of collective identity with regard to yet another important form of social behaviour, namely volunteerism (Simon, Stürmer & Steffens, 2000). Volunteerism is generally considered a socially desirable, pro-social form of action in which people actively seek out opportunities to help others in need and make considerable commitments to offer assistance, often in stressful circumstances and for long periods of time (Bierhoff, 2002; Omoto & Snyder, 1995; Snyder & Omoto, 2001).

From an identity perspective, AIDS volunteerism, at least in modern Western societies, is a particularly interesting phenomenon because it involves a number of different, often mutually exclusive, identities. More specifically, at the time when we conducted our study (summer 1997), gay men were (and still are) the largest subgroup among people living with AIDS or HIV in Germany, while both gay and heterosexual people were engaged in AIDS volunteerism. In terms of the self-aspect 'sexual orientation', the recipients of AIDS volunteerism were thus mostly ingroup members for gay volunteers, but outgroup members for heterosexual volunteers. Because collective identification usually fosters favourable treatment of ingroup members and discriminatory treatment of outgroup members (Tajfel & Turner, 1986; Mummendey & Otten,

2001), we hypothesized that, for gays, willingness to volunteer (i.e. willingness to help ingroup members) should increase with stronger collective identification in terms of sexual orientation. For heterosexuals, however, willingness to volunteer (i.e. willingness to help outgroup members) was expected to decrease with stronger collective identification. We also examined the relationship between strength of individual identity and willingness to volunteer. In line with the assumption that identification as an individual counteracts differential ingroup–outgroup treatment (Gaertner et al., 1989; Turner et al., 1987), we expected that, for gays, identification as an individual and willingness to volunteer would be negatively related, whereas a positive relationship was expected for heterosexuals. Finally, because all research participants were registered members of the German AIDS volunteer service organization AIDS-Hilfe (AH), we also expected identification with this particular organization to be positively related to willingness to volunteer, irrespective of sexual orientation.

Forty-six gay and 54 heterosexual members of the target organization (AH) completed a questionnaire containing the critical variables. Multiple regression analyses with willingness to participate in 10 future volunteer activities (Cronbach's $\alpha = .80$) as the criterion confirmed our predictions (see table 7.2).

Table 7.2 Regression analyses with willingness to engage in AIDS volunteerism as criterion

	Identification with AIDS volunteer service organization	Identification as individual	Identification with ingroup
Homosexuals			
ß	0.30	−0.29	0.41
t	2.19*	−2.11*	3.06***
	$R^2 = .27$, $F(3, 42) = 5.16$, $p < .01$.		
Heterosexuals			
ß	0.31	0.24	−0.20
t	2.26*	1.85*	−1.44(*)
	$R^2 = .16$, $F(3, 50) = 3.16$, $p < .05$.		

(*) $p < .10$, * $p < .05$, ** $p < .01$ (one-tailed t-tests)

Source: From Simon et al., 2000, Table 4. Copyright © 2000 by the Society for Personality and Social Psychology, Inc. Reprinted by Permission of Sage Publications, Inc.

In line with the other research reported in this chapter, organizational identification was positively related to willingness to volunteer, both in the gay sample and in the heterosexual sample. Also as expected, in the gay sample, collective identification in terms of sexual orientation was a positive predictor, whereas identification as an individual emerged as a negative predictor. The opposite antagonism was found in the heterosexual sample. Thus, in both samples, collective identity (in terms of sexual orientation) and individual identity seemed to push willingness to volunteer in opposite directions, but the specific form of antagonism depended on whether the potential helper and recipient of help shared a common group membership or belonged to two different groups. However, in keeping with the elaboration of the relationship between individual and collective identities in chapters 3 and 4, such an antagonism at the level of behavioural effects does not necessarily imply an incompatibility at the level of self-interpretation. In fact, collective identification in terms of sexual orientation and identification as an individual were uncorrelated in this study. To use an analogy, the observation that hunger and thirst prompt different behaviours (i.e. eating or drinking, respectively) does not imply that hunger and thirst are incompatible experiences.

It is also noteworthy that the results did not change when more specific motives, such as gaining knowledge about AIDS or expressing one's humanitarian values (Omoto & Snyder, 1995), were included as additional predictors. That is, identification processes contributed to (or detracted from) willingness to volunteer above and beyond more specific incentives. It thus seems that the dual-pathway model developed in the context of social movement participation, with its identification and calculation pathways, is also applicable to volunteerism. However, it may be useful to broaden the identification pathway in order to include individual-identity processes as well. Our results suggest that identification as an individual can promote pro-social behaviour in favour of people that are otherwise more likely to be the recipients of mistreatment (i.e. outgroup members). Though not tested in this research, it stands to reason that this desirable effect is primarily due to the more universalistic (independence) component of individual identity (Simmel, 1908, 1984; Simon & Kampmeier, 2001, pp. 210–11; see also chapter 3). In so far as this component prevails in individual identity, there should be less reason to lament over increasing individualism in modern society.

Summary

In this chapter, I have examined the influence of identity on various forms of social behaviour. The major part of the chapter was concerned with the role of collective identity in social movement participation, which is an important collective strategy for members of disadvantaged groups to improve their lot. Analysing the various steps towards actual social movement participation, I examined how a strong collective identity increases the likelihood that one becomes part of the mobilization potential, becomes a target of mobilization attempts, develops the motivation to participate and actually overcomes barriers to participation in social movement activities such as collective protest. I argued that collective identity plays an important mediating role in the mobilization and participation process in that it connects macro- and micro-level antecedents of social movement participation and transforms these into collective action aimed at initiating macro-level social changes. More specifically, I reviewed research on several different new social movements, such as the older people's movement, the gay movement and the fat acceptance movement, and concluded that collective identification is another important pathway to social movement participation, in addition to and largely independent of the calculation of specific costs and benefits. This conclusion was supported not only by correlational data from cross-sectional designs, but also by data from experimental and longitudinal designs. Our programme of research further demonstrated that it is usually the specific social movement or its formal organization that provides its members with a mobilizing collective identity. However, it was also found that, under particularly politicizing circumstances, the collective identity derived from membership in the broader social category of aggrieved people, from which the social movement (organization) typically recruits its members, can also emerge as a unique mobilizing force.

A similar role was uncovered for collective identity concerning several other forms of social behaviour that are less controversial than participation in collective protest and often even considered pro-social. For instance, our research suggests that collective identification with the social movement organization facilitates not only participation in outward-directed collective-protest activities, but also more inward-directed organizational participation. More generally, collective identification was found to foster (intended) intragroup cooperation and volunteerism in favour of the ingroup and its members. Examining the role of intragroup respect in collective-identity processes and intragroup cooperation, I further argued that collective identity and its mobilizing power are also critically shaped by intragroup relations in the immediate (meso-level) interaction situation. Finally, in the context of AIDS volunteerism, I also discussed the role of individual identity in social action and suggested that identification as an individual can promote pro-social behaviour in favour of outgroup members that are otherwise likely targets of mistreatment.

NOTES

1. Klandermans (1997, p. 26) refers to this incentive as the 'social' incentive (or social motive). Because the other incentives can also involve costs and benefits that are social, though perhaps in a different sense (e.g. gaining or losing social status, making new friends), I prefer the term 'normative' to the term 'social' in this context.
2. When not reported in the original publications, the findings discussed in this chapter are based on subsequent re-analyses of the original data (see also Stürmer et al., 2003).
3. When we started this research SVD was an almost exclusively male organization with less than 5% female members. It later adopted a more inclusive policy and changed its name to 'Lesben-und Schwulenverband in Deutschland' (LSVD).
4. Examples of respectful and disrespectful commentaries are respectively: 'Your suggestions are in. I find them all interesting and will check them carefully, before I come up with a final opinion. Hence it will take some time, please understand, I will try hard' and 'I have read your suggestions, because I have to. But actually I'd rather have done something else. Concerning this topic, I am pretty opinionated.'

Chapter 8

Conclusions and Future Directions

This book is a report on my scientific inquiry into identity – its foundations, dynamics and outgrowths. The inquiry started from, and was directed by, the basic premise that identity results from interaction in the social world and in turn guides interaction in the social world. As shown in chapter 1, this premise, which ascribes identity a critical mediating role, is consistent with insights provided by anthropological and cultural studies concerning the social conditions of human existence as well as with insights provided by the disciplines of philosophy and cognitive neuroscience concerning human consciousness. The review of sociological and psychological contributions to the analysis of identity presented in chapter 2 then laid open the relational, socially constructed and socially structured nature of identity. Also, it further specified the function of identity as a crucial social-cognitive mediator that enables people to make sense of, and to act in, their social worlds as self-conscious and motivated agents.

The theoretical heart of the book beats in chapter 3. It contains the outline for an integrative social psychological approach to identity which revolves around a self-aspect model of identity (SAMI). Undoubtedly, SAMI was inspired by social identity or self-categorization theory (Tajfel & Turner, 1986; Turner et al., 1987) in important ways, and I would therefore like to consider it an offspring of the social identity perspective. However, SAMI enabled me to approach important (under-researched) identity issues in novel and promising, and sometimes also provocative, ways. In particular, it helped me refine the concept of individual identity and clarify the relation between individual identity and collective identity in modern society.

In line with SAMI, the empirical research reported in chapter 4 started with the working assumption that individual identity is predicated on de-centrated self-interpretation involving a complex configuration of multiple self-aspects, whereas collective identity results from self-interpretation that is focused or concentrated on a single socially shared (social categorical) self-aspect. It was indeed found that factors or variables that were assumed to be conducive to either the de-centration or concentration process (e.g. low or high personal importance of a self-aspect) fostered individual identity or collective identity, respectively. So far, the research thus pointed to, and was in fact guided by the assumption of, an antagonistic relation between individual identity and collective identity. That is, these identity variants seemed to function as opponents, with each trying to drive away the other from the battlefield of self-interpretation. Soon, however, interesting anomalies emerged. They prompted further research which revealed a more dynamic interplay of individual and collective identity including both antagonistic and harmonious interrelations. It was shown that, under appropriate circumstances, the two identity variants can be mutually compatible and may even operate as partners. I further argued that individuality or individual identity functions as an ideological or cultural ideal in modern society so that, rather than driving individual identity completely away, (readiness to adopt a) collective identity often presupposes at least some level of individual identity. In this sense, one may say that collective identity is a provocation not only for, but also of, individual identity.

Research on (numerical) minority and majority groups turned out to be particularly informative as to the functioning of individual and collective identities and their interrelation. It appears that, in many ways, the minority group approximates the paradigmatic case of a social group which provides its members with an ideal-type collective identity, whereas the majority group offers fertile soil for individual identity. The respective consequences for minority and majority members' cognition, affect and behaviour were reviewed in chapter 5. Overall, it appears that collective identity is usually in the limelight for members of minority groups and individual identity in the limelight for members of majority groups. However, although minority members' individual identity and majority members' collective identity may be in the dark, these identity variants are not necessarily inactive or at least they can easily be awakened. The systematic interplay between individual and collective identities observed in minority-majority contexts (see chapters 4 and 5) clearly supports this conclusion. Because minority and majority groups exhibit such a clear dividing line between identities in the limelight and those in the shade, they should also be a promising starting-point for a systematic analysis of the role of implicit identities and their interplay with explicit identities, which is an important task for future research on identity.

Identity in the context of intercultural contact also deserves high priority on social psychologists' future research agenda. The question of cultural identity, including issues such as the preservation or change of one's own cultural identity as well as respect or disrespect for other people's cultural identities, is of increasing relevance to modern society owing to processes of globalization and mass (im)migration. These developments offer a challenging research context in which social psychology can prove its capacity to contribute to evidence-based social intervention and problem solving in direct contact with the hopes and worries of an increasing number of people. At the same time, it is an important opportunity for social psychologists, especially those interested in identity, to further develop and refine their conceptual and methodological tools. The analysis presented in chapter 6, which is no more than a first step in this direction, highlighted the advantages of an articulation of social psychology with cross-cultural psychology and pointed to the pivotal role of collective identity, both as a means and an end, in the process of social integration as well as in the resistance against immigration.

In chapter 7, I discussed the role of identity in social behaviour directed towards goals that transcend the individual (self-)interest of the person. I demonstrated that collective identity is an important determinant of participation in collective action (e.g. social movement participation) and that it has a motivating power that seems to be independent of specific cost–benefit calculations. I suggested considering collective identity a meso-level variable because it is critically shaped in the immediate interaction situation where influences from multiple levels (i.e. from macro, meso and micro levels) meet and articulate. As a mediating variable, collective identity then translates these influences into action, or at least, functions as an important link in a chain of mediating processes. Although the focus in chapter 7 was clearly on collective identity, there was also some indication from research on volunteerism that individual identity may play a similar role.

After this brief recap, I wish to conclude the book with some thoughts on two identity themes that, although touched upon in several of the preceding chapters, deserve more thorough investigation in the future. These are (1) the relationship between identity and action and (2) the relationship between identity and power. To be sure, they are not the only themes that have been dealt with incompletely in the book. For instance, although chapters 4 to 7 contain ample evidence for the various identity functions proposed in chapter 3, a systematic analysis thereof is still outstanding. The reason why I focus on 'identity and action' and 'identity and power' in my concluding comments is that I expect these themes to underlie and guide my own research in years to come.

Identity and Action

The research discussed in this book strongly suggests that identity is a reliable predictor of social behaviour. The role of identity in social behaviour was examined especially in the collective realm, where collective identification turned out to be an important determinant of collective action, including both intergroup and intragroup behaviour (see especially chapter 7; but also chapters 5 and 6). However, there was also evidence for a second pathway to collective action. In addition to, and independent of, collective identification, the expected costs and benefits of collective action affected behavioural intentions as well as actual behaviour. Accordingly, I suggested a dual-pathway model with collective identification and calculation of costs and benefits as two independent psychological routes to collective action. This dual-pathway model of collective action, or more precisely, this variant of a dual-pathway model of collective action, implies that the collective-identification and calculation pathways can operate simultaneously and in parallel, that they can be singly sufficient, but also that a weak impulse from one pathway can be compensated by a strong impulse from the other. Because the particular contexts in which the research was conducted, as well as the specific methodology that was used (e.g. regression models based on 'between-subjects' co-variation of variables; see Schmitz, 2000), may have favoured this particular variant of a dual-pathway model, it is useful to also consider alternative variants. In addition to the independence variant, a dominance variant and a compatibility variant seem plausible (and possibly others as well; see Gilbert, 1999).

A dominance variant of the dual-pathway model is conceivable that would predict that people who strongly identify with their group engage in collective action without paying much attention to possible costs and benefits of their actions. This is not to say that such action has no goal or direction. After all, it is action on behalf of the ingroup and thus in the service of one's ingroup's interests. Rather, the important point is that strong collective identification should be enacted without much on-line calculation of costs and benefits. For example, strong collective identification could make ingroup norms highly accessible which then guide behaviour largely irrespective of costs and benefits (Haslam, 2001; Stürmer et al., 2002; Turner et al., 1987). Strong collective identification may thus give access to ready-made choices (which may partly be the crystallized products of past calculation processes) and produce die-hards who support their group in word and deed against all odds. Conversely, under conditions of weak collective identification, the calculation process should take over and its dominance should be closely related to individual identity which also comes to the fore under such conditions. Whereas collective identity prescribes conformity in line with the one-dimensional differentiation between 'us' and 'them' and between 'our interests' and 'their interests' and thus affords simple behavioural guidelines, individual identity reflects and highlights one's embeddedness in a more complex network of interdependent individuals. This complexity necessitates more careful deliberation of one's interests and actions in relation to the interests and actions of multiple others, and hence a 'calculative spirit' (Weber, 1978). Note that this dominance variant of the dual-pathway model does not exclude the possibility that the calculative spirit associated with individual identity also considers collective costs and benefits. It may very well do so if, but only if, such costs and benefits are also of instrumental relevance to individual identity. For example, despite low identification with her current company, an employee may still work very hard for the company because its success also increases her chance of receiving an offer from a better-paying company.

Turning to the compatibility variant of the dual-pathway model, it is also conceivable that the interplay of identification and calculation processes follows a compatibility or matching principle with regard to the (collective or individual) level on which these processes can operate. More specifically, strong collective identification may foster and actually merge with the consideration of collective costs and benefits and simultaneously lead to the neglect of individual costs and benefits, whereas strong identification as an individual may result in the exclusive consideration of individual costs and benefits. Strictly speaking, the dual-*pathway* model then turns into a dual-*level* model, with identification and calculation processes being closely interwoven, if not identical, on each level. I have gone to some pains in this book to elaborate the distinction between collective and individual identity, but the compatibility variant hinges also on a sound differentiation of collective costs and benefits versus individual costs and benefits. More conceptual and empirical work is necessary in the future to advance also our understanding of the individual–collective distinction in the realm of costs and benefits. Azzi's (1992) differentiation between 'individual-level resources' that are redistributable among individuals and can be consumed by them (e.g. food or money) and 'group-level resources' that are of a more intangible or symbolic nature (e.g. religious holidays or official language) seems to provide a promising starting-point for progress in this direction.

Two other issues are noteworthy. The first concerns the differential nature of collective-identification and calculation processes, the second concerns their interrelation. First, especially with respect to the independence and dominance variants of the dual-pathway model, it may be tempting to interpret the distinction between collective-identification and calculation processes in terms of social psychological dual-process theories that distinguish between automatic, spontaneous or heuristic processes, on the one hand, and controlled, strategic or systematic processes, on the other (for an overview, see Chaiken & Trope, 1999). For example, strong collective identification could be viewed as (indicative of) a highly accessible positive attitude towards one's ingroup which biases the perception or definition of the situation and thus automatically elicits approach or avoidance behaviour on behalf of the ingroup without much deliberate reflection or calculation. Conversely, when calculating costs and benefits, people can be expected to engage in a more effortful analysis of the 'raw data' (Fazio, 1990; Fazio & Towles-Schwen, 1999).

However, this interpretation has its limits because the calculation process is not without automatic components, nor does collective identification render cognitive control necessarily superfluous. For instance, the evaluative meaning of 'raw data' used for the calculation of costs and benefits usually becomes automatically available to the information processor (Ajzen & Fishbein, 2000), and cognitive control is needed to align one's concrete actions with the more abstract group norms prescribed by one's collective identity, especially in the absence of relevant collective habits or traditions. The articulation of the (collective-)identification–calculation distinction with the distinction between automatic and controlled processes is a challenge for future research which will certainly benefit from further elaboration of the notion of automaticity and its various aspects (Bargh, 1989) and a more fine-grained analysis of the different phases of self-regulation (Gollwitzer, 1990).

Finally, although the discussion of possible variants of the dual-pathway model of collective action suggests that collective-identification and calcula-tion processes can have independent or even mutually exclusive effects on social behaviour, I propose that both processes are closely intertwined in a more fundamental sense. They are fundamentally intertwined because the values on the basis of which people define costs and benefits are part and parcel of people's more fundamental, and often implicit, collective identities. If I know who I am, I also know what I want (and possibly also vice versa). For example, identity as a socialist provides people with a set of values (e.g. equality and solidarity) which in turn enable them to define what are important costs and benefits for them (e.g. losing or winning comrades) and what aren't (e.g. losing or winning money). Fundamental collective identities are also fertile soil for the emergence of more specific and (socially) less inclusive collective identities. My socialist identity may induce me to become a member of a specific left-wing political party, and at least to some extent this choice may be a calculated one based on my beliefs as to what party is most instrumental in achieving goals in line with my socialist values (Simon & Klein, 2003). Although never completely independent of more inclusive or fundamental collective identification processes, identification with the less inclusive group or collective unfolds its own mobilizing power which may eventually combine, in various ways, with that of the immediate calculation process to guide social behaviour. Again, the calculation process and the underlying values point to the involvement of implicit and more fundamental collective identities, with the complexity of the calculation process reflecting the multiplicity of implicitly involved collective identities.

In conclusion, if people know what or who they are, they also know – one (path)way or the other – what they have or want to do. Because the opposite seems to be true as well (Bem, 1972), it appears that, in the final analysis, to be is to do and to do is to be (Stets & Burke, 2000).

Identity and Power

The analysis of identity presented in this book has repeatedly led, and required, me to consider power issues. For example, the cognitive–affective crossfire which turns people with a minority identity into unhappy group members seems to be particularly fierce for members of powerless minority groups. Conversely, majority members often enjoy themselves as happy individuals, and this may be so especially when they can rely on an implicit power advantage (chapter 5). The role of identity in phenomena such as intergroup discrimination and (self-)stereotyping also needs to be analysed with an eye on power. Otherwise the role of identity is both overestimated and underestimated.

As argued in chapter 5, outgroup discrimination or ingroup favouritism is a function not only of the search for a positive collective identity, but also of the opportunities granted by the power structure (see also Mummendey & Otten, 2001, p. 127). Similarly, unfavourable self-stereotyping on the part of members of disadvantaged minority groups is not simply the result of 'immaculate' collective-identity construction, but of collective-identity construction constrained by the stereotypes held by powerful outgroups. However, power not only affects, but is also affected by, identity and its functioning. Intergroup discrimination and (self-)stereotyping are again good examples. Both are identity-driven phenomena that contribute to changes or stability in the power hierarchy. Depending on the position of one's ingroup in the power hierarchy, ingroup favouritism may be a direct attempt either to change or to defend this hierarchy, while stereotyping as well as self-stereotyping contributes to the (de-)legitimization of, and the (de-)mobilization for, this struggle. The interrelation of identity issues and power issues became most evident probably in the discussion of the role of identity in intercultural contexts (chapter 6) and in social movement participation (chapter 7). In both cases, I dealt with struggles in which identity and power are closely intertwined in that one serves as a resource or means to attain the other as an end, and vice versa.

How identity is shaped by power and how power is exercised by identity are two important questions, among others, that deserve more systematic attention in future social psychological research. With regard to the first question, I suggest, as a starting-point for further inquiry, that identity depends on power in a fundamental sense. Because no one is an island, people and their identities need recognition and respect from others (James, 1890/1950; Moscovici, 1976). However, in order not to be at the transient mercy of other people, recognition of and respect for one's identity presuppose entitlements or rights as a more or less explicitly codified or institutionalized basis, which in turn need to be backed up by power. Therefore, identity ultimately depends on power and is shaped by power relations between and within social groups.

Turning to the second question, identity can be involved in the exercise of power in many ways. Because identity is shaped by power relations, power manifests itself in identity which then either contributes to the reproduction of the power structure or becomes a source of resistance (Tajfel, 1978b, 1981). Another perhaps more interesting, because more subtle, way in which power is exercised by means of identity has to do with the role of identity placeholders discussed in chapter 3. Different people can fill the cognitive placeholder for the collective identity derived from the same group membership quite differently, but still share the assumption of a deeper underlying and unifying, though not necessarily known, identity essence. This allows fuzzy identity definitions and symbolizations that gloss over conflicting opinions and interests within the group (Edelman, 1977; Wimmer, 2002, pp. 31–2). Drawing on conformity processes fuelled by collective identification, 'entrepreneurs of identity' can thus exercise subtle, but still highly effective disciplinary power over other ingroup members (Reicher & Hopkins, 1996a, 1996b). This way of exercising power should be particularly subtle and effective because it is very likely perceived as influence rather than coercion, with the latter being usually associated with the exercise of power by and over outgroups (Haslam, 2001). It seems to me that the only antidote against (mis)use of such intragroup power is a system or culture of participation within the group that not only symbolizes democracy (Edelman, 1977, p. 126), but enables, encourages and respects the contribution of each group member to all aspects of group life (Simon & Stürmer, 2003).

In conclusion, a complete analysis of identity definitely requires articulation with an analysis of power. In this sense, and certainly other senses as well, this book is admittedly incomplete and should be seen as an interim report, but hopefully also as a useful springboard for future scientific inquiries into identity. In any case, I have not written this book in order to then stop working.

References

Abrams, D., & Hogg, M. A. (1988). Comments on the motivational status of self-esteem in social identity and intergroup discrimination. *European Journal of Social Psychology*, *18*, 317–334.

Adam, B. D. (1987). *The rise of a gay and lesbian movement (Twayne's social movements series)*. Boston: Twayne Publishers.

Ajzen, I., & Fishbein, M. (1980). *Understanding attitudes and predicting social behavior*. Englewood Cliffs, NJ: Prentice Hall.

Ajzen, I., & Fishbein, M. (2000). Attitudes and the attitude–behavior relation: Reasoned and automatic processes. In W. Stroebe & M. Hewstone (Eds.), *European Review of Social Psychology* (Vol. 11, pp. 1–33). Chichester, England: Wiley.

Ajzen, I., & Madden, T. J. (1986). Prediction of goal-directed behavior: Attitudes, intentions, and perceived behavioral control. *Journal of Experimental Social Psychology*, *22*, 453–474.

Allport, F. H. (1924). *Social psychology*. New York: Houghton Mifflin.

Allport, F. H. (1962). A structuronomic conception of behavior: Individual and collective. *Journal of Abnormal and Social Psychology*, *64*, 3–30.

Allport, G. W. (1955). *Becoming* (pp. 36–56). New Haven, CT: Yale University Press.

Allport, G. W. (1961). *Pattern and growth in personality* (pp. Chapter 6). New York: Holt, Rinehart, and Winston.

Allport, G. W. (1968). Is the concept of self necessary? In C. Gordon & K. J. Gergen (Eds.), *The self in social interaction:* (Vol.1) Classic and contemporary perspectives (pp. 25–32). New York: Wiley.

Allport, G. W. (1954/1979). *The nature of prejudice*. Reading, MA: Addison-Wesley Publ. Company.

Anderson, B. (1983). *Imagined communities*. London: Verso.

Andersen, S. M., Klatzky, R. L., & Murray, J. (1990). Traits and social stereotypes: Efficiency differences in social information processing. *Journal of Personality and Social Psychology*, *59*, 192–201.

Aron, A., Aron, E. N., & Norman, C. (2001). Self-expansion model of motivation and cognition in close relationships and beyond. In M. Clark & G. J. O. Fletcher (Eds.),

Blackwell Handbook of Social Psychology: Interpersonal Processes. Oxford, England: Basil Blackwell.

Ashmore, R. D., & Jussim, L. (1997). Self and identity. Fundamental issues. In R. D. Ashmore & L. Jussim (Eds.), *Rutgers series on self and social identity* (Vol. 1). Oxford: University Press.

Assmann, A. (1994). Zum Problem der Identität aus kulturwissenschaftlicher Sicht. In R. Lindner (Ed.), *Die Wiederkehr des Regionalen. Über neue Formen kultureller Identität.* Frankfurt: Campus Verlag.

Aufderheide, B. (2000). *Zum Einfluss der Wahrnehmung von Ähnlichkeiten und Unterschieden zwischen Personen auf die aktuelle Selbst-Interpretation.* Unveröffentlichte Dissertation, Universität Kiel. (*The influence of perceived interpersonal similarities and differences on self-interpretation.* Unpublished dissertation, University of Kiel.)

Azzi, A. E. (1992). Procedural justice and the allocation of power in intergroup relations: Studies in the United States and South Africa. *Personality and Social Psychology Bulletin, 18,* 736–747.

Azzi, A. E. (1993). Implicit and category-based allocations of decision-making power in majority–minority relations. *Journal of Experimental Social Psychology, 29,* 203–228.

Bandura, A. (1997). *Self-efficacy: The exercise of control.* New York: Freeman.

Barchas, P. R. (1986). A sociophysiological orientation to small groups. In E. J. Lawler (Ed.), *Advances in group processes. A research annual* (Vol. 3, pp. 209–246). Greenwich, CT: JAI Press Inc.

Bargh, J. A. (1989). Conditional automaticity: Varieties of automatic influence in social perception and cognition. In J. S. Uleman & J. A. Bargh (Eds.), *Unintended thought* (pp. 3–51). New York: Guilford Press.

Barsalou, L. W. (1987). The instability of graded structure: Implications for the nature of concepts. In U. Neisser (Ed.), *Concepts and conceptual development: Ecological and intellectual factors in categorization* (pp. 101–140). Cambridge, England: Cambridge University Press.

Bassili, J. N., & Provencal, A. (1988). Perceiving minorities: A factor-analytic approach. *Personality and Social Psychology Bulletin, 14,* 5–15.

Baumeister, R. F. (1986). *Identity: Cultural change and the struggle for the self.* New York: Oxford University Press.

Baumeister, R. F., & Leary, M. R. (1995). The need to belong: Desire for interpersonal attachments as a fundamental human motivation. *Psychological Bulletin, 117,* 497–529.

Beck, U. (1994). Jenseits von Stand und Klasse? (Beyond rank and class?). In U. Beck & E. Beck-Gernsheim (Eds.), *Riskante Freiheiten* (Risky freedoms) (pp. 43–60). Frankfurt am Main, Germany: Suhrkamp.

Bell, D. (1973). *The coming of post-industrial society.* New York: Basic Books.

Bem, D. J. (1972). Self-perception theory. In L. Berkowitz (Ed.), *Advances in experimental social psychology* (Vol. 6, pp. 1–62). New York: Academic Press.

Berry, J. W. (1997). Immigration, acculturation, and adaption. *Applied Psychology: An International Review, 46,* 5–68.

Berry, J. W. (2001). A psychology of immigration. *Journal of Social Issues, 57,* 615–631.

Bettencourt, B. A., Charlton, K., & Kernahan, C. (1997). Numerical representation of groups in cooperative settings: Social orientation effects on ingroup bias. *Journal of Experimental Social Psychology, 33*, 630–659.

Bettencourt, B. A., Miller, N., & Hume, D. L. (1999). Effects of numerical representation within cooperative settings: Examining the role of salience in in-group favouritism. *British Journal of Social Psychology, 38*, 265–287.

Bierhoff, H. W. (2002). *Prosocial behaviour*. Hove: Psychology Press.

Biernat, M., & Vescio, T. K. (1993). Categorization and stereotyping: Effects of group context on memory and social judgment. *Journal of Experimental Social Psychology, 29*, 166–202.

Billig, M. (1995). *Banal nationalism*. London: Sage.

Blumer, H. (1969). *Symbolic interactionism: Perspective and method*. Englewood Cliffs, NJ: Prentice-Hall.

Bodenhausen, G. V., Macrae, C. N., & Sherman, J. S. (1999). On the dialectics of discrimination: Dual processes in social stereotyping. In S. Chaiken & Y. Trope (Eds.), *Dual-process theories in social psychology* (pp. 271–290). New York: Guilford Press.

Branscombe, N. R., Schmitt, M. T., & Harvey, R. D. (1999). Perceiving pervasive discrimination among African-Americans: Implications for group identification and well-being. *Journal of Personality and Social Psychology, 77*, 135–149.

Breakwell, G. M. (1986). *Coping with threatened identities*. London: Methuen.

Brewer, M. B. (1979). In-group bias in the minimal intergroup situation: A cognitive-motivational analysis. *Psychological Bulletin, 86*, 307–324.

Brewer, M. B. (1988). A dual process model of impression formation. In T. K. Srull & R. S. Wyer (Eds.), *Advances in social cognition* (Vol. 1, pp. 1–36). Hillsdale, NJ: Erlbaum.

Brewer, M. B. (1991). The social self: On being the same and different at the same time. *Personality and Social Psychology Bulletin, 17*, 475–482.

Brewer, M. B. (1998). Category-based vs. person-based perception in intergroup contexts. In W. Stroebe & M. Hewstone (Eds.), *European Review of Social Psychology* (Vol. 9, pp. 77–106). Chichester, England: Wiley.

Brewer, M. B., & Gaertner, S. L. (2001). Toward reduction of prejudice: Intergroup contact and social categorization. In R. Brown & S. L. Gaertner (Eds.), *Blackwell Handbook of Social Psychology: Intergroup processes* (pp. 238–257). Oxford, UK: Blackwell Publishers Inc.

Brewer, M. B., & Harasty Feinstein, A. S. (1999). Dual processes in the cognitive representation of persons and social categories. In S. Chaiken & Y. Trope (Eds.), *Dual-process theories in social psychology* (pp. 255–270). New York: Guilford Press.

Brewer, M. B., Manzi, J. M., & Shaw, J. S. (1993). In-group identification as a function of depersonalization, distinctiveness, and status. *Psychological Science, 4*, 88–92.

Brewer, M. B., & Miller, N. (1984). Beyond the contact hypothesis: Theoretical perspectives on desegregation. In N. Miller & M. B. Brewer (Eds.), *Groups in contact: The psychology of desegregation*. New York: Academic Press.

Brewer, M. B., & Roccas, S. (2001). Individual values, social identity, and optimal distinctiveness. In C. Sedikides & M. B. Brewer (Eds.), *Individual self, relational self, and collective self*. Philadelphia, PA: Taylor & Francis, Inc.

Brewer, M. B., & Silver, M. (1978). Ingroup bias as a function of task characteristics. *European Journal of Social Psychology, 8,* 393–400.

Brewer, M. B., & Weber, J. G. (1994). Self-evaluation effects of interpersonal versus intergroup social comparison. *Journal of Personality and Social Psychology, 66,* 268–275.

Brewer, M. B., Weber, J. G., & Carini, B. (1995). Person memory in intergroup contexts: Categorization versus individuation. *Journal of Personality and Social Psychology, 69,* 29–40.

Brown, R. (1986). *Social Psychology (2nd ed.).* New York: The Free Press.

Brown, R. J. (1995). *Prejudice: Its social psychology.* Oxford, England: Blackwell Publishers Ltd.

Brown, R. J. (2000). Social identity theory: Past achievements, current problems and future challenges. *European Journal of Social Psychology, 30,* 745–778.

Brown, R. J., Hinkle, S., Ely, P. G., Fox-Cardamone, L., Maras, P., & Taylor, L. A. (1992). Recognizing group diversity: Individualist-collectivist and autonomous-relational social orientations and their implications for intergroup processes. *British Journal of Social Psychology, 31,* 327–342.

Brown, R. J., & Turner, J. C. (1981). Interpersonal and intergroup behaviour. In J. C. Turner & H. Giles (Eds.), *Intergroup behaviour* (pp. 33–65). Oxford, England: Basil Blackwell.

Brown, R. J., Vivian, J., & Hewstone, M. (1999). Changing attitudes through inter-group contact: The effects of group membership salience. *European Journal of Social Psychology, 10,* 399–414.

Brown, R. W. (1954). Mass phenomena. In G. Lindzey (Ed.), *Handbook of social psychology* (pp. 833–876). Reading, MA: Addison-Wesley.

Bruner, J. S. (1957a). On perceptual readiness. *Psychological Review, 64,* 123–152.

Bruner, J. S. (1957b). Going beyond the information given. In H. E. Gruber, K. R. Hammond, & R. Jessor (Eds.), *Contemporary approaches to cognition* (pp. 41–69). Cambridge, MA: Harvard University Press.

Bruner, J. S. (1994). The 'remembered' self. In U. Neisser & R. Fivush (Eds.), *The remembering self: Constructions and accuracy in the self-narrative* (pp. 41–54). New York: Cambridge University Press.

Byrne, D. (1971). *The attraction paradigm.* New York: Academic Press.

Cadinu, M. R., & Rothbart, M. (1996). Self-anchoring and differentiation processes in the minimal group setting. *Journal of Personality and Social Psychology, 70,* 661–677.

Calvin, W. H. (1990). *The cerebral symphony: Seashore reflections on the structure of consciousness.* New York: Bantam.

Cameron, J. E. (1999). Social identity and the pursuit of possible selves: Implications for the psychological well-being of university students. *Group Dynamics, 3,* 179–189.

Campbell, B. G. (1985). *Human Evolution: An introduction to man's adaptions.* Chicago, IL: Aldine.

Caporael, L. R. (2001). Parts and wholes: The evolutionary importance of groups. In C. Sedikides & M. B. Brewer (Eds.), *Individual self, relational self, collective self* (pp. 241–258). Philadelphia: Psychology Press.

Cartwright, D. (1959b). A field theoretical conception of power. In D. Cartwright (Ed.), *Studies in social power* (pp. 183–220). Ann Arbor, MI: University of Michigan Press.

Cartwright, D. (1959a). Power: A neglected variable in social psychology. In D. Cartwright (Ed.), *Studies in social power* (pp. 1–14). Ann Arbor, MI: University of Michigan Press.

Catellani, P., Milesi, P., & Crescentini, A. (2003). Collective identity and perceived injustice in Italian right-wing parties. In B. Klandermans & N. Mayer (Eds.), *Through the magnifying glass: The world of right-wing extremism.* (Forthcoming).

Chaiken, S., & Trope, Y. (Eds.) (1999). *Dual-process theories in social psychology.* New York: Guilford Press.

Chryssochoou, R. (2000). Multicultural societies: Making sense of new environments and identities. *Journal of Community and Applied Psychology, 10*, 343–354.

Cialdini, R. B., Borden, R. J., Thorne, A., Walker, M. R., Freeman, S., & Sloan, L. R. (1976). Basking in the reflected glory: Three (football) field studies. *Journal of Personality and Social Psychology, 34*, 366–375.

Codol, J. P. (1984). Social differentiation and nondifferentiation. In H. Tajfel (Ed.), *The social dimension* (Vol. 1, pp. 314–337). Cambridge, England: Cambridge University Press.

Coenders, M., Scheepers, P., Sniderman, P. M., & Verberk, G. (2001). Blatant and subtle prejudice: Dimensions, determinants and consequences; some comments on Pettigrew and Meertens. *European Journal of Social Psychology, 31*, 281–298.

Côté, J. E., & Levine, C. G. (2002). Identity formation, agency, and culture. Mahwah, NJ: Lawrence Erlbaum Associates.

Cousins, S. (1989). Culture and selfhood in Japan and the United States. *Journal of Personality and Social Psychology, 56*, 124–131.

Crocker, J., & Major, B. (1989). Social stigma and self-esteem: The self-protective properties of stigma. *Psychological Review, 96*, 608–630.

Crocker, J., Major, B., & Steele, C. (1998). Social stigma. In: D. T. Gilbert, S. T. Fiske, & G. Lindzey (Eds.), *The handbook of social psychology.* New York: Oxford University Press.

Crocker, J., & Quinn, D. M. (2001). Psychological consequences of devalued identities. In R. Brown & S. Gaertner (Eds.), *Blackwell Handbook of Social Psychology: Intergroup processes* (pp. 238–257). Oxford, UK: Blackwell Publishers Inc.

Cruikshank, M. (1992). *The gay and lesbian liberation movement.* New York: Routledge, Chapman & Hall, Inc.

DeCharms, R. (1968). *Personal causation: The internal-affective determinants of behavior.* New York: Academic Press.

Deci, E. L., & Ryan, R. M. (1985). *Intrinsic motivation and self-determination in human behavior.* New York: Plenum.

Deci, E. L., & Ryan, R. M. (1991). A motivational approach to self: Integration in personality. In R. A. Dienstbier (Ed.), *Nebraska symposium on motivation* (Vol. 38). Perspectives on motivation. Current theory and research in motivation (pp. 237–288). Lincoln, NE: University of Nebraska Press.

Deci, E. L., & Ryan, R. M. (1995). Human agency: The basis for true self-esteem. In M. H. Kernis (Ed.), *Efficacy, agency, and self-esteem* (pp. 31–50). New York: Plenum.

Dekker, T., Helsloot, J., & Wijers, C. (2000). Introduction. In T. Dekker, J. Helsloot, & C. Wijers (Eds.), *Roots and rituals. The construction of ethnic identity.* Amsterdam: Het Spinhuis.

Dennett, D. (1989). The origins of selves. *Cogito, 2*, 163–173.

Dennett, D. (1991). *Consciousness explained*. New York: Little Brown.

Dépret, E. F., & Fiske, S. T. (1993). Social cognition and power: Some cognitive consequences of social structure as a source of control deprivation. In G. Weary, F. Gleicher, & K. Marsh (Eds.), *Control motivation and social cognition* (pp. 176–202). New York: Springer-Verlag.

Dépret, E., & Fiske, S. T. (1999). Perceiving the powerful: Intriguing individuals versus threatening groups. *Journal of Experimental Social Psychology, 35*, 461–480.

De Weerd, M., & Klandermans, B. (1999). Group identification and social protest: Farmers' protest in the Netherlands. *European Journal of Social Psychology, 29*, 1073–1095.

Dewey, J. (1890). On some current conceptions of the term 'Self'. *Mind, 15*, 58–74.

Diamond, J. (1992). *The third chimpanzee: The evolution and future of the human animal*. New York: HarperCollins Publisher.

Ditto, P. H., & Jemmott, J. B. I. (1989). From rarity to evaluative extremity: Effects of prevalence information on evaluations of positive and negative characteristics. *Journal of Personality and Social Psychology, 57*, 16–26.

Doosje, B., Ellemers, N., & Spears, R. (1995). Perceived intragroup variability as a function of group status and identification. *Journal of Experimental Social Psychology, 31*, 410–436.

Dovidio, J. F., & Esses, V. M. (2001). Immigrants and immigration: Advancing the psychological perspective. *Journal of Social Issues, 57*, 375–387.

Dovidio, J. F., Kawakami, K., & Beach, K. R. (2001). Implicit and explicit attitudes: Examination of the relationship between measures of intergroup bias. In R. Brown & S. Gaertner (Eds.), *Blackwell Handbook of Social Psychology: Intergroup processes* (pp. 175–197). Oxford, UK: Blackwell Publishers Inc.

Drury, J., & Reicher, S. (1999). The intergroup dynamics of collective empowerment: Substantiating the social identity model of crowd behavior. *Group Processes and Intergroup Relations, 2*, 381–402.

Drury, J., & Reicher, S. (2000). Collective action and psychological change: The emergence of new social identities. *British Journal of Social Psychology, 39*, 579–604.

Dubé, L., & Guimond, S. (1986). Relative deprivation and social protest: The personal group issue. In J. M. Olson, C. P. Herman, & M. P. Zanna (Eds.), *The Ontario symposium: Vol.4. Relative deprivation and social comparison* (pp. 201–216). Hillsdale, NJ: Erlbaum.

Durkheim, E. (1893/1960). *The division of labor*. Glencoe, IL: Free Press.

Durkheim, E. (1895/1976). *Die Regeln der soziologischen Methode (The rules of the sociological method), 5th ed.* Darmstadt, Germany: Luchterhand.

Duval, S., & Wicklund, R. A. (1972). *A theory of objective self-awareness*. New York: Academic Press.

Edelman, M. (1977). *Political language: Words that succeed and politics that fail*. New York, NY: Academic Press.

Eiser, J. R., & Stroebe, W. (1972). *Categorization and social judgement*. London: Academic Press.

Elias, N. (1988). *Die Gesellschaft der Individuen (The society of the individuals)*. Frankfurt am Main, Germany: Suhrkamp.

Elias, N. (1990). *Über den Prozess der Zivilisation. (Translated into English by Edmund Jephcott: The civilizing process. Vol.1, New York: Urizen Books, 1978; Vol. 2, New York: Pantheon Books, 1982)*. Frankfurt am Main, Germany: Suhrkamp.

Elias, N. (1992). *Studien über die Deutschen*. Frankfurt am Main, Germany: Suhrkamp.

Ellemers, N. (1993). The influence of socio-structural variables on identity management strategies. In W. Stroebe & M. Hewstone (Eds.), *European Review of Social Psychology* (pp. 27–57). Chichester, England: John Wiley & Sons.

Ellemers, N., & Barreto, M. (2001). The impact of relative group status: Affective, perceptual and behavioral consequences. In R. Brown & S. Gaertner (Eds.), *Blackwell Handbook of Social Psychology: Intergroup processes* (pp. 324–343). Oxford, UK: Blackwell Publishers Inc.

Ellemers, N., Doosje, B., van Knippenberg, A., & Wilke, H. (1992). Status protection in high status minority groups. *European Journal of Social Psychology, 22,* 123–140.

Ellemers, N., Kortekaas, P., & Ouwerkerk, J. W. (1999). Self-categorization, commitment to the group and group self-esteem as related but distinct aspects of social identity. *European Journal of Social Psychology, 29,* 371–389.

Ellemers, N., van Knippenberg, A., & Wilke, H. (1990). The influence of permeability of group boundaries and stability of group status on strategies of individual mobility and social change. *British Journal of Social Psychology, 29,* 233–246.

Emerson, R. (1960). *From empire to nation*. Cambridge: Harvard University Press.

Epstein, S. (1973). The self-concept revisited: Or a theory of a theory. *American Psychologist, 28,* 404–416.

Erikson, E. H. (1968). *Identity: Youth and crisis*. New York: W. W. Norton.

Espinoza, J. A., & Garza, R. T. (1985). Social group salience and interethnic cooperation. *Journal of Experimental Social Psychology, 21,* 380–392.

Esser, H. (1988). Ethnische Differenzierung und moderne Gesellschaft (Ethnic differentiation and modern society). *Zeitschrift für Soziologie, 17,* 235–248.

Esser, H. (1993). *Soziologie – Allgemeine Grundlagen*. Frankfurt a. M., Germany: Campus.

Farley, J. (1982). *Majority–minority relations*. Englewood, NJ: Prentice Hall.

Farr, R. M., & Moscovici, S. (1984). *Social representations*. Cambridge, England: Cambridge University Press.

Fazio, R. H. (1990). Multiple processes by which attitudes guide behavior: The MODE model as an integrative framework. In M. P. Zanna (Ed.), *Advances in experimental social psychology* (Vol. 23, pp. 75–109). San Diego, CA: Academic Press.

Fazio, R. H., & Towles-Schwen, T. (1999). The MODE model of attitude-behavior processes. In S. Chaiken & Y. Trope (Eds.), *Dual-process theories in social psychology* (pp. 97–116). New York: Guilford Press.

Fenigstein, A., Scheier, M. F., & Buss, A. H. (1975). Public and private self-consciousness: Assessment and theory. *Journal of Consulting and Clinical Psychology, 43,* 522–527.

Festinger, L. (1954). A theory of social comparison processes. *Human Relations, 7,* 117–140.

Fiske, S. (2000). Stereotyping, prejudice, and discrimination at the seam between the centuries: Evolution, culture, mind, and brain. *European Journal of Social Psychology, 30*, 299–322.

Fiske, S. T. (1993). Controlling other people: The impact of power on stereotyping. *American Psychologist, 48*, 621–628.

Fiske, S. T., & Neuberg, S. L. (1990). A continuum of impression formation, from category-based to individuating processes: Influences of information and motivation on attention and interpretation. In M. P. Zanna (Ed.), *Advances in experimental social psychology* (Vol. 23, pp. 1–74). New York: Random House.

Fiske, S. T., Morling, B., & Stevens, L. E. (1996). Controlling self and others: A theory of anxiety, mental control, and social control. *Personality and Social Psychology Bulletin, 22*, 115–123.

Fiske, S. T., & Taylor, S. E. (1991). *Social cognition (2nd Ed.).* New York: McGraw-Hill.

Flanagan, O. (1994). *Consciousness reconsidered.* Cambridge, MA: The MIT Press.

Foucault, M. (1982). Afterword: The subject and power. In H. L. Dreyfus & P. Rabinow, *Michel Foucault: Beyond structuralism and hermeneutics* (pp. 208–226). Chicago: The University of Chicago Press.

Frable, D. E. S., Platt, C., & Hoey, S. (1998). Concealable stigmas and positive self-perceptions: Feeling better around similar others. *Journal of Personality and Social Psychology, 74*, 909–922.

French, J. R. P., & Raven, B. H. (1959). The bases of social power. In D. Cartwright (Ed.), *Studies in social power* (pp. 118–149). Ann Arbor, MI: Institute of Social Research.

Freud, S. (1922/1989). *Group psychology and the analysis of the ego.* New York: W. W. Norton & Company.

Friedman, D., & McAdam, D. (1992). Collective identity and activism: Networks, choices, and the life of a social movement. In A. D. Morris & C. M. Mueller (Eds.), *Frontiers in social movement theory* (pp. 156–173). New Haven, CT: Yale University Press.

Frisch, M. (1964). *Andorra (English translation by Michael Bullock).* New York: Hill and Wang.

Fromm, E. (1942). *Fear of freedom.* London: Routledge & Kegan Paul.

Gaertner, S. L., & Dovidio, J. F. (2000). *Reducing intergroup bias. The common ingroup identity model.* Philadelphia, PA: Psychology Press.

Gaertner, S. L., Mann, J., Murrell, A., & Dovidio, J. F. (1989). Reducing intergroup bias: The benefits of recategorization. *Journal of Personality and Social Psychology, 57*, 239–249.

Gaertner, S. L., Rust, M. C., Dovidio, J. F., Bachman, B. A., & Anastasio, P. A. (1994). The Contact Hypothesis: The role of a common ingroup identity on reducing intergroup bias. *Small Groups Research, 25*, 224–249.

Gamson, W. A. (1992a). *Talking politics.* Cambridge, England: University of Cambridge Press.

Gamson, W. A. (1992b). The social psychology of collective action. In A. D. Morris & C. M. Mueller (Eds.), *Frontiers in social movement theory* (pp. 53–76). New Haven, CT: Yale University Press.

Gerard, H. (1985). When and how the minority prevails. In S. Moscovici, G. Mugny, & E. van Avermaet (Eds.), *Perspectives on minority influence* (pp. 171–186). Cambridge, England: Cambridge University Press.

Gerard, H., & Hoyt, M. F. (1974). Distinctiveness of social categorization and attitude toward ingroup members. *Journal of Personality and Social Psychology, 29*, 836–842.

Gergen, K. J. (1971). *The concept of self.* New York: Holt, Rinehart and Winston, Inc.

Gergen, K. J. (1991). *The saturated self.* New York: Springer.

Giddens, A. (1990). *The consequences of modernity.* Cambridge: Polity Press.

Giddens, A. (1991). *Modernity and self-identity.* Cambridge: Polity Press.

Gilbert, D. T. (1999). What the mind's not. In S. Chaiken & Y. Trope (Eds.), *Dual-process theories in social psychology* (pp. 3–11). New York: Guilford Press.

Gollwitzer, P. M. (1990). Action phases and mind-sets. In T. E. Higgins & R. M. Sorrentino (Eds.), *Handbook of motivation and cognition: Foundations of social behavior* (Vol. 2, pp. 53–92). New York: Guilford Press.

Gollwitzer, P. M., & Kirchhof, O. (1998). The willful pursuit of identity. In: J. Heckhausen & C. S. Dweck (Eds). Motivation and self-regulation across the life span (pp. 389–423). New York: Cambridge University Press.

González, R., & Brown, R. (2003). Generalization of positive attitude as a function of subordinate group identifications in intergroup contact. *European Journal of Social Psychology, 33*, 195–214.

Gordon, C. (1968). Self-conceptions: Configurations of content. In C. Gordon & K. J. Gergen (Eds.), *The self in social interaction* (Vol. 1: Classic and contemporary perspectives, pp. 115–136). New York: John Wiley & Sons, Inc.

Graumann, C. F. (1996). Introduction to a history of social psychology. In M. Hewstone, W. Stroebe, & G. M. Stephenson (Eds.), *Introduction to social psychology.* Oxford: Blackwell.

Greenwald, A. G., & Pratkanis, A. R. (1984). The self. In R. S. Wyer Jr. & T. K. Srull (Eds.), *Handbook of social cognition* (Vol. 3, pp. 129–178). Hillsdale, NJ: Erlbaum.

Grice, H. P. (1975). Logic and conversation. In P. Cole & J. C. Morgan (Eds.), *Syntax and semantics* (Vol. 3: Speech acts, pp. 41–58). New York: Academic Press.

Guimond, S., & Dubé-Simard, L. (1983). Relative deprivation theory and the Quebec nationalist movement: The cognition–emotion distinction and the personal-group deprivation issue. *Journal of Personality and Social Psychology, 44*, 526–535.

Guinote, A., Judd, C. M., & Brauer, M. (2002). Effects of power on perceived and objective group variability: Evidence that more powerful groups are more variable. *Journal of Personality and Social Psychology, 82*, 708–721.

Gurin, P., & Townsend, A. (1986). Properties of gender identity and their implications for gender consciousness. *American Political Science Review, 67*, 514–539.

Habermas, J. (1992). *Die Moderne – ein unvollendetes Projekt. Philosophisch-politische Aufsaetze 1977–1992.* Leipzig: Reclam-Verlag.

Hall, S. (1992). The question of cultural identity. In S. Hall & T. McGrew (Eds.), *Modernity and its futures* (pp. 273–326). Cambridge: Polity Press.

Hamilton, D. L., Gibbons, P. A., Stroessner, S. J., & Sherman, J. W. (1992). Stereotypes and language use. In G. R. Semin & K. Fiedler (Eds.), *Language, interaction and social cognition* (pp. 102–128). London: Sage.

Harris, M. (1987). *Cultural anthropology (second edition)*. New York: Harper & Row Publishers Inc.

Harvey, D. (1989). *The condition of postmodernity*. Oxford: Basil Blackwell.

Haslam, S. A. (2001). *Psychology in organizations. The social identity approach*. London: Sage Publications Ltd.

Haslam, S. A., Turner, J. C., Oakes, P. J., McGarty, C., & Hayes, B. K. (1992). Context-dependent variation in social stereotyping 1: The effects of intergroup relations as mediated by social change and frame of reference. *European Journal of Social Psychology, 22*, 3–20.

Hastedt, C. (1998). *Selbstkomplexität, Individualität und soziale Kategorisierung*. Münster, Germany: Waxmann.

Hegarty, P., & Pratto, F. (2001). The effects of social category norms and stereotypes on explanations for ingroup differences. *Journal of Personality and Social Psychology, 80*, 723–735.

Hewstone, M. (1996). Contact and categorization: Social-psychological interventions to change intergroup relations. In C. N. Macrae, C. Stangor, & M. Hewstone (Eds.), *Foundations of stereotypes and stereotyping* (pp. 323–368). New York: Guilford.

Hewstone, M., & Brown, R. (1986). Contact is not enough: An intergroup perspective on the 'Contact Hypothesis'. In M. Hewstone & R. Brown (Eds.), *Contact and conflict in intergroup encounters* (pp. 1–44). Oxford, England: Basil Blackwell.

Hewstone, M., Islam, M. R., & Judd, C. M. (1993). Models of crossed categorization and intergroup relations. *Journal of Personality and Social Psychology, 64*, 779–793.

Higgins, E. T. (1987). Self-discrepancy: A theory relating self and affect. *Psychological Review, 94*, 319–340.

Higgins, E. T., & May, D. (2001). Individual self-regulatory functions: It's not 'we' regulation, but it's still social. In C. Sedikides, & M. B. Brewer (Eds.), *Individual self, relational self, collective self* (pp. 47–67). Philadelphia: Psychology Press.

Hobsbawm. E., & Ranger, T. (Eds.) (1983). *The invention of tradition*. Cambridge: Cambridge University Press.

Hofstede, G. (1980). *Culture's consequences. International differences in work-related values*. Beverly Hills, CA: Sage.

Hogg, M. A., & Turner, J. C. (1987). Intergroup behaviour, self stereotyping and the salience of social categories. *British Journal of Social Psychology, 26*, 325–340.

Holland, D., Lachicotte, W., Skinner, D., & Cain, C. (1998). *Identity and agency in cultural worlds*. Cambridge: Harvard University Press.

Hornsey, M. J., & Hogg, M. A. (2000). Sub-group relations: Two experiments comparing subgroup differentiation and common ingroup identity models of prejudice reduction. *Personality and Social Psychology Bulletin, 28*, 242–256.

Hornstein, H. A. (1972). Promotive tension: The basis of prosocial behaviour from a Lewinian perspective. *Journal of Social Issues, 28*, 191–218.

Hoyle, R. H., Kernis, M. H., Leary, M. R., & Baldwin, M. W. (1999). *Selfhood. Identity, esteem, regulation*. Boulder, CO: Westview Press.

Huntington, S. P. (1996). *The clash of civilizations and the remaking of world order*. New York: Simon and Schuster.

Ignazi, P. (1992). The silent counter-revolution: Hypotheses on the emergence of extreme right-wing parties in Europe. *European Journal of Political Research, 22*, 3–34.

Ignazi, P. (1997). The extreme right in Europe: A survey. In P. H. Merkl & L. Weinberg (Eds.), *The revival of right-wing extremism in the nineties*. London: Frank Cass.

Inglehart, R., & Baker, W. E. (2000). Modernization, cultural change, and the persistence of traditional values. *American Sociological Review, 65*, 19–51.

Islam, M. R., & Hewstone, M. (1993). Dimensions of contact as predictors of intergroup anxiety, perceived out-group variability, and out-group attitude: An integrative model. *Personality and Social Psychology Bulletin, 19*, 700–710.

Jackson, J. W. (1999). How variations in social structure affect different types of intergroup bias and different dimensions of social identity in a multi-intergroup setting. *Group Processes and Intergroup Relations, 2*, 145–173.

Jackson, J. W., & Smith, E. R. (1999). Conceptualizing social identity: A new framework and evidence for the impact of different dimensions. *Personality and Social Psychology Bulletin, 25*, 120–135.

James, W. (1890/1950). *The principles of psychology (Vol. 1)*. Cambridge, MA: Harvard University Press.

James, W. (1892/1961). *Psychology: The briefer course*. New York: Harper and Row.

Johnson-Laird, P. N. (1988). *The computer and the mind: An invitation to cognitive science*. Cambridge: Harvard University Press.

Jones, J. R. (1972). *Prejudice and racism*. Reading, MA: Addison-Wesley.

Judd, C. M., & Park, B. (1988). Out-group homogeneity: Judgments of variability at the individual and group levels. *Journal of Personality and Social Psychology, 54*, 778–788.

Judd, C. M., & Park, B. (1993). Definition and assessment of accuracy in social stereotypes. *Psychological Review, 100*, 109–128.

Jussim, L. (1991). Social perception and social reality: A reflection-construction model. *Psychological Review, 98*, 54–73.

Kahneman, D., & Miller, D. T. (1986). Norm theory: Comparing reality to its alternatives. *Psychological Review, 93*, 136–153.

Kampmeier, C. (2001). *Individualität und psychologische Gruppenbildung: Eine sozialpsychologische Perspektive*. Wiesbaden: Deutscher Universitäts-Verlag.

Kampmeier, C., & Simon, B. (2001). Individuality and group formation: The role of independence and differentiation. *Journal of Personality and Social Psychology, 81*, 448–462.

Kampmeier, C., Simon, B., & Hastedt, C. (2000). Das Gedanken-Sortier-Verfahren: Ein alternatives Meßinstrument zur Erhebung der Selbstkomplexität (The thought-sorting task: An alternative measure of self-complexity). *Unpublished manuscript*, University of Kiel.

Kant, I. (1781/1997). *Critique of pure reason*. Cambridge: University Press.

Kashima, Y., Kashima, E., & Aldridge, J. (2001). Toward cultural dynamics of self-conceptions. In C. Sedikides & M. B. Brewer (Eds.), *Individual self, relational self, collective self* (pp. 277–298). Philadelphia: Psychology Press.

Kawakami, K., & Dion, K. L. (1993). The impact of salient self-identities on relative deprivation and action intentions. *European Journal of Social Psychology, 23*, 525–540.

Kawakami, K., & Dion, K. L. (1995). Social identity and affect as determinants of collective action. Toward an integration of relative deprivation and social psychology theories. *Theory and Psychology, 5,* 551–577.

Kelly, C. (1993). Group identification, intergroup perceptions and collective action. In W. Stroebe & M. Hewstone (Eds.), *European Review of Social Psychology* (Vol. 4, pp. 59–83). Chichester, England: John Wiley & Sons.

Kelly, C., & Breinlinger, S. (1995). Identity and injustice: Exploring women's participation in collective action. *Journal of Community & Applied Social Psychology, 5,* 41–57.

Kelly, C., & Breinlinger, S. (1996). *The social psychology of collective action: Identity, injustice and gender.* London: Taylor & Francis Ltd.

Kessler, T., & Mummendey, A. (2001). Is there any scapegoat around? Determinants of intergroup conflicts at different categorization levels. *Journal of Personality and Social Psychology, 81,* 1090–1102.

Klandermans, B. (1984). Mobilization and participation: Social psychological expansions of resource mobilization theory. *American Sociological Review, 49,* 583–600.

Klandermans, B. (1997). *The social psychology of protest.* Oxford, England: Basil Blackwell.

Klandermans, B. (2002). How group identification helps to overcome the dilemma of collective action. *American Behavioral Scientist, 45,* 887–900.

Klandermans, B., & Mayer, N. (Eds.) (2003). *Through the magnifying glass: The world of right-wing extremism.* (Forthcoming).

Klandermans, B., & Oegema, D. (1987). Potentials, networks, motivations, and barriers: Steps towards participation in social movements. *American Sociological Review, 52,* 519–531.

Klauer, K. C., & Wegener, I. (1998). Unraveling social categorization in the 'Who said what?' paradigm. *Journal of Personality and Social Psychology, 75,* 1155–1178.

Klauer, K. C., Wegener, I., & Ehrenberg, K. (2002). Perceiving minority members as individuals: The effects of relative group size in social categorization. *European Journal of Social Psychology, 32,* 147–292.

Klein, S. B. (2001). A self to remember: A cognitive neuropsychological perspective on how self creates memory and memory creates self. In C. Sedikides & M. B. Brewer (Eds.), *Individual self, relational self, collective self* (pp. 25–46). Philadelphia, PA: Psychology Press.

Klein, L. (2003). *Rechtsextremismus und kollektive Identität. Eine sozialpsychologische Studie über ,Republikaner' und Redakteure der ,Jungen Freiheit'.* Unveröffentlichte Dissertation, Universität Kiel. (*Right-wing extremism and collective identity. A social psychological study of 'Republicans' and editors of 'Junge Freiheit'.* Unpublished dissertation, University of Kiel.)

Kohlberg, L. (1976). Moral stages and moralization: The cognitive-developmental approach. In T. Lickona (Ed.), *Moral development and behavior* (pp. 31–53). New York: Holt, Rinehart & Winston.

Koopmans, R. (1996). Explaining the rise of racist and extreme right violence in Western Europe: Grievances or opportunities? *European Journal of Political Research, 30,* 185–216.

Koopmans, R., & Statham, P. (1999). Challenging the liberal nation-state? Postnation-alism, multiculturalism, and the collective claims making of migrants and ethnic minorities in Britain and Germany. *American Journal of Sociology, 105*, 652–696.

Krech, D., & Crutchfield, R. S. (1948). *Theory and problems of social psychology.* New York: McGraw-Hill.

Kreckel, R. (1989). Ethnische Differenzierung und 'moderne' Gesellschaft: Kritische Anmerkungen zu Hartmut Essers Aufsatz in der Zeitschrift für Soziologie, Jg. 17 (1988), S. 235–248. *Zeitschrift für Soziologie, 18*, 162–167.

Kriesi, H., Koopmans, R., Duyvendak, J. W., & Giugni, M. G. (1995). *New social movements in Western Europe. A comparative analysis.* London, England: UCL Press.

Kuhn, M. H. (1964). Major trends in symbolic interaction theory in the past twenty-five years. *Sociological Quarterly, 5*, 61–84.

Kunda, Z. (1990). The case for motivated reasoning. *Psychological Bulletin, 108*, 480–498.

Lalonde, R. N., & Silverman, R. A. (1994). Behavioral preferences in response to social injustice: The effects of permeability and social identity salience. *Journal of Personality and Social Psychology, 66*, 78–85.

Lash, S. (1990). *The sociology of postmodernism.* London: Routledge.

Le Bon, G. (1903). *The crowd: A study of the popular mind.* London, England: Unwin.

Leary, M. R., & Baumeister, R. F. (2000). The nature and function of self-esteem: Sociometer theory. In M. Zanna (Ed.), *Advances in experimental social psychology* (Vol. 32, pp. 1–62). San Diego. CA: Academic Press.

Leary, M. R., Tambor, E. S., Terdal, S. K., & Downs, D. L. (1995). Self-esteem as an interpersonal monitor: The sociometer hypothesis. *Journal of Personality and Social Psychology, 68*, 518–530.

Leonardelli, G. J., & Brewer, M. B. (2001). Minority and majority discrimination: When and why. *Journal of Experimental Social Psychology, 37*, 468–485.

Lewin, K. (1948). *Resolving social conflicts.* New York: Harper.

Lewin, K. (1951). *Field theory in social science.* New York: Harper.

Lijphart, A. (1977). *Democracy in plural societies: A comparative exploration.* New Haven, CT: Yale University Press.

Lijphart, A. (1984). *Democracies: Patterns of majoritarian and consensus government in twenty-one countries.* New Haven, CT: Yale University Press.

Lind, E. A., & Tyler, T. R. (1988). *The social psychology of procedural justice.* New York: Plenum.

Linville, P. W. (1985). Self-complexity and affective extremity: Don't put all your eggs in one cognitive basket. *Social Cognition, 3*, 94–120.

Linville, P. W. (1987). Self-complexity as a cognitive buffer against stress-related illness and depression. *Journal of Personality and Social Psychology, 52*, 663–676.

Long, K., & Spears, R. (1997). The self-esteem hypothesis revisited: Differentiation and the disaffected. In R. Spears, P. J. Oakes, N. Ellemers, & S. A. Haslam (Eds.), *The social psychology of stereotyping and group life* (pp. 296–317). Oxford, England: Basil Blackwell Publishers, Inc.

Lorenzi-Cioldi, F. (1998). Group status and perceptions of homogeneity. In W. Stroebe & M. Hewstone (Eds.), *European Review of Social Psychology* (Vol. 9, pp. 31–75). Chichester, England: John Wiley & Sons.

Luhtanen, R., & Crocker, J. (1992). A collective self-esteem scale: Self-evaluation of one's social identity. *Personality and Social Psychology Bulletin, 18*, 302–318.

Lücken, M. (2002). *Das kognitiv-affektive Kreuzfeuer im Minoritäts-Majoritäts-Kontext*. Unveröffentlichte Dissertation, Universität Kiel. (*The cognitive-affective cross-fire in minority–majority contexts*. Unpublished dissertation, University of Kiel.)

Lücken, M., & Simon, B. (2003). Unhappy group members and happy individuals: The cognitive-affective crossfire in minority–majority contexts. *Unpublished manuscript*, University of Kiel.

Lyotard, J. -F. (1984). *The postmodern condition*. Manchester: Manchester University Press. -

Maass, A., Salvi, D., Arcuri, L., & Semin, G. (1989). Language use in intergroup contexts: The linguistic intergroup bias. *Journal of Personality and Social Psychology, 57*, 981–993.

Mackie, D., & Cooper, J. (1984). Attitude polarization: Effects of group membership. *Journal of Personality and Social Psychology, 46*, 575–585.

Major, B., & Crocker, J. (1993). Social stigma: The consequences of attributional ambiguity. In D. M. Mackie & D. L. Hamilton (Eds.), *Affect, cognition, and stereotyping: Interactive Processes in group perception* (p.. 345–370). San Diego, CA: Academic Press.

Markus, H. (1977). Self-schemata and processing information about the self. *Journal of Personality and Social Psychology, 35*, 63–78.

Markus, H., & Kunda, Z. (1986). Stability and malleability of the self-concept. *Journal of Personality and Social Psychology, 51*, 858–866.

Markus, H. R., & Kitayama, S. (1991). Culture and the self: Implications for cognition, emotion, and motivation. *Psychological Review, 98*, 224–253.

Markus, H. R., & Nurius, P. (1986). Possible selves. *American Psychologist, 41*, 954–969.

Markus, H., & Smith, J. (1981). The influence of self-schemata on the perception of others. In N. Cantor & J. F. Kihlstrom (Eds.), *Personality, cognition, and social interaction* (pp. 233–262). Hillsdale, NJ: Lawrence Erlbaum Associates.

Markus, H. R., & Wurf, E. (1987). The dynamic self-concept: A social psychological perspective. *Annual Review of Psychology, 38*, 299–337.

Markus, H., Smith, J., & Moreland, R. L. (1985). Role of the self-concept in the perception of others. *Journal of Personality and Social Psychology, 49*, 1494–1512.

Marx, K., & Engels, F. (1978). *The Marx–Engels Reader* (edited by R. C. Tucker). New York: W. W. Norton & Company.

Maslow, A. (1970). *Motivation and personality (rev. ed.)*. New York: Harper & Row.

Mayer, K. U., & Müller, W. (1994). Individualisierung und Standardisierung im Strukturwandel der Moderne. Lebensverläufe im Wohlfahrtsstaat. In U. Beck & E. Beck-Gernsheim (Eds.), *Riskante Freiheiten* (Risky freedoms) (pp. 265–295). Frankfurt a. M.: Suhrkamp.

McAdam, D., McCarthy, J. D., & Zald, M. N. (1988). Social movements. In N. J. Smelser (Ed.), *Handbook of Sociology* (pp. 695–737). Newbury Park, CA: Sage.

McAdams, D. P. (1997). The case for unity in the (post)modern self: A modest proposal. In R. D. Ashmore & L. Jussim (Eds.), *Rutgers series on self and social identity (Volume 1). Self and identity: Fundamental issues* (pp. 46–78). New York: Oxford University Press.

McCarthy, J. D., & Zald, M. N. (1973). *The trend of social movements in America: Professionalization and resource mobilization*. Morristown, NJ: General Learning Press.

McCarthy, J. D., & Zald, M. N. (1977). Resource mobilization and social movements: A partial theory. *American Journal of Sociology, 82*, 1212–1241.

McDougall, W. (1920). *The group mind.* Cambridge: Cambridge University Press.

McGrew, A. (1992). A global society? In S. Hall & T. McGrew (Eds.), *Modernity and its futures* (pp. 61–116). Cambridge: Polity Press.

McGuire, W. J., & McGuire, C. V. (1988). Content and process in the experience of self. In L. Berkowitz (Ed.), *Advances in experimental social psychology* (Vol. 21, pp. 97–144). New York: Academic Press, Inc.

Mead, G. H. (1934/1993). *Mind, self and society.* Chicago: University of Chicago Press.

Medin, D. L. (1989). Concepts and conceptual structure. *American Psychologist, 44*, 1469–1481.

Medin, D. L., Goldstone, R. L., & Gentner, D. (1993). Respects for similarity. *Psychological Review, 100*, 254–278.

Medin, D. L., & Ortony, A. (1989). Psychological essentialism. In S. Vosniadou & A. Ortony (Eds.), *Similarity and analogical reasoning* (pp. 179–195). Cambridge, England: Cambridge University Press.

Merton, R. K. (1948). The self-fulfilling prophecy. *The Antioch Review, 8*, 193–210.

Messick, D. M., & Mackie, D. M. (1989). Intergroup relations. *Annual Review of Psychology, 40*, 45–81.

Miller, D. T., & Ross, M. (1975). Self-serving biases in the attribution of causality. Fact or fiction? *Psychological Bulletin, 82*, 213–225.

Morgan, H. J., & Janoff-Bulman, R. (1994). Positive and negative self-complexity: Patterns of adjustment following traumatic versus non-traumatic life experiences. *Journal of Social and Clinical Psychology, 13*, 63–85.

Moscovici, S. (1976). *Social influence and social change.* London: Academic Press.

Moscovici, S., & Paicheler, G. (1978). Social comparison and social recognition: Two complementary processes of identification. In H. Tajfel (Ed.), *Differentiation between social groups* (pp. 251–266). London, England: Academic Press.

Mullen, B. (1991). Group composition, salience, and cognitive representations: The phenomenology of being in a group. *Journal of Experimental Social Psychology, 27*, 297–323.

Mullen, B., Brown, R., & Smith, C. (1992). Ingroup bias as a function of salience, relevance, and status: An integration. *European Journal of Social Psychology, 22*, 103–122.

Mummendey, A., Kessler, T., Klink, A., & Mielke, R. (1999). Strategies to cope with negative social identity: Predictions by social identity theory and relative deprivation theory. *Journal of Personality and Social Psychology, 76*, 229–245.

Mummendey, A., & Otten, S. (2001). Aversive discrimination. In R. Brown & S. Gaertner (Eds.), *Blackwell Handbook of Social Psychology: Intergroup processes* (pp. 112–132). Oxford, UK: Blackwell Publishers Inc.

Mummendey, A., & Simon, B. (Eds.) (1997). *Identität und Verschiedenheit.* Bern: Hans Huber.

Mummendey, A., Simon, B., Dietze, C., Grünert, M., Haeger, G., Kessler, S., Lettgen, S., & Schäferhoff, S. (1992). Categorization is not enough: Intergroup discrimination in negative outcome allocation. *Journal of Experimental Social Psychology, 28*, 125–144.

Neidhardt, F., & Rucht, D. (1993). Auf dem Weg in die 'Bewegungsgesellschaft'? Über die Stabilisierbarkeit sozialer Bewegungen (On the way to a 'movement society'?). *Soziale Welt, 44,* 305–326.

Nemeth, C. J. (1997). Beziehungen zwischen Minoritäten: Der Wert von Vielfalt und abweichenden Meinungen. In A. Mummendey & B. Simon (Eds.), *Selbst, Identität und Verschiedenheit.* Bern: Verlag Hans Huber.

Noelle-Neumann, E., & Köcher, R. (1987). *Die verletzte Nation: Über den Versuch der Deutschen, ihren Charakter zu ändern.* Stuttgart: Deutsche Verlags-Anstalt.

Ng, S. H. (1982). Power and intergroup discrimination. In H. Tajfel (Ed.), *Social identity and intergroup relations* (pp. 179–206). Cambridge: University Press.

Ng, S. H., & Cram, F. (1988). Intergroup bias by defensive and offensive groups in majority and minority conditions. *Journal of Personality and Social Psychology, 55,* 749–757.

Oakes, P. J., Haslam, S. A., & Turner, J. C. (1994). *Stereotyping and social reality.* Oxford: Blackwell.

Oakes, P. J., & Reynolds, K. J. (1997). Asking the accuracy question: Is measurement the answer? In R. Spears, P. J. Oakes, N. Ellemers, & S. A. Haslam (Eds.), *The social psychology of stereotyping and group life.* Oxford: Blackwell Publishers Ltd.

Oakes, P. J., Turner, J. C., & Haslam, S. A. (1991). Perceiving people as group members: The role of fit in the salience of social categorizations. *British Journal of Social Psychology, 30,* 125–144.

Oakes, P. J., & Turner, J. C. (1980). Social categorization and intergroup behaviour: Does minimal intergroup discrimination make social identity more positive. *European Journal of Social Psychology, 10,* 295–301.

Oakes, P. J., & Turner, J. C. (1986). Distinctiveness and the salience of social category memberships: Is there a perceptual bias towards novelty? *European Journal of Social Psychology, 16,* 325–344.

Oakes, P. J., & Turner, J. C. (1990). Is limited information processing capacity the cause of social stereotyping? In W. Stroebe & M. Hewstone (Eds.), *European Review of Social Psychology* (Vol. 1, pp. 111–135). Chichester: John Wiley & Sons.

Omoto, A. M., & Snyder, M. (1995). Sustained helping without obligation: Motivation, longevity of service, and perceived attitude change among AIDS volunteers. *Journal of Personality and Social Psychology, 68,* 671–686.

Onorato, R. S., & Turner, J. C. (2001). The 'I,' the 'me,' and the 'us': The psychological group and self-concept maintenance and change. In C. Sedikides & M. B. Brewer (Eds.), *Individual self, relational self, and collective self.* Philadelphia, PA: Taylor & Francis, Inc.

Opp, K.-D. (1989). *The rationality of political protest.* Boulder: Westview.

Otten, S., Mummendey, A., & Blanz, M. (1996). Intergroup discrimination in positive and negative outcome allocations: Impact of stimulus valence, relative group status, and relative group size. *Personality and Social Psychology Bulletin, 22,* 568–581.

Perdue, C. W., Dovidio, J. F., Gurtman, M. B., & Tyler, R. B. (1990). 'Us' and 'Them': Social categorization and the process of intergroup bias. *Journal of Personality and Social Psychology, 59,* 475–486.

Pettigrew, T. F. (1971). *Racially separate or together?* New York: McGraw Hill.

Pettigrew, T. F. (1996). *How to think like a social scientist*. New York: Harper Collins.

Pettigrew, T. F. (1997). Generalized intergroup contact effects on prejudice. *Personality and Social Psychology Bulletin, 23*, 173–185.

Pettigrew, T. F. (1998). Intergroup contact theory. *Annual Review of Psychology, 49*, 65–85.

Pettigrew, T. F., & Meertens, R. W. (1995). Subtle and blatant prejudice in Western Europe. *European Journal of Social Psychology, 25*, 57–76.

Pettigrew, T. F., & Meertens, R. W. (2001). In defense of the subtle prejudice concept: A retort. *European Journal of Social Psychology, 31*, 299–310.

Phinney, J. S. (1990). Ethnic identity in adolescents and adults: Review of research. *Psychological Bulletin, 108*, 499–514.

Popper, K. R. (1982). *Logik der Forschung (7. Auflage)*. Tübingen: Mohr.

Popper, K. R., & Eccles, J. C. (1977). *The self and its brain*. Berlin: Springer International.

Preston, P. W. (1997). *Political/cultural identity. Citizens and nations in a global era*. London: Sage Publications.

Rabbie, J. M., & Horwitz, M. (1988). Categories versus groups as explanatory concepts in intergroup relations. *European Journal of Social Psychology, 18*, 117–123.

Reicher, S. (1982). The determination of collective behaviour. In H. Tajfel (Ed.), *Social identity and intergroup relations* (pp. 41–83). Cambridge: Cambridge University Press.

Reicher, S., & Hopkins, N. (1996a). Seeking influence through characterising self-categories: An analysis of anti-abortionist rhetoric. *British Journal of Social Psychology, 35*, 297–311.

Reicher, S., & Hopkins, N. (1996b). Self-category constructions in political rhetoric: An analysis of Thatcher's and Kinnock's speeches concerning the British Miners' Strike (1984–5). *European Journal of Social Psychology, 26*, 353–372.

Reynolds, K. J., Oakes, P. J., Haslam, S. A., Nolan, M. A., & Dolnik, L. (2000). Responses to powerlessness: Stereotyping as an instrument of social conflict. *Group Dynamics, 4*, 275–290.

Rogers, C. R. (1959). A theory of therapy, personality and interpersonal relationships, as developed in the client-centered framework. In S. Koch (Ed.), *Psychology: A study of a science* (Vol. 3, pp. 184–256). Toronto: McGraw-Hill.

Rogers, T. B. (1981). A model of the self as an aspect of the human information processing system. In N. Cantor & J. F. Kihlstrom (Eds.), *Personality, cognition, and social interaction* (pp. 193–214). Hillsdale: NJ: Lawrence Erlbaum Associates.

Rosch, E. (1978). Principles of categorization. In E. Rosch & B. B. Lloyd (Eds.), *Cognition and categorization* (pp. 27–48). Hillsdale, NJ: Erlbaum.

Rothbart, M., & Taylor, M. (1992). Category labels and social reality: Do we view social categories as natural kinds? In G. R. Semin & K. Fiedler (Eds.), *Language, interaction and social cognition* (pp. 11–36). London: Sage.

Royce, J. (1895). Self-consciousness, social consciousness and nature. *Philosophical Review, 4*, 577–602.

Rucht, D. (1995). Kollektive Identität: Konzeptuelle Überlegungen zu einem Desiderat der Bewegungsforschung. *Forschungsjournal Neue Soziale Bewegungen, 8*, 9–23.

Sachdev, I., & Bourhis, R. Y. (1984). Minimal majorities and minorities. *European Journal of Social Psychology, 14*, 35–52.

Sachdev, I., & Bourhis, R. Y. (1985). Social categorization and power differentials in group relations. *European Journal of Social Psychology, 15,* 415–434.

Sachdev, I., & Bourhis, R. Y. (1991). Power and status differentials in minority and majority group relations. *European Journal of Social Psychology, 21,* 1–24.

Sampson, E. E. (1993). Identity politics. Challenges to psychology's understanding. *American Psychologist, 48,* 1219–1230.

Schacter, D. L., & Tulving, E. (Eds.) (1994). *Memory systems.* Cambridge, MA: MIT Press.

Schank, R. C., & Abelson, R. P. (1977). *Scripts, plans, goals, and understanding: An inquiry into human knowledge structures.* Hillsdale, NY: Erlbaum.

Schimank, U. (1985). Funktionale Differenzierung und reflexiver Subjektivismus: Zum Entsprechungsverhältnis von Gesellschafts-und Identitätsform (Functional differentiation and reflexive subjectivism: On the correspondence between forms of society and identity). *Soziale Welt, 4,* 447–465.

Schimank, U. (1996). *Theorien gesellschaftlicher Differenzierung (Theories of societal differentiation).* Opladen, Germany: Leske + Budrich.

Schlenker, B. (1980). *Impression management: The self-concept, social identity, and interpersonal relations.* Monterey, CA: Brooks/Cole.

Schmitt, M. T., & Branscombe, N. R. (2002). The meaning and consequences of perceived discrimination in disadvantaged and privileged social groups. In: W. Stroebe & M. Hewstone (Eds.), *European Review of Social Psychology* (Volume 12, pp. 167–199). Chichester: John Wiley & Sons.

Schmitz, B. (2000). Auf der Suche nach dem verlorenen Individuum: Vier Theoreme zur Aggregation von Prozessen. *Psychologische Rundschau, 51,* 83–92.

Schopenhauer, A. (1819/1995). *The world as will and idea.* London: J. M. Dent.

Schopler, J., & Insko, A. (1992). The discontinuity effect in interpersonal and intergroup relations: Generality and mediation. In W. Stroebe & M. Hewstone (Eds.), *European Review of Social Psychology* (Volume 3, pp. 121–151). Chichester: John Wiley & Sons.

Sedikides, C. (1993). Assessment, enhancement, and verification determinants of the self-evaluation process. *Journal of Personality and Social Psychology, 65,* 317–338.

Sedikides, C. (1997). Differential processing of ingroup and outgroup information: The role of relative group status in permeable boundary groups. *European Journal of Social Psychology, 27,* 121–144.

Sedikides, C., & Brewer, M. B. (Eds.) (2001). *Individual self, relational self, collective self.* Philadelphia: Psychology Press.

Sedikides, C., & Strube, M. J. (1997). Self-evaluation: To thine own self be good, to thine own self be sure, to thine own self be true, and to thine own self be better. In M. P. Zanna (Ed.), *Advances in experimental social psychology* (Vol. 29, pp. 209–269). New York: Academic.

Semin, G. R., & Fiedler, K. (1988). The cognitive functions of linguistic categories in describing persons: Social cognition and language. *Journal of Personality and Social Psychology, 54,* 558–568.

Sherif, M. (1966). *The psychology of social norms.* New York: Harper Torchbook.

Sherif, M. (1967). *Group conflict and co-operation: Their social psychology.* London, England: Routledge & Kegan Paul.

Simmel, G. (1908). *Soziologie: Untersuchungen über die Formen der Vergesellschaftung (Sociology: Investigations into forms of society)*. Leipzig, Germany: Duncker & Humblot.

Simmel, G. (1955). *The web of group-affiliations (Translation of 'Die Kreuzung sozialer Kreise', Soziologie. Muenchen: Duncker & Humblot, edited by Reinhard Bendix)*. New York: The Free Press.

Simmel, G. (1984). *Grundfragen der Soziologie: Individuum und Gesellschaft (Basic issues of sociology: Individual and society) (4th edition)*. Berlin, Germany: Walter de Gruyter, Sammlung Göschen.

Simon, B. (1992). The perception of ingroup and outgroup homogeneity: Re-introducing the intergroup context. In W. Stroebe & M. Hewstone (Eds.), *European Review of Social Psychology* (Vol. 3, pp. 1–30). Chichester: John Wiley & Sons.

Simon, B. (1993). On the asymmetry in the cognitive construal of ingroup and outgroup: A model of egocentric social categorization. *European Journal of Social Psychology, 23,* 131–147.

Simon, B. (1997). Self and group in modern society: Ten theses on the individual self and the collective self. In R. Spears, P. J. Oakes, N. Ellemers, & S. A. Haslam (Eds.), *The social psychology of stereotyping and group life* (pp. 318–335). Oxford, England: Basil Blackwell.

Simon, B. (1998a). The self in minority–majority contexts. In W. Stroebe & M. Hewstone (Eds.), *European Review of Social Psychology* (Vol. 9, pp. 1–31). Chichester, England: Wiley.

Simon, B. (1998b). Individuals, groups, and social change: On the relationship between individual and collective self-interpretations and collective action. In C. Sedikides, J. Schopler, & C. Insko (Eds.), *Intergroup cognition and intergroup behavior* (pp. 257–282). Mahwah, NJ: Lawrence Erlbaum.

Simon, B. (1999). A place in the world: Self and social categorization. In T. R. Tyler, R. M. Kramer, & O. P. John (Eds.), *The psychology of the social self* (pp. 47–69). Mahwah, NJ: Lawrence Erlbaum Associates, Publishers.

Simon, B., Aufderheide, B., & Hastedt, C. (2000). The double negative effect: The (almost) paradoxical role of the individual self in minority and majority members' information processing. *British Journal of Social Psychology, 39,* 73–93.

Simon, B., Aufderheide, B., & Kampmeier, C. (2001). The social psychology of minority–majority relations. In R. Brown & S. Gaertner (Eds.), *Blackwell Handbook of Social Psychology: Intergroup processes* (pp. 303–323). Oxford, England: Basil Blackwell.

Simon, B., & Brown, R. (1987). Perceived intragroup homogeneity in minority–majority contexts. *Journal of Personality and Social Psychology, 53,* 703–711.

Simon, B., Glässner-Bayerl, B., & Stratenwerth, I. (1991). Stereotyping and self-stereotyping in a natural intergroup context: The case of heterosexual and homosexual men. *Social Psychology Quarterly, 54,* 252–266.

Simon, B., & Hamilton, D. L. (1994). Self-stereotyping and social context: The effects of relative ingroup size and ingroup status. *Journal of Personality and Social Psychology, 66,* 699–711.

Simon, B., & Hastedt, C. (1997). When misery loves categorical company: Accessibility of the individual self as a moderator in category-based representation of attractive and unattractive in-groups. *Personality and Social Psychology Bulletin, 23,* 1254–1264.

Simon, B., & Hastedt, C. (1999). Self-aspects as social categories: The role of personal importance and valence. *European Journal of Social Psychology, 29*, 479–487.

Simon, B., Hastedt, C., & Aufderheide, B. (1997). When self-categorization makes sense: The role of meaningful social categorization in minority and majority members' self-perception. *Journal of Personality and Social Psychology, 73*, 310–320.

Simon, B., & Kampmeier, C. (2001). Revisiting the individual self: Toward a social-psychological theory of the individual self and the collective self. In C. Sedikides & M. B. Brewer (Eds.), *Individual self, relational self, collective self* (pp. 199–218). Philadelphia, PA: Taylor & Francis, Inc.

Simon, B., & Kampmeier, C. (2002). *Abschlussbericht zum Projekt 'Integration und Respekt'* (gefördert von der Landesregierung Schleswig-Holstein). Kiel: Christian-Albrechts-Universität.

Simon, B., & Klandermans, B. (2001). Politicized collective identity. A social psychological analysis. *American Psychologist, 56*, 319–331.

Simon, B., & Klein, L. (2003). Identity in German right-wing extremism: Levels, functions, and processes. In B. Klandermans & N. Mayer (Eds.), *Through the magnifying glass: The world of right-wing extremism*. (Forthcoming).

Simon, B., Loewy, M., Stürmer, S., Weber, U., Freytag, P., Habig, C., Kampmeier, C., & Spahlinger, P. (1998). Collective identification and social movement participation. *Journal of Personality and Social Psychology, 74*, 646–658.

Simon, B., & Mummendey, A. (1997). Selbst, Identität und Gruppe: Eine sozialpsychologische Analyse des Verhältnisses von Individuum und Gruppe. In A. Mummendey & B. Simon (Eds.), *Identität und Verschiedenheit: Zur Sozialpsychologie der Identität in komplexen Gesellschaften* (pp. 11–38). Bern, Schweiz: Huber.

Simon, B., Pantaleo, G., & Mummendey, A. (1995). Unique individual or interchangeable group member? The accentuation of intragroup differences versus similarities as an indicator of the individual self versus the collective self. *Journal of Personality and Social Psychology, 69*, 106–119.

Simon, B., & Pettigrew, T. F. (1990). Social identity and perceived group homogeneity: Evidence for the ingroup homogeneity effect. *European Journal of Social Psychology, 20*, 269–286.

Simon, B., & Stürmer, S. (2003). Respect for group members: Intragroup determinants of collective identification and group-serving behavior. *Personality and Social Psychology Bulletin, 29*, 183–193.

Simon, B., Stürmer, S., & Steffens, K. (2000). Helping individuals or group members? The role of individual and collective identification in AIDS volunteerism. *Personality and Social Psychology Bulletin, 26*, 497–506.

Smith, E. R., Coats, S., & Walling, D. (1999). Overlapping mental representations of self, in-group, and partner. *Personality and Social Psychology Bulletin, 25*, 873–882.

Smith, E. R., & Mackie, D. M. (2000). *Social psychology*. Philadelphia: Psychology Press.

Smith, H., Spears, R., & Oyen, M. (1994). 'People like us': The influence of personal deprivation and group membership salience on justice evaluations. *Journal of Experimental Social Psychology, 30*, 277–299.

Smith, H., Tyler, T. R., Huo, Y. J., Ortiz, D. J., & Lind, E. A. (1998). The self-relevant implications of the group-value model: Group membership, self-worth, and treatment quality. *Journal of Experimental Social Psychology, 34*, 470–493.

Snyder, M. (1984). When belief creates reality. In L. Berkowitz (Ed.), *Advances in experimental social psychology* (Vol. 18, pp. 247–305). New York: Academic Press.

Snyder, M. (1987). *Public appearances/private realities: The psychology of self-monitoring.* New York: Freeman.

Snyder, C. R., & Fromkin, H. L. (1980). *Uniqueness: The human pursuit of difference.* New York: Plenum Press.

Snyder, M., & Omoto, A. M. (2001). Basic research and practical problems: Volunteerism and the psychology of individual and collective action. In W. Wosinska, R. B. Cialdini, J. Reykowski, & D. W. Barrett (Eds.), *The practice of social influence in multiple cultures.* Hillsdale, NJ: Erlbaum.

Spears, R. (2001). The interaction between the individual and the collective self: Self-categorization in context. In C. Sedikides & M. B. Brewer (Eds.), *Individual self, relational self, collective self* (pp. 171–198). Philadelphia: Psychology Press.

Stephan, W. G. (1987). The contact hypothesis in intergroup relations. In C. Hendrick (Ed.), *Review of Personality and Social Psychology, Vol. 9: Group processes and intergroup relations* (pp. 13–40). Beverly Hills, CA: Sage.

Stephan, W. G. & Stephan, C. W. (1984). The role of ignorance in intergroup relations. In N. Miller & M. B. Brewer (Eds.), *Groups in contact: The psychology of desegregation* (pp. 229–257). New York: Academic Press.

Stephan, W. G. & Stephan, C. W. (1985). Intergroup anxiety. *Journal of Social Issues, 41*, 157–175.

Stets, J. E., & Burke, P. J. (2000). Identity theory and social identity theory. *Social Psychology Quarterly, 63*, 224–237.

Strawson, G. (1997). The self. *Journal of Consciousness Studies, 4*, 405–428.

Struch, N., & Schwartz, S. H. (1989). Intergroup aggression: Its predictors and distinctness from in-group bias. *Journal of Personality and Social Psychology, 56*, 364–373.

Stryker, S. (1977). Developments in two social psychologies: Toward an appreciation of mutual relevance. *Sociometry, 40*, 145–160.

Stryker, S. (1980). *Symbolic interactionism: A social structural version.* Menlo Park, CA: Benjamin/Cummings.

Stryker, S. (1987). Identity theory: Developments and extensions. In K. Yardley & T. Honess (Eds.), *Self and identity: Psychosocial perspectives* (pp. 89–103). New York: Wiley.

Stryker, S., & Burke, P. (2000). The past, present, and the future of an identity theory. *Social Psychology Quaterly, 63*, 284–297.

Stryker, S., & Serpe, R. T. (1982). Commitment, identity salience, and role behavior: Theory and research example. In W. Ickes & E. S. Knowles (Eds.), *Personality, roles, and social behavior* (pp. 199–218). Springer: New York.

Stryker, S., & Statham, A. (1985). Symbolic interactionism and role theory. In G. Lindzey & E. Aronson (Eds.), *Handbook of social psychology* (3rd edition, pp. 311–378). New York: Random House.

Stürmer, S., & Simon, B. (in press). The role of collective identification in social movement participation: A panel study in the context of the German gay movement. *Personality and Social Psychology Bulletin.*

Stürmer, S., Simon, B., Loewy, M., & Jörger, H. (2003). The dual-pathway model of social movement participation: The case of the fat acceptance movement. *Social Psychology Quarterly, 66,* 71–82.

Sumner, W. C. (1906). *Folkways.* Boston, MA: Ginn.

Swann, W. B. (1996). *Self-traps: The elusive quest for higher self-esteem.* New York: W. H. Freeman.

Swann, W. B., Griffin, J. J., Predmore, S. C., & Gaines, B. (1987). The cognitive-affective crossfire: When self-consistency confronts self-enhancement. *Journal of Personality and Social Psychology, 52,* 881–889.

Tajfel, H. (1970). Experiments in intergroup discrimination. *Scientific American, 223, 5,* 96–102.

Tajfel, H. (1974). Social identity and intergroup behaviour. *Social Science Information, 13,* 65–93.

Tajfel, H. (1976). Against 'biologism'. *New Society, 29,* 240–242.

Tajfel, H. (1978a). Social categorization, social identity and social comparison. In H. Tajfel (Ed.), *Differentiation between social groups: Studies in the social psychology of intergroup relations* (pp. 61–76). London, England: Academic Press.

Tajfel, H. (1978b). Interindividual behaviour and intergroup behaviour. In H. Tajfel (Ed.), *Differentiation between social groups: Studies in the social psychology of intergroup relations* (pp. 27–60). London, England: Academic Press.

Tajfel, H. (1978c). *The social psychology of minorities.* London: Minority Rights Group (No. 7).

Tajfel, H. (1981). *Human groups and social categories: Studies in social psychology.* Cambridge: Cambridge University Press.

Tajfel, H. (1982). Social psychology of intergroup relations. *Annual Review of Psychology, 33,* 1–39.

Tajfel, H., Billig, M. G., Bundy, R. P., & Flament, C. (1971). Social categorization and intergroup behaviour. *European Journal of Social Psychology, 1,* 149–178.

Tajfel, H., & Turner, J. C. (1979). An integrative theory of intergroup conflict. In W. G. Austin & S. Worchel (Eds.), *The social psychology of intergroup relations* (pp. 33–47). Monterey, CA: Brooks/Cole.

Tajfel, H., & Turner, J. C. (1986). The social identity theory of intergroup behavior. In S. Worchel & W. G. Austin (Eds.), *Psychology of intergroup relations* (pp. 07–24). Chicago: Nelson-Hall.

Tarrow, S. (1995). *Power in movement. Social movements, collective action and mass politics in the modern state.* Cambridge: Cambridge University Press.

Taylor, D. M. (1997). The quest for collective identity: The plight of disadvantaged ethnic minorities. *Canadian Psychology, 38,* 174–190.

Taylor, S. E., & Brown, J. D. (1988). Illusion and well-being: A social psychological perspective on mental health. *Psychological Bulletin, 103,* 193–210.

Taylor, S. E., Fiske, S. T., Etcoff, N. L., & Ruderman, A. J. (1978). Categorical and contextual bases of person memory and stereotyping. *Journal of Personality and Social Psychology, 36,* 778–793.

Terry, D. J., & Hogg, M. A. (1996). Group norms and the attitude–behavior relationship: A role for group identification. *Personality and Social Psychology Bulletin, 22,* 776–793.

Tesser, A. (1988). Toward a self-evaluation maintenance model of social behavior. In L. Berkowitz (Ed.), *Advances in experimental social psychology* (Volume 21, pp. 181–227). New York: Academic Press.

Thoits, P. A. (1983). Multiple identities and psychological well-being: A reformulation and test of the social isolation hypothesis. *American Sociological Review, 48,* 174–187.

Thoits, P. A. (1986). Multiple identities: Examining gender and marital status differences in distress. *American Sociological Review, 51,* 259–272.

Tice, D. M., & Baumeister, R. F. (2001). The primacy of the interpersonal self. In C. Sedikides & M. B. Brewer (Eds.), *Individual self, relational self, collective self* (pp. 71–88). Philadelphia: University Press.

Toch, H. (1965). *The social psychology of social movements.* Indianapolis: Bobbs-Merrill.

Tougas, F., & Veilleux, F. (1988). The influence of identification, collective relative deprivation, and procedure of implementation on women's response to affirmative action: A causal modeling approach. *Canadian Journal of Behavioral Science, 20,* 15–27.

Tönnies, F. (1887/1957). *Community and society.* (Translated and edited by Ch. P. Loomis). East Lansing: Michigan State University Press.

Triandis, H. C. (1989). The self and social behavior in differing cultural contexts. *Psychological Review, 96,* 506–520.

Triandis, H. C. (1990). Cross-cultural studies of individualism and collectivism. In J. Berman (Ed.), *Nebraska Symposium on Motivation* (1989, pp. 41–133). Lincoln, NE: University of Nebraska Press.

Triandis, H. C. (1995). *Individualism and collectivism.* Boulder, CO: Westview Press.

Triandis, H. C., Bontempo, R., Villareal, M. J., Asai, M., & Lucca, N. (1988). Individualism and collectivism: Cross-cultural perspectives on self-ingroup relationships. *Journal of Personality and Social Psychology, 54,* 323–338.

Trivers, R. (1985). *Social evolution.* Menlo Park, CA: Benjamin/Cummings.

Trope, Y. (1983). Self-assessment in achievement behavior. In J. M. Suls & A. G. Greenwald (Eds.), *Psychological perspectives on the self* (Vol. 2, pp. 93–121). New York: Erlbaum.

Tulving, E. (1993). Human memory. In P. Anderson, O. Hvalby, & B. Hokfelt (Eds.), *Memory concepts – 1993: Basic and clinical aspects* (pp. 27–45). Amsterdam: Elsevier Science.

Turner, B. S. (1990). *Theories of modernity and postmodernity.* London: Sage.

Turner, J. C. (1982). Towards a cognitive redefinition of the social group. In H. Tajfel (Ed.), *Social identity and intergroup relations* (pp. 15–40). Cambridge, England: Cambridge University Press.

Turner, J. C. (1991). *Social influence.* Pacific Grove, CA: Brooks/Cole.

Turner, J. C., Hogg, M. A., Oakes, P. J., Reicher, S. D., & Wetherell, M. S. (1987). *Rediscovering the social group. A self-categorization theory.* Oxford, England: Basil Blackwell.

Turner, J. C., Oakes, P. J., Haslam, S. A., & McGarty, C. (1994). Self and collective: Cognition and social context. *Personality and Social Psychology Bulletin, 20,* 454–463.

Turner, J. C., & Onorato, R. S. (1999). Social identity, personality, and the self-concept: A self-categorization perspective. In T. R. Tyler, R. M. Kramer, & O. P. John (Eds.), *The psychology of the social self* (pp. 11–46). Mahwah, NJ: Erlbaum.

Turner, J. C., & Reynolds, K. J. (2001). The social identity perspective in intergroup relations: Theories, themes, and controversies. In R. Brown & S. Gaertner (Eds.), *Blackwell Handbook of Social Psychology: Intergroup processes* (pp. 133–152). Oxford, UK: Blackwell Publishers Inc.

Tversky, A. (1977). Features of similarity. *Psychological Review, 84*, 327–352.

Tyler, T. R., & Blader, S. (2000). *Cooperation in groups. Procedural justice, social identity and behavioral engagement.* Philadelphia, PA: Psychology Press.

Tyler, T. R., Boeckmann, R. J., Smith, H. J., & Huo, Y. J. (1997). *Social justice in a diverse society.* Boulder, CO: Westview.

Tyler, T. R., Kramer, R. M, & John, O. P. (Eds.) (1999). *The psychology of the social self.* Mahwah, NJ: Lawrence Erlbaum Associates, Publishers.

Tyler, T. R., & Lind, E. A. (1992). A relational model of authority in groups. In M. Zanna (Ed.), *Advances in experimental social psychology* (Vol. 25, pp. 115–191). New York: Academic Press.

Tyler, T. R., & Smith, H. (1998). Social justice and social movements. In D. T. Gilbert, S. T. Fiske, & G. Lindzey (Eds.), *The Handbook of Social Psychology* (4th. ed.). Oxford: McGraw-Hill.

Tyler, T. R., & Smith, H. J. (1999). Justice, social identity, and group processes. In T. R. Tyler, R. M. Kramer, & O. P. John (Eds.), *The psychology of the social self* (pp. 223–264). Mahwah, NJ: Lawrence Erlbaum Associates, Publishers.

Van Oudenhoven, J. P., Groenewoud, J. T., & Hewstone, M. (1996). Cooperation, ethnic salience, and generalization of interethnic attitudes. *European Journal of Social Psychology, 26*, 649–661.

Van Twuyver, M., & Van Knippenberg, A. (1999). Social categorization as a function of relative group size. *British Journal of Social Psychology, 38*, 135–156.

Veenstra, K., & Haslam, S. A. (2000). Willingness to participate in industrial protest: Exploring social identification in context. *British Journal of Social Psychology, 39*, 153–172.

Verkuyten, M. (1995). Self-esteem, self-concept stability, and aspects of ethnic identity among minority and majority youth in the Netherlands. *Journal of Youth and Adolescence, 24*, 155–173.

Viney, L. (1969). Self: The history of a concept. *Journal of the History of the Behavioral Sciences, 5*, 349–359.

Vivian, J., Hewstone, M., & Brown, R. J. (1997). Intergroup contact: Theoretical and empirical developments. In R. Ben-Ari & Y. Rich (Eds.), *Enhancing education in heterogeneous schools* (13–46), Ramat-Gan: Bar-Ilan University Press.

Von Krockow, C. (1987). Symbolbildung und politische Identität. In Bundeszentrale für politische Bildung, Bonn (Ed.), *Wappen und Flaggen der Bundesrepublik Deutschland und ihrer Länder.*

Wallman, S. (1983). Identity options. In C. Fried (Ed.), Minorities: Community and identity. Berlin: Springer-Verlag.

Was macht eigentlich Martina Navratilova? (By the way, how is Martina Navratilova?) (1996). *Stern, 44*, 250.

Weber, M. (1978). The disintegration of the household: The rise of the calculative spirit and of the modern capitalist enterprise. In G. Roth & C. Wittich (Eds.), *Max Weber: Economy and Society* (Vol. I). Berkeley, CA: University of California Press.

Weinstein, E. A., & Deutschberger, P. (1963). Some dimensions of altercasting. *Sociometry, 26,* 454–466.

White, R. W. (1959). Motivation reconsidered: The concept of competence. *Psychological Review, 66,* 297–333.

Wicklund, R. A., & Gollwitzer, P. M. (1982). *Symbolic self-completion.* Hillsdale, NJ: Erlbaum.

Wilder, D., & Simon, A. F. (1998). Categorical and dynamic groups: Implications for social perception and intergroup behavior. In: C. Sedikides, J. Schopler, & C. A. Insko (Eds.), *Intergroup cognition and intergroup behavior* (pp. 27–44). Mahwah, NJ: Lawrence Erlbaum Associates.

Wilder, D., & Simon, A. F. (2001). Affect as a cause of intergroup bias. In R. Brown & S. Gaertner (Eds.), *Blackwell Handbook of Social Psychology: Intergroup processes* (pp. 153–172). Oxford, UK: Blackwell Publishers Inc.

Wilson, T. D., Lindsey, S., & Schooler, T. Y. (2000). A model of dual attitudes. *Psychological Review, 107,* 101–126.

Wimmer, A. (2002). *Nationalist exclusion and ethnic conflict. Shadows of modernity.* Cambridge, UK: Cambridge University Press.

Woolfolk, R. L., Novalany, J., Gara, M. A., Allen, L. A., & Polino, M. (1995). Self-complexity, self-evaluation, and depression: An examination of form and content within the self-schema. *Journal of Personality and Social Psychology, 68,* 1108–1120.

Wright, S. C. (2001a). Strategic collective action: Social psychology and social change. In R. Brown & S. Gaertner (Eds.), *Blackwell Handbook of Social Psychology: Intergroup processes* (pp. 409–430). Oxford, UK: Blackwell Publishers Inc.

Wright, S. C. (2001b). Restricted intergroup boundaries: Tokenism, ambiguity and the tolerance of injustice. In J. Jost & B. Major (Eds.), *The psychology of legitimacy: Emerging perspectives on ideology, justice, and intergroup relations.* Cambridge: Cambridge University Press.

Wright, S. C., Aron, A., McLaughlin-Volpe, T., & Ropp, S. A. (1997). The extended contact effect: Knowledge of cross-group friendships and prejudice. *Journal of Personality and Social Psychology, 73,* 73–90.

Yzerbyt, V., Rocher, R., & Schadron, G. (1997). Stereotypes and explanations: A subjective essentialistic view of group perception. In R. Spears, P. J. Oakes, N. Ellemers, & S. A. Haslam (Eds.), *The social psychology of stereotyping and group life* (pp. 20–50). Oxford, UK: Blackwell Publishers Ltd.

Author Index

Subject Index